THE

Fabulous Fanny

☆

THE STORY OF
Fanny Brice

THE
Fabulous Fanny

✧

THE STORY OF

✧ *Fanny Brice* ✧

✧

by NORMAN KATKOV

Alfred A. Knopf: New York
1953

L. C. catalog card number: 52–6419

THIS IS A BORZOI BOOK,
PUBLISHED BY ALFRED A. KNOPF, INC.

FIRST EDITION

80447
6-53

TO *Betty*, MY WIFE

WITH LOVE

☆   ☆   ☆

I saw her once, a year before she died, in her eighteen-room California home with its acre of putting-green lawn, its half-moon drive from the street, its swimming-pool and bathhouse, its lovely, lovely furnishings, its quiet . . . and Fanny herself.

Walking across the room tall and straight and stately, as though she were granting audience to her prime minister.

She was fifty-nine years old, wearing slacks that fitted her the way ski pants fit a Vassar sophomore. She wore a simple, no-frills blouse and tiny, unadorned earrings. Her hands were magnificent: white, with no veins showing, slender, soft as soft but not flabby; long-fingered and exquisitely manicured.

I had those five or six seconds to watch her as she came toward me, remembering what little I knew about her, while I studied this stranger who was my hostess. In my years as a newspaperman I'd interviewed more "celebrities" than I could count. With some it was hard to break the ice, with others it was not so hard, and with a rare few it was easy.

But nobody was ever so easy as Fanny. She said: "All my

life it's been a problem, how to spell my name: Fanny with an 'ie,' or with a 'y.' I sign my checks with a 'y.' In my book I'm writing it's going to be Fanny with a 'y.' What are you doing in California, kid?"

I'd come to Hollywood to write a motion picture, finished it, and been asked by my agent to see Fanny before I left California, because she was thinking of having her biography written. Since I was a writer, he said, and she wanted a book done; well, after all, and why not? I told him I had a full schedule, but he insisted.

I'd heard about the book. There'd been a parade of writers calling on Fanny that was slightly less numerous than the salesmen who appear at the door of a sweepstakes winner. For one reason and another she hadn't found anyone with whom she was *sympatico*.

Now I was another writer, sitting with this woman who had been a Ziegfeld Follies star before I was born, who had made "My Man" as familiar to the country as, say, "My Old Kentucky Home," whose protuberant nose and conniving leer were as well known as Sir Harry Lauder's kilt, or Charlie Chaplin's cane, or Maurice Chevalier's straw sailor, or Eddie Cantor's eyes.

It was a pleasant day. Fanny mostly talked and I mostly listened, she gave me an excellent lunch, and later she walked to the door with me. I thanked her and I thanked my agent and left California a day or two later.

But I kept thinking of her all the way across the country. Like her or dislike her, she had impressed me. Here was this woman who had sat like a queen and could talk like a truck driver. Maybe more so; maybe she could have taught the driver a few things. Nobody had the flair for downright earthiness that Fanny Brice was blessed with. She didn't just swear, she created her own language.

And I didn't mind it.

In a curious, inexplicable way her profanity was Fanny's as much as the impeccable clothes, the superb grooming, and the faultlessly furnished home. She made only one reference to her language. As we sat at lunch before an early Spode service, she said: "Anyone who can't say blank is deceitful."

I remembered one more dominant feature of that day: Fanny's obsession with her age. She was fifty-nine then, she looked forty-nine, and she could not stop talking about her falling hair, her lined face, her baggy eyes. She talked of old age without sadness, without bitterness, and without regret, as an enemy against whom she knew she must lose, but against whom she would never slacken the fight.

She talked not at all with self-pity but with anger. There was a feeling of need about her, a wanting to live: to taste, to feel, to experience, to understand. She was into old age that day but she had youth, real youth, and the eagerness and zest that are youth's characteristics.

So I left California. I read of Fanny's death in the newspapers, remembering a handsome woman in her handsome home, and in the summer following—1951—came back to California to write another motion picture. I finished *that* one, went to my agent's office to say good-bye, and he asked me how I'd like to write Fanny's biography.

Just like that.

Me with train tickets and a packed suitcase and plans for a smooth summer's fishing in Minnesota.

He told me I wouldn't be starting from scratch, because from time to time in these last years Fanny had been setting down notes for her memoir.

While he told me I'd have the notes I thought of all my well-laid plans; I started to say no ten times and never made it because her image kept intruding and her story kept my lips closed and the book—the unwritten, unplanned, unresearched book—began to take its vague shape in my mind.

So I said: "Yes."

Just like that.

I said I'd like to do it. Five minutes later I was standing in the California sun wondering how to do it. All I knew about Fanny was what I've told you. The stories are the kind that attach themselves to anyone who is in the public eye and public press long enough, particularly show people.

For here in America show people are the only kind of royalty we have. They are the princes and princesses, the kings and queens, of our country and their *mots* are repeated the next day over the back fence, the saloon bar, and the bridge table across the length and breadth of the republic.

I knew the stories. I knew she had divorced Nick Arnstein, the gambler and confidence-man, loving him as much on the day she got the decree as she had ever loved him, for she had told me so.

But that was all. Fanny Brice had been wife, mother, and grandmother. She had been married three times and divorced three times. She had been a Broadway immortal, and a London favorite. She had been a burlesque soubrette and Baby Snooks. She had made friends and enemies. She had laughed and wept. She had lived into her sixtieth year and she had been as real as rain, as alive as anyone who ever drew breath. She had started poor and ended rich, and now I had agreed to write a book about her, *all* about her.

And I didn't know where to begin.

I had to talk to people: Fanny's children, her husbands, her brother, her sister, her agents, her lawyers, her business managers, her radio writers, her old, old friends in New York and her not-so-old friends in California.

There were newspaper morgues to visit and court files to examine in Los Angeles and Chicago and New York and Newark, New Jersey.

There were Fanny's notes to read and hundreds and hun-

dreds of pictures to look at. Later I would have to go to San
Francisco, and Las Vegas, and Dallas, Texas, and St. Mark's
Avenue, Brooklyn.

I stood there under the blue skies of California. For a
moment I didn't know where to start, or what to do, or how
to do it.

Then I went into a drugstore and telephoned Lew Brice
and made an appointment for the next morning.

I had to start learning about Fanny somewhere.

St. Paul
October, 1952

THE
Fabulous Fanny

THE STORY OF
Fanny Brice

LEW BRICE: *"I'm the People's Choice."*

Keeney's Theatre in Brooklyn," said Lew Brice, "that's where Fanny started. Fourteen years old. I'm a year younger. She out front singing in amateur night and me back behind the curtain, fighting the stagehands for pennies.

"Say you're in the audience and you like Fanny's pipes. So you throw her a coin. But if you're Fanny, you're going to finish that song. You figure you'll get the pennies and nickels later. Except there's no later.

"Those stagehands would raise the curtains six inches," Lew said. "Just enough for the coins to roll through. You had to be fast. I was fast. I'm still fast," breaking into a buck and wing there in the small, one-room apartment above Hollywood Boulevard, with its two studio couches, its maple chair, its maple desk, its worn, faded carpet.

"Yeah," he snarled, lunging forward, his forefinger jabbing the air, "and don't you forget it, see? I'm as tough as I ever was, see?" grimacing in imitation of Edward G. Robinson. "Mess around with Lew Brice and you get your ears pinned back, see?" and stopped, his hands on his hips, smiling, his eyelid dropping in the wink that had become his sister's signature.

In that moment the resemblance to Fanny was startling. In that moment you could almost see Fanny, and then Lew became Lew, walking impatiently around the room. He is a tall, thin man with tiny feet and tiny hands whose fistic adventures have kept his name and the sister's name, by which he has always been identified, in the newspapers for years. You would not believe it to look at Lew Brice, who seems frail and fragile, who laughs easily and smiles always, but the evidence in knockdowns is recorded on a hundred front pages.

There was the night a few years ago when Lew was a guest of Fanny's, recuperating from a slight case of pari-mutuel poverty. After a stag evening devoted to good fellowship, Lew returned by taxi to Fanny's home about three a.m., alighted uncertainly from the cab, and dug into his pockets for fare and tip.

"How much?" asked Lew.

The driver, disgruntled after an evening of bad business, and hoping to make the night a profitable one, mentioned a figure something in excess of the true fee.

Lew, who had made the trip from Hollywood to Fanny's home hundreds of times in hundreds of cabs, waved an admonishing finger at the driver. "You're out of line, pal," he said, dropping the correct fare and a substantial tip into the front seat. He turned away from the taxi and began the swaying journey to Fanny's front door.

"I want my money!" cried the driver.

Lew continued.

The driver sprang from the cab and followed Lew, who shook him off, reached for the key and let himself into the house.

While the driver began shouting that he had been cheated, Lew made his way slowly up the staircase.

Fanny, wakened by the driver, who was shouting and

pressing the doorbell, sat up in bed. "What the hell is going on here?" she demanded.

Lew froze at the head of the stairs.

"Lew!" she shouted.

"I want my money!" the driver wailed.

"LEW!" Fanny shouted.

And the doorbell sounded.

Lew turned slowly and started down the stairs, Fanny's shouts behind him and the driver's yells ahead of him. Carefully, taking each step carefully, he made it to the first floor. He got to the door, opened it carefully, doubled his tiny fingers into a tiny fist, and hit the driver one shot, waiting until he fell before closing the door.

Then, as he passed Fanny's bedroom on the way to his, she said: "Lew, what's going on at this time of night?"

"Some drunk, Fanny," Lew said, and continued carefully toward his bedroom.

Now, in his one-room apartment, Lew laughed as he remembered that night, and laughing, remembered that Fanny had won her first amateur contest. "She got ten bucks," he said. "I made half as much behind the curtain and I never even opened my mouth. That was the beginning, right there, and we made every amateur night in Brooklyn from then on."

They lived then on St. Mark's Avenue, around the corner from Vanderbilt Avenue in south Brooklyn, in an eight-family tenement house that Fanny's mother had bought. While the amateur night was Fanny's first professional appearance, it occurred to Lew that his sister's career had begun long before.

"Twice a year," Lew said, "my Mom used to take us out to Coney Island, all dressed up, and parade the boardwalk. Lunch was two shoeboxes full of sandwiches. No spun candy, no loop-the-loop, no roller-coaster, no ice cream. Like being in the five and dime store with your hands tied behind your back.

"*Twice* a year. Fanny wanted to go twice a day, but we've got no money, we're just a pair of punks then. But Fanny's a schemer. A block from our house is Bergen Street, where you can transfer to the Vanderbilt Avenue trolley to Coney Island. First Fanny gets a white handkerchief, fills it full of little stones, and ties it in a knot. Then she takes me down to the corner of Bergen and Vanderbilt, and watches to see who throws away their transfers when they get off the trolley.

"Now we got two transfers and we're on the trolley for Coney Island. But I heard that the conductor collects a second fare when you go over a bridge. So I grab Fanny, I whisper to her about the second fare. She says shut up. Now I see the conductor coming up the aisle. I'm real worried, but Fanny is smiling and waving the handkerchief back and forth, back and forth, and the conductor is coming closer, and all of a sudden the handkerchief is out of the window, and Fanny is crying like somebody stole the rent money.

"I mean crying. Real salt tears. Fanny was a born weeper. 'That was our fare,' she bawls. 'I was supposed to take my little brother to visit Grandma.' Well, figure it. You think anybody was going to let that sweet little kid and her sweet little brother get put off the trolley? There was always somebody riding to put up for us."

Arrived at Coney Island, there was the problem of getting money for rides, for hot dogs, for salt-water taffy, for the thousand delights of this children's paradise. Holding Lew's hand in hers, Fanny would walk through the crowds until she saw a fat man eating. Approaching him, Fanny would say: "Excuse me, please, mister, but what is the shortest way to walk . . ." and the tears would come, faster and bigger than before, ". . . back to St. Mark's and Vander . . . Vander . . . Vander . . ." clutching Lew to her bosom, pressing her cheek to his, and weeping bitterly until the money had been put into her reluctant fingers.

Thus, carefully canvassing the area, working first one end of the boardwalk, then the other; later, both ends of the beach; later still, the hardened pitchmen and performers themselves—provided always that she wailed before fat men —Fanny would weep them into enough food and rides to bloat a Boy Scout encampment.

At last, with twilight imminent, with Lew weary and footsore, Fanny would lead him to the trolley stalls. There she would wait for the last obese citizen of the day to appear. Then, a final tear, a final plea, and the pair were on their way home.

"Now, the next morning," Lew said, "Fanny is outside with another handkerchief, loading it with stones. I says to her: 'What's that for?' She tells me we're going to Coney Island.

"We go that day, the next and the next. All of a sudden I got it figured. All Fanny wants to do is cry. It's not Coney Island any more. It's the weeping. She's in love with her act."

Lew wore a thin, blue bathrobe, and now he paused, pulled the belt tight around his middle, and moved his shoulders like a prizefighter waiting for the bell. Lew Brice is fifty-eight years old, with thinning, graying hair, and a pencil mustache.

He looked at himself carefully in the mirror above the maple desk before turning. "Not bad," he said. "Not bad at all," grinning suddenly and doing a time step, finishing with a flourish and bowing, right arm extended as he waited for the applause.

"We were together from then on," Lew said. "They loved

me. I was the people's choice, brother."

Lew cannot remember a time when Fanny wasn't performing. Her first, her very first, act was a show she conceived, produced, directed, and starred in. Admission was a penny, and the theater was a shed beside the tenement.

When she had collected twenty pennies, a sum mysteriously arrived at in the secret corners of her child's mind, Fanny would lock the door of the shed, walk before her audience, drape a shawl over her head and around her shoulders, bend forward so that she was an aged woman, and announce that this was a bridge over a black river at midnight.

And the rain was pouring over the bridge and into the black river and on the baby she held in her arms. And her baby was starving and freezing and dying of pneumonia because Fanny had no money for milk or coal.

If Fanny's tears were matched by her audience's, the performance was forthwith ended, the door flung open, the shawl folded carefully until her next appearance.

However, if the customers were dry-eyed, the rain continued to pour, the baby continued to starve for milk and die of pneumonia until the shed was filled with the wailing of twenty-one lachrymose children, for in any chorus of crying Fanny was a hands-down winner.

On summer nights Fanny and her audience would gather on her front stoop for an evening of singing. Within a few weeks she noticed that they were attracting more and more adults who would stand around the group listening to the songs. One night Fanny counted the house. The following evening, when her gang gathered, she led them seven or eight blocks away from St. Mark's Avenue.

Stopping at last in the rear of a likely-looking tenement, Fanny ordered the others to be still and broke into, "When You Know You're Not Forgotten by the Girl You Can't Forget," seasoning the lyric with a generous portion of tears.

She sang it loud and clear and mournfully. When she had finished, she stepped back, ran her sleeve over her eyes, and waited.

There was a brief, scattered shower of pennies, followed by a brief flurry of fisticuffs, which Fanny arbitrated immediately by electing herself treasurer of the choir.

With the pennies securely tied in her white handkerchief, Fanny led the choristers through an alley, across another block, and into another back yard. At the end of an hour, having infrequently allowed someone else to sing, Fanny called a halt to the evening's concert, stopping below an arc light to open the handkerchief.

"Nobody ever got a short count from Fanny," Lew said. "She divided it even all the way around, keeping fifteen cents in a pile near her. When she was finished, one of the kids says: 'What's the fifteen cents for?'

" 'For a flashlight, you dope,' Fanny yells at him. 'I heard more pennies fall than what we got here. Tomorrow night we're not leaving any behind.' "

Lew lit a half-smoked cigar as though the match were a dollar bill. "One night the kids show up around our stoop and everybody's going to Keeney's Theatre for the amateur night. Fanny and I never even heard of it. They tell us it costs a quarter to get in, so Fanny takes me and the flashlight and we make a couple of back yards, her singing and me collecting. In an hour we got the price for both of us."

Except that when they arrived at the theater, all the quarter seats were sold. Only fifty-cent tickets remained. Taking Lew's hand, Fanny led him to the stage door, stopping a few feet away to give him instructions. They would tell the man they wanted to appear on amateur night. She was a singer, Lew was a dancer, and they worked together. That way they would get into the theater. Once inside, they would see as much of the show as they could. When it was their turn to perform, they would sneak out, and still have their half dollar.

"Next thing I know," Lew said, "we're in the wings behind Frank Keeney, and we're watching those amateurs. He's got our names, but I'm not too worried. I'm fast on my feet. Then I see that the curtain is up about six inches from the floor and I spot those stagehands picking up the coins.

"Next thing I know," Lew continued, "Keeney announces some guy, but nobody makes a move. The audience is clapping their hands and stamping feet and Keeney grabs Fanny by the arm and shoves her out there."

Most of the audience knew the thin, gawky girl, and not a few had heard her sing. They saw her shaking with fear, and they shouted: "Stick with it, Fanny!" They saw her crying real tears, and they yelled: "You can do it, Fan! Go on, show them, Fanny!" but she could only stand with her fists clenched, her fingernails digging into her palms, too far from the wings to run for it, too frightened to sing anything.

Until someone shouted: "When You Know You're Not Forgotten!" First one shouted it and then a second asked for the song. A third and fourth and fifth took it up. Soon the gallery was pleading for the tune. The orchestra leader raised his baton, and led the musicians into the chorus.

Still she could not sing. She put one shoe atop the other, she twisted her fingers behind her back, she sniffled in a vain attempt to stop her tears, as someone yelled: "If you're going to jump, then jump!"

And she sang. She sang, and later she told Lew that she had closed her eyes and imagined nobody in the theater but herself and her mother.

With her eyes closed Fanny imagined her mother wearing a straw hat with a blue, ostrich plume. Her mother wore white, canvas shoes with high heels, and a beautiful, velvet dress.

Fanny made it up that her mother had come to hear her sing. She made it up that she had arranged all this for her mother because she was a big star and made fifty dollars a week. She had built her mother a house in the country, she imagined as she sang that night. She had bought her mother a car and hired a chauffeur with a mustache who drove her mother all over the United States in the beautiful car.

"You should have heard her that night," Lew said. "She never had to learn a thing about singing a ballad, she had that from the beginning. That theater quieted down like somebody had hung a smallpox sign over the door.

"They started with the money. I hear it falling and I take a deep breath and go past Frank Keeney and I'm behind there with the stagehands."

After the show Frank Keeney learned that Fanny had never been in an amateur night before. He told her he owned two other theaters and wanted her to appear there the following Wednesday and Thursday nights.

She won those. Within a month Fanny had won a dozen amateur shows. The prize money, together with half of what Lew picked up behind the curtain, brought her weekly income to between sixty and seventy dollars.

As for Fanny's school days, Lew remembers her as the kind of student who spent most of her time in the coat closet, having been ordered there by the teacher for disturbing the other pupils. On one such instance, when she was in the second grade, Fanny appeared at the entrance to the classroom, hand raised high over her head. The teacher ordered her back.

Within a few minutes Fanny was once more in the entrance.

The teacher announced that Fanny would remain for thirty minutes after school.

Fanny disappeared, to return shortly, waving her hand frantically at the teacher.

Who raised the stay-after period to an hour.

Whereupon Fanny, who was near the bursting-point in more ways than one, spied the teacher's galoshes, filled them, and ran home.

Now that she was winning contests, Fanny decided to quit school. She had never liked it and had never been a good student. When she showed her mother the money she was making, Fanny was an ex-student.

Lew put the cigar in one corner of his mouth and got out of the chair, rubbing the small of his back with both hands. He walked to the door of the one-room apartment, opened it, and stepped back, setting the cigar carefully into an ashtray.

"She won the first time she ran, remember that," he said. "Fanny never stopped winning. I never stopped picking up the pennies."

✻ 2 ✻

CAROLYN SAUL: *"Pinochle Charlie Was a Fascinating Bastard."*

WHEN she was eighteen years old and in love with an improvident tailor, Rosie Stern, Fanny's mother, married Charles Borach, a bartender earning eighty dollars a week in the largest saloon on the Bowery.

For Rosie Stern, whose eight years alone in America had been 2,922 days of eighteen hours' work out of twenty-four; of boarding with one family after another in the fetid back bedrooms of a dozen lower East Side flats; of friendlessness and loneliness and always . . . always and always of poverty; for her the bartender with the black mustache was something more real than love.

Pinochle Charlie, as he was called, was as real as the sewing-machine in the cold fur-factory, with its damp walls, where Rosie Stern worked. He was as real as the food in the pushcarts she passed daily; as real as the apartment of her own on Second Street, with its steam heat, which he promised her.

From a village near Budapest, Rosie's mother had sent her to America with the child's aunt, giving three feather-beds in payment of passage from Hungary to Ellis Island. Her mother wanted something more for Rosie than her own hut with its leaking roof, dirt floors, and the cow in the kitchen. Years later, Rosie told her children that she had not wanted to leave her parents; her brothers and sisters; her familiar, safe world for the new world. But her mother had said go and she had gone.

To live first with an East Side family as cook, maid, and nurse for the infant of the house.

Following which she found a job in a dress factory, where she earned enough to share a room with the daughter of another family.

She moved again and again and again in an unceasing search for warmer, cleaner, more private lodging, until at last she found a bedroom of her own in the home of Frank Grant and his wife, who was Pinochle Charlie's sister.

Rosie had known Seymour Cohen for almost a year then. He was a short, sallow youth, making two dollars a week, which was almost enough for himself and the aged mother who lived with him. He was thin, badly dressed, and ungainly. When he walked the East Side with Rosie, buying her a bag of sunflower seeds, holding her hand in his hand, speaking softly and tenderly, her heart turned over and her eyes shone.

Oh, he could talk, could Seymour Cohen, and while he talked, Rosie waited.

Waited and worked and walked the East Side with Seymour Cohen until the night Pinochle Charlie came to visit his sister and saw Rosie going out to meet her tailor.

Until then, Pinochle Charlie had been a sometime guest at the Grants. Now he became as frequent a visitor as a bill-collector, and there was a night when Seymour Cohen could not make her listen, when Rosie could no longer wait, when two dollars every seven days was not enough for a youth and a girl and an old woman. She gave him back his sun-flower seeds that night and turned away from him on Houston Street. When she came home the Grants were in the kitchen, drinking beer with Pinochle Charlie.

Mrs. Grant insisted that Rosie join them. After several minutes of silence, the two men went into another room, and Mrs. Grant said: "He wants to marry you, Rosie."

"No."

"It's time you were married. He's a good man. He makes good money."

"No."

"Think about it," Mrs. Grant said before joining the men.

Rosie thought about it for a week. Pinochle Charlie came every night, sitting in the parlor with Frank Grant.

Rosie Borach never told anyone what happened during those seven days, but at the end of the week she agreed to marry Pinochle Charlie.

"You could say she wanted the security," said Carolyn Saul, Fanny's older sister, remembering now, on a dismal New York winter's day, her mother's stories. "Mom's been dead sixteen years, she died in California, but I remember what she told me like it was yesterday.

"I would remember where the others wouldn't. You see, I had a better education than the other children, and I have a tendency toward facts.

"There were four of us. My brother, Phil, was the oldest. He died young, when he was in his twenties. I come next. I'm sixty-two. Then Fanny. Then Lew, the baby. There aren't many of us . . ." stopping to dab at her eyes with a handkerchief.

When she had recovered, Carolyn said: "I never had to ask Fanny for money. In all our years she always sent me enough and in death I was not forgotten, not Lew and not me."

Of Lew, Fanny said once: "I loved my brother. We have something more in common than I have with my sister, Carolyn. I send my sister money every month. I don't send Lew one cent, because I know he gambles it. I just couldn't give him anything, knowing it's all going for the races. When I'm gone, he will get more than he ever got from me. But I don't want to give it to him now because I know it will go on the card tables and the betting-windows at the tracks.

"Lew hurt me," Fanny continued, "because he threw away his talent. The most precious thing in this world is talent; to be gifted. Lew was very gifted. He was a wonderful dancer. He would go into a show, rehearse, work hard. Until a race track would open and, pffffftttt, no more Lew.

"He liked the bottle. I know he would have gotten way up in show business if he really wanted to. I loved Lew but he disappointed me. I stopped giving Lew any money, but all the money I gave my mother she would give to him. He would get every cent she had. He was just wonderful to my mother, took her out all the time. He really loved my mother and was always sweet to her."

Carolyn twisted her handkerchief, then squeezed it into a ball between her fingers.

"The doctors made me give up smoking," Carolyn continued. "It's been so many long years since I felt myself. I have good days and bad days. Right now I'm recovering from a cold, that's why I'm home now, you know. But you surely don't want to hear about my troubles.

"We were all born on the East Side. Very soon after Lew came, we moved to Newark, where my father bought a saloon across from the Pennsylvania station. He bought it and Mom ran it. She could tap a keg of beer better than any man. She couldn't read or write but she could figure per-

2: *Carolyn Saul* (17)

centages like an adding-machine. Fanny adored my mother. She was always with Fanny in later years.

"So it was Mom who was boss. Pinochle Charlie was too busy playing cards in the back. Everybody who knew him loved that man. Everybody except my mother. She never liked him, but Pinochle Charlie was a fascinating bastard, forgive my French."

Fanny wrote of her father: "He liked his liquor. He said it made him feel good. He had asthma and he couldn't breathe sometimes. He never slept in bed. He used to put a pillow on the table and sleep on his arm. Because he said if he laid down he would choke. He said the whisky would let him breathe. On Sunday the saloons were closed. We would all sit down in the saloon after breakfast on Sunday. I remember there was a pool table and it would be covered with a cloth. And I would get up on the bar and sing and dance. And my mother would be mad, but my father would say: 'No, let her sing, let her dance.'

" 'What are you going to do for us, my actress?' he would ask.

"So I would tell him. 'I'm a princess in a big castle,' I'd say. 'The bad king has me locked up. I can't escape.' I would do a whole routine, and my father would applaud and throw me a nickel or a dime. Then I would sing a song and he would throw me another coin. It's funny, Mom made all the money and there he sat throwing nickels and dimes at me.

"All the men I can remember as a kid were kings in their house. We had neighbors, I forgot their name, but I hung around with the girl. I would be there at supper time and her mother would feed me when she fed the kids. Then her father would come home from work. And there was always something special for him to eat. Something different and better than what we had. And I can still see him—let's say she is bringing in a steak for him—putting it down in front of him. I can see her looking at him while he is eating it, wishing she had a piece of it. And when I was at their house, in the kitchen, we couldn't talk when he got home.

" 'Sssshhhh,' the mother would say. 'Papa's eating.'

"Then after dinner she'd say: 'Sssshhhh, Papa's taking a nap.'

"And I thought: 'That sour-looking guy, why does he act like that to such a sweet woman?' And I thought it was awful. The master of the house. I could see this woman's face when she looked at him while he ate, and I used to think: 'Why doesn't he give her a *taste* of that?'

"When I was about ten years old in Newark, I had another girl friend. I'm at her house one day, sitting in the kitchen and her mother is on the back porch hanging up clothes. First she puts the clothes up on the line. I'm talking to my girl friend and now I see the mother is taking all the clothes off the line. Then I see she is putting them back *on* the line.

"I said: 'I must tell you something terrible is happening to your mother. She has been taking the clothes off and on that line for the last half hour; putting them on, taking them off, putting them on again.'

"So we ran three or four blocks to relatives and told them. So they called their doctor and they had to take my friend's mother away. She went insane. And I would go with my girl friend to the crazy house to see her mother.

"And I loved going there because I loved to study those people. When you went there, you'd all go in one big room: the crazies and the visitors who came to see them. And I remember one very young girl who wouldn't eat. Her family would come up there and try to make her eat. I remem-

ber one day they brought her a charlotte russe. They wanted
her to have that. But she closed her lips tight, wouldn't open
her lips. I thought: 'If she won't eat it, why don't they give
it to me?' But I couldn't ask for it, because it was in a crazy
house.

"Well, maybe a year later, I was visiting my girl friend's
mother and she said: 'Mama, don't you remember Fanny?'

"The woman shook her head.

" 'Fanny Borach,' my girl friend said. 'Borach. Borach.'

"And the woman smiled. She had not smiled for a year.
She said: 'I remember Fanny Borach. She used to bring me
bread.' And she reached out and touched me. My girl friend
started crying, but I smiled at her mother. I held her hand
and talked with her, because she was right. They were very
poor and I used to sneak bread out of our house and bring
it to them. She remembered. So I thought: 'Maybe I can
get her well.' I tried talking with her about everything, but
she only said: 'Bread, bread.' Now why does it have to happen to people like that?"

In the New York apartment Carolyn Saul brought her
guest an ashtray. "You know, Fanny was a crook as a kid,"
she said. "Really! When she was eight years old, she would
steal money and buy toys to give to babies on the block. We
had a charge account at a shoe store. One month my mother
got a bill for seven pairs of shoes. She saw that only Phil and
Lew had new shoes, so she went to the store. She found out
that Fanny had come in with five kids and bought them all
shoes.

"Here is a strange thing. When we were young, Fanny
would always say: 'I'm going to marry a blind man.' I would
ask her why. She'd tell me so she could take care of him.

"Now how do you put that together with the stealing?
It's a funny psychology she had. Fanny didn't need to steal,

because Mom was very good in business. Once we had seven saloons in Newark. Mom would go from one to the other. Still Fanny stole. Whenever Mom would visit people, she never took Fanny or Lew because they would go right into the kitchen to the sugar bowl where the money was."

The pair became adept shoplifters. Fanny would take only pencils, crayons, and erasers, tearing the lining in the pocket of her coat so she would have more room for loot. Lew stole only candy.

After many months of such successful forays against law and order, Fanny decided they were being watched with more than ordinary interest by several blue-suited sentinels in the department stores they visited.

On the afternoon of their next scheduled venture, Fanny dragged Lew into the bedroom she shared with her sister and told him to get out of his clothes.

"Huh?" Lew said, staring at his sister.

"You're going to wear Carrie's clothes," Fanny decided. "They won't recognize us."

"Who?" Lew asked.

"We'll fool them," Fanny said, tugging at Lew's shirt.

"Fool who?" Lew said. "I'm not wearing girls' clothes. Mom!" he shouted, breaking for the door. But Rosie was at the saloon and Fanny blocked his path to the door.

"Get them off," she commanded.

An hour later two small girls dressed in matching white made their way into a department store. They held hands as they walked shyly along the aisles, smiling at salesgirls and stealing whatever they could lay their grubby little hands on.

Until, looking up, they saw a pair of store detectives standing before them.

"We're waiting for mother," Fanny said.

Lew was pale, shaken, and speechless.

"We've got a special waiting-room," one of the detectives

announced, getting a firm hold on each. Fanny and Lew were quickly transported to a room upstairs and separated. While Lew was taken through a door by one detective, Fanny was kept outside by the other.

Fanny noticed that the wall behind which Lew was held did not extend to the ceiling. She saw the lamp cords extending down into the room as the detective said: "Empty your pockets."

"Me?" Fanny asked.

"Come on, kid, empty them," the detective ordered, and Fanny emptied.

Even the detective was amazed at the amount of his employer's merchandise which Fanny had been able to secret about her person. "How'd you steal all this, kid?" the detective asked.

"I didn't steal nothing."

"Look, kid, don't get smart with me," the detective warned.

"I didn't steal nothing," Fanny insisted.

"Now, listen . . ." the detective began, as Lew screamed: "She made me do it!"

Fanny heard him and the detective heard him. "She made me do it!" Lew repeated. "I didn't want to, mister, honest I didn't. It was her!"

Always thereafter, twenty and thirty and forty years later, Fanny would suddenly remember that day, and point the accusing finger at Lew. "You sonofabitch, you sold me out!" she would remind him.

Fanny loved flowers. They were living in a rather dingy neighborhood in Newark, in one of three identical buildings, each with a janitor. Often Fanny led Lew into the outlying districts of the city, where they would make their way into the private gardens behind fine homes to steal flowers. One summer day Fanny saw a music box on the back porch of a

house. Within seconds the device was off the porch and the
two were running as fast as they could. Since they could not
bring the music box into their own home without submitting
to questions for which Fanny had no answers, she showed
it to the janitor of the building next door. Fanny sold it to
him for two dollars, watching as he carried it down into the
cellar. When he appeared without the music box and went
into the building, Fanny reasoned that the janitor had hidden it until he left for the day. Leading the trusting Lew,
she made her way into the basement, where she found the
instrument in the cold furnace.

Before ten minutes passed, Fanny had sold it to the janitor of the building beyond. Loitering near the stoop, they
saw the second purchaser take it into *his* cellar, waited until *he* was gone, and this time sold it to a music store for ten
dollars.

You had to give her this: In those years Fanny didn't care
whether the money could be made within or beyond the
pale; all she wanted was a chance at it. She was ten years
old when she learned, a few weeks before Christmas, that
a Newark department store was hiring wrappers for the holiday season at $2.50 a week. Unable to recruit Lew, who sus-
pected another stealing scheme and for once preferred frac-
tions to five-fingering, Fanny left school immediately and
was hired the same day. Mom was busy in the saloon from
morning to night, the children had to make do for themselves, and Fanny swore the others to secrecy.

One morning, a few days later, while Carolyn dressed for
school, she was startled to see Fanny putting on her best
Sunday dress: a pink organdy with white lace. Since the
temperature was a few degrees above zero and since Fanny
announced that she was going to work in nothing but the
dress, Carolyn began to doubt whether her sister was in full
possession of her faculties. When Fanny not only put on her

own diamond-studded earrings, but commandeered her sister's matching set, so that each small lobe held two ornaments, Carolyn insisted on being told the reason for this lunacy.

As she gulped her breakfast, Fanny explained. Standing at the wrapping-table the day before, she began to imagine that she was very poor, that her mother was dead and her father blind, that she was the sole support of the family.

The fantasy continued, with Fanny refining and reshaping the original ingredients: Carolyn was epileptic (Fanny had once seen someone in a seizure); Phil had to have a brace for his crippled leg; Pinochle Charlie was not only blind but needed a set of false teeth.

The other girls around the wrapping-table soon noticed Fanny's sad face. When one asked if anything was troubling her, Fanny reluctantly shared her imaginary grief with the others, giving her recitation precisely the same shading and emphasis she was later to employ in the Ziegfeld Follies.

That evening when she finished work and opened the locker that had been assigned her in the department store, she found several stale rolls that her colleagues had bought for her to take home to her blind, toothless father, her epileptic sister, and her crippled brother. Fanny was horrified. She wanted to tell them then and there that it was all a joke and that her family owned saloons; but she was hit suddenly with this plan for a more theatrical disclosure. The next morning Carolyn warned Fanny she would catch cold wearing nothing but the organdy, but she was running through the house on her way to work.

When the other wrappers saw Fanny in all her elegance, they could only stare at her. Finally one found her voice and asked Fanny if she had come into a legacy, whereupon they were all told that the Borach family was as rich as any in Newark. Yesterday's performance was only a comedy act, and they were all a pack of ninnies for believing what she had told them.

One of the girls stole away to report the incident to the section manager. He immediately asked Fanny to repeat the story, which she did with alacrity, shaking her four earrings triumphantly. The section head went from the wrapping-table to the store's main office, where he quickly learned that Fanny's mother not only had a charge account at the store, but was a very good customer. He thought it wise to telephone Rosie Borach.

That night, as they lay in bed together, Fanny told Carolyn what had followed. Rosie appeared at the department store within the hour and was led to the wrapping-table. She seized Fanny's ear with one hand and slapped her with the other.

"You disgraced me!" cried Rosie.

Slap!

"You told lies!" cried Rosie.

"Mom, please . . ."

"Shut up!"

Slap!

As she held on to the ear, pulling Fanny through the store.

"Mama's dead," Rosie remembered, "and Papa's . . ."

Slap!

". . . blind!"

Slap!

"You're hurting me," Fanny wailed.

"Good."

Slap!

Now, more than fifty years later, Carolyn chuckled as she remembered Fanny's bruised ear and puffed face. "The week after Christmas the store sent Mom a check for $2.50," Carolyn said, "and she wouldn't give it to Fanny. It was a big, standing joke in the family. Years and years afterward, when

Fanny was living in California, she would say to Mom: 'You owe me $2.50 and I want my money.'

"Just about that time we went abroad, you know," Carolyn continued. "Yes, Fanny, Mom, and I traveled first-class to see Mom's family in Budapest, Hungary."

Fanny remembered the journey clearly in her notes. "There was a big park in Budapest," Fanny wrote, "and there was an American show playing in the park. In between the performances, the actors would sit on the benches. Carolyn and I sat with them. They thought we were Hungarian kids. We sat there listening to them and heard all the things they were saying. That was when the cakewalk was the big thing. My uncles belonged to a club in Budapest that was giving a big affair. I told my uncles Carolyn and I danced the cakewalk. So they got a dress for her and pants for me. I was the boy in the act, and we did the cakewalk at the affair. The next day my mother made us dress up in the costumes and have our pictures taken so she could hang them behind the bar in Newark.

"After we had been in Hungary a couple of weeks, my mother took us to her home where she was born, some Godforsaken hole about eight hours from Budapest. And in this village all the roofs were straw. The Hungarian gypsy children, ten and twelve years old, used to go around naked, so primitive was this village. And my mother took us through the woods, and said: 'Now here is a place where I always used to go when I was a little girl. I used to find eggs here.' The chickens used to run wild, see, and the kids would run all over looking for eggs. And as we came to the spot where she used to find eggs, you guessed it . . . we found two eggs there!

"My mother had an aunt in this village who was a hundred and two years old. My mother would buy beer and give it to the old aunt, and the old aunt would put sugar in it and then put her finger in the glass and stir it. I never could enjoy beer after that.

"I had to take the old aunt to the bathroom that was outside. She was blind. When she was forty years old, she was milking a cow, and the cow swished her tail across the old aunt's eyes and blinded her. My mother bought food and gave a party for the whole town, and I sang songs and danced for them. I had a real time.

"Coming back to Budapest, the train stopped at a small station. I looked out of the window and saw a whole field of poppies. Now all I heard in school was poppies, poppies, poppies, so I ran out to pick some. And while I'm out in the field, the train leaves. And my mother screams and gets them to stop the train. They stopped it and they backed it up. The conductor came to get me, and when he brought me to my mother, *bam!* Not a word out of her, just beat the pants off me."

Carolyn's account of the trip to Europe was substantially the same as Fanny's. You had the feeling, as you listened, that she enjoyed this accustomed role of Fanny's biographer. She talked as though she had, in a hundred ways, helped her sister. She was like the willing witness at a highway accident, offering unsolicited statistics: rate of speed, length of skid, exact location of impact; spelling name, repeating address, and declaring herself available any time for further questioning and, should it become necessary, testimony.

"Yes, well, we didn't stay in Newark long after we came home," Carolyn continued. "Not because of Fanny, oh, no. Mom just got tired of my father's ways, I suppose you would say. She would work from dark to dark and he would be losing all the money playing poker and betting on the horses. There was a Sunday morning, I remember it very well, when

Pinochle Charlie was watching Fanny perform up on the bar. I was there and Lew, and Mom came in with Phil. Being the oldest, he was with her a lot in those days."

The saloon, Carolyn recalls, was hot and muggy and dark that summer's day. Fanny was singing as Rosie came through the front door. Waving at her mother, Fanny continued her ballad.

"Enough," Rosie said.

Fanny sang on.

Holding Phil's hand, Rosie walked across the saloon to her husband, who sat facing his daughter, legs crossed as though he were in the front row of a music hall.

"Charlie, I . . ." Rosie began, but he didn't turn his head. He didn't look at his wife, but put his forefinger to his lips, cautioning against any interruption of his daughter's efforts.

Rosie walked to the bar, her back to Pinochle Charlie. "Get down, Fanny," she said. "It isn't our bar any more."

And reached up for her daughter, lifting her from the bar.

"Wait," Pinochle Charlie said. He rose from the chair. "Wait a minute, please. What do you mean, it isn't our bar?" He walked to his wife's side. "What do you mean, Rose?"

"You," Rosie said, pointing at Fanny, "go home." She pointed at Phil. "Take them home, Phil," she ordered, but nobody moved.

"I'm asking you, Rose," Pinochle Charlie said.

"I'm telling you," Rosie answered. "I sold the saloons today."

"You sold!"

"Me," Rosie said, and nodded. "Me. I sold," she said, tapping her chest. "Me, myself, Mr. Borach."

"Since when are you the boss, please?" he demanded.

"Since I opened the first saloon. Since I stand behind the bar. Since I work from morning to midnight, Mr. Borach," and turning to her children who stood together like waifs in the snow, she said: "Go home. All of you. Phil, take them," she said, but nobody moved.

"I'll stop the sale," Pinochle Charlie declared.

"You'll stop nothing," Rosie told him. "You're not the boss, Mr. Borach. I'm the boss, and I sold."

"Sold, sold, sold," he repeated. "And now what? We have children to support. How will we support the children?"

"I'll support them. I did and I will," she said.

Lew began to cry. They could hear him.

Rosie said: "Keep still, you," and Carolyn began to cry.

Rosie said: "Come, I'll give you dinner," but Pinochle Charlie took her arm.

"And what happens now, Rose?"

She turned to him. She looked at her handsome husband, with the black mustache. She stared at him, remembering, for a fleeting, heartbreaking moment, the walks with Seymour Cohen. She remembered the promises Seymour Cohen had made. She remembered again, could almost taste again, the sunflower seeds Seymour Cohen had bought for her, and then she said: "We are moving to Brooklyn. I bought a building in Brooklyn."

"I don't want to move to Brooklyn," Pinochle Charlie declared.

She pushed his hand from her arm. "You're not going," she told him. "I'm going. The children and me. I'm tired of lazy bums. I'm tired of working for you. I won't work for you any more," walking away from him to her children, whom she embraced as a hen collects her brood, sweeping them toward the front door.

"Rose," Pinochle Charlie called.

"Rose, stop!" he demanded.

"I warn you, Rose," he said, but spoke now to an empty saloon, where he stood motionless for a moment before turning to his chair.

He sat down in the chair and looked at the bar. He sat for a time without moving and then stretched his arm out on the table and dropped his head on his arm and tried to remember Fanny's song.

When Rosie moved her brood, Pinochle Charlie did not move with them. Rosie learned that he had followed them to Brooklyn, taking a room far out in Gravesend where he became a bookmaker, but she did not tell the children. Rosie plunged into the real estate business, leaving her children in the care of a housekeeper during the day.

Carolyn remembers that she and Fanny were on the stoop in front of the St. Mark's Avenue house one day, when Pinochle Charlie came around the corner. She remembers that Fanny saw him first, offering a wild, ecstatic scream to the Brooklyn skies as she hurled herself at Pinochle Charlie.

Who dropped the packages he carried to the sidewalk while Fanny held him with both hands, her skinny arms around his middle.

Now Carolyn was upon him, the pair holding and kissing their father whom they had not seen for months, until he straightened up, laughing, to tell them how beautiful they were.

"I grew," Fanny announced.

"I grew too," Carolyn declared.

"You are both very beautiful," Pinochle Charlie told them. "You are my beautiful daughters."

"Me too," Fanny said. "Do you want to hear me sing, Daddy?"

"Of course I want to hear you sing. I want to hear Carolyn sing. And I want you to show me your presents."

"Presents!" Fanny shrieked.

And, "Where?" Carolyn demanded, as Pinochle Charlie bent to pick up the packages on the sidewalk. He held the packages and led them to the stoop, where he sat while the girls tore at the paper wrappings.

There was a doll for each. Twin, beautiful dolls, as big as babies, with long blonde curls, and white silk dresses, and blue silk sashes, and black patent-leather shoes. They had tiny pink hands and creamy white skin, and Pinochle Charlie told Fanny that her doll's name was Baby Annie.

"Baby Annie," Fanny repeated reverently.

"Carolyn's doll is named Baby Jane," Pinochle Charlie said, as his daughters held their dolls close to them.

Until Fanny saw the other two packages and reached for one. "Another doll!" she said, but her father shook his head.

"These are drums for Phil and Lew," he said. "Where are my sons?"

"I'll get them," Fanny said. She sprang from the stoop, and set off down St. Mark's Avenue, holding Baby Annie tightly.

"Phil!" she screamed, and "Lew! Lew, Daddy's home!" she screamed.

She saw a friend and screamed: "My Daddy's home!" She announced it to shopkeepers and shoppers and friends of her mother and strangers on the street. She found Lew and held him with one hand, held the doll with the other, as both searched for Phil until they found him.

Each son had a drum. A big, red-painted, boom-boom-boom-booming drum that he pounded in front of the house while Fanny sang and waltzed with her doll and Carolyn sat happily beside her father until the sun had dropped behind the buildings and Pinochle Charlie rose from the stoop, brushing the dust from his trousers.

"Have we had fun?" he asked his children.

Who watched him carefully, the drums silent, the singing finished, the laughter ended.

"Have we?" he asked, smiling at them.

They nodded, watching him.

"You'll have to get ready for supper," he said. "Your mother will be home soon."

"Aren't you hungry?" Fanny asked.

"I have already had my supper."

"When?" Fanny asked.

"Oh, before I came."

"You could watch us," Fanny said, holding the doll by one patent-leather shoe.

"But I have to go now, Fanny."

"Why?" she asked.

"I have an appointment."

"When is your appointment?" she asked.

"It is now."

"Why?"

"Come kiss your father good-bye," he said, kneeling before his children.

Carolyn kissed him first. Carolyn and then Phil and last Lew.

But Fanny stood apart, holding her doll by its shoe until Pinochle Charlie came to her, bending to kiss the top of her head, before backing away, smiling, and waving his hand; walking backward for a time, until he turned without warning, hurrying to the corner and disappearing from sight.

Phil picked up his drum from the stoop and he walked into the house. Carolyn held her doll and followed him. Lew picked up his drum and he walked into the house. But Fanny dropped her doll, her Baby Annie, on the stoop and began to walk to the corner. She walked slowly and then she quickened her steps. She walked quickly and then she began to run.

Running to Vanderbilt Avenue where she stopped to look.

Did not see him and ran for the trolley stop. Did not see him and retraced her route, looking in each saloon, but could not find Pinochle Charlie.

Nor could Rosie find Fanny. When she had returned from the day's business, and fed her children, and sent Phil to find his sister, and waited for his return without Fanny, Rosie ordered the others to bed.

She sat alone in the kitchen until nearly midnight when Fanny came home. "Your supper," Rosie said, and led her daughter to the table, where she had propped Baby Annie against the sugar bowl.

She didn't ask Fanny where she had been. She didn't ask why she had been away so late. She didn't order her daughter to wash her hands. She set food before Fanny and watched her eat and didn't insist that the child eat more.

For a time Fanny pecked at her food and then she reached for Baby Annie and slid off her chair. "I'm going to sleep," Fanny said, holding her doll.

"All right," Rosie said.

Fanny was nearly out of the kitchen when Rosie said: "Do you want to kiss me good night?"

Fanny turned. She walked to her mother and lifted her face. She let her mother kiss her cheek. "Good night, darling," Rosie said.

"Good night," Fanny said.

"Go to bed," Rosie said gently.

Fanny nodded. She started for the door. "Sleep well," Rosie said, as Fanny walked across the kitchen.

"Sleep well, darling," Rosie said, in the empty room, as she lifted Fanny's plate from the table.

In her apartment Carolyn moved her hand over her eyes. "He came back now and then," she said. "Pinochle Charlie would come to see us. Always with presents, and always during the day, when Mom was away on business. That's when he'd come: handsome and tall and dressed like the king of Rumania. Oh, he was gallant, Pinochle Charlie. We would beg him to stay home with us. All except Fanny. After that first time, whenever he came she would leave; she would disappear after a few minutes. I don't know why. She would get her present and take it in the house and go out the back door. Not us: not Phil and Lew and me. We would just plead with him to stay, but he never did. Never came home to live."

Carolyn crossed the room to a framed picture of Fanny taken a dozen years ago, lifting it from the end-table on which it rested. She turned, holding the picture up as a newsboy displays his paper.

"You can see the resemblance, can't you?" Carolyn asked, a woman of medium height with graying hair. "We were very similar. Very similar. I was on the stage too, you know. Oh, certainly. Once Fanny and I applied for burlesque in the old Bryant Hall on Sixth Avenue and 42nd Street. The man said: 'We'll take you,' pointing at me. I said: 'How about my sister?' He said he just wanted me, so I told him: 'No sister, no me.'

"I suppose my brother, Phil, was the only one of us who wasn't theatrically inclined, but Fanny was the one who made something of herself. Do you know why? Because she had ambition. Her ambition was the biggest part of Fanny."

✡ 3 ✡

IDA CANTOR: *"She Liked to Talk About the Old Days."*

I N any national popularity contest Ida Cantor would be a cinch to finish ahead of Bess Truman. Ahead of Bess, ahead of Margaret, and maybe ahead of Betty Grable. The white-haired woman, who is as slim as any of her five daughters, as chic as Valentina, and as without pretense as Sam Levenson, is probably the best-known mother in the world. On a tri-umphal journey to Israel a few years ago, Ida was startled to see the crowds that gathered about her and her famous hus-band, who is perhaps responsible for saving the lives of more refugees than any single human being through his fund-raising activities.

"Who are they looking at?" she asked Eddie as the crowds stared at them.

"At us, Ida."

"Why?" she asked.

She really didn't understand what all the shouting was about during that trip. It seemed to her no more than hu-mane that her husband should do what he could on behalf of the struggling state and the thousands who sought refuge there. He'd been doing it for years; for any cause, and for people of any creed.

In the Hollywood apartment that Fanny decorated for the Cantors after they sold the big Beverly Hills house, Ida was knitting a baby's cap for her youngest daughter, Janet. Her daughter, Edna, was visiting that evening, since Eddie was entertaining in an Army hospital upstate.

"You'll be lucky if you *ever* see Eddie," Ida said. "I never see him. He can't say no, that man. If they asked him to play a benefit in Iceland, he'd leave tomorrow.

"I was never close to Fanny until we all came to California," Ida continued. "Fanny couldn't even recall me from the days that Eddie was with her in the Follies. I never hung around the stage door. I never used to talk to Fanny. Out here we were close because she liked to be with people from the old days. She would come to the big house and bring her own supper, a sandwich or something. 'Don't fuss with me,' she'd say, 'I've got mine.' So it wound up that she was sitting at the table and eating ours. To tell the truth she tired me out when she came to my house."

Daughter Edna interrupted. "The reason she tired Mother," Edna said, "was because she and Mother, when they had a conversation, talked at the same time and neither one ever listened to the other one."

"Listen," Ida said, "I liked Fanny like a sister. I know definitely that she was very fond of me, and wanted to be with us a lot. She found in our family the same honesty which she had. There were a lot of people she knew who were phonies, pretending they were something they weren't. The kids opened up with Fanny. She would talk to them. She would go to the icebox with them and chew on a leg of chicken. Then off would come the shoes. Then she would be completely relaxed. Then she would start talking about the old days."

When she had won every amateur night in Brooklyn,
Fanny began to cross the East River into Manhattan. She
won contests as far uptown as the Harlem Opera House on
125th Street. Three and four nights a week she was out winning contests and every night she was badgering her mother
to move to New York.

To Rosie Borach, who had turned her back on love for
Pinochle Charlie's eighty dollars a week, Fanny's bring-home
pay was a convincing argument. Soon she and her brood occupied an apartment in uptown New York.

Fanny was rapidly losing her amateur status, and wanted
to break into real show business. For a time she worked as
pianist, ticket-taker, and sweeper in a motion-picture theater
on Third Avenue and 83rd Street. She had long ago promised
John Brice, a hearty, Irish friend of the family, that she
would one day take his name as hers. In applying for the
job, she called herself Fanny Brice. She was done with
Borach forever. Rosie, who considered her separation from
Pinochle Charlie a lifetime arrangement, followed suit, as
did the other children.

For her varied chores at the movie house, Fanny received
eight dollars a week. But for the gawky girl of fourteen it
was only a way-station. Carolyn recalls that Fanny considered her job at the nickelodeon as required training for the
future. She was not unlike the West Point plebe who regards
his hazing as necessary indoctrination for the office of Chief
of Staff that he expects to occupy half a century hence.

One night a few weeks later Fanny read an advertisement
in the theatrical section of one of the newspapers calling for
chorus girls the following day. It bore the name of George M.
Cohan and Sam Harris, who were about as familiar to Fanny
then as are Martin and Lewis to an Eskimo. Fanny didn't
care who was in need of chorus girls; she just knew she
wanted to be one.

"But I'm thinking to myself," she wrote in her notes, " 'If I don't get *that* job, I don't want to lose the job in the movie house.' That night I say to Carolyn: 'You call the nickelodeon in the morning and tell them I'm sick.'

" 'You're not sick,' she says.

" 'I know I'm not sick. Just tell them I'm sick.'

" 'That's a lie,' she says.

" 'I know it's a lie,' I told her. 'I don't want to lose my job in case I don't get hired at this other place.'

" 'I won't do it,' Carolyn says.

"So I told my Mom to call. Mom did it. She had brains."

While Rosie called the nickelodeon the next morning to announce that her daughter was in bed with a high fever, Fanny was on her way to the offices of Cohan and Harris.

Taking her place at the end of the line, Fanny made her way slowly, pausing at last before a young man who looked at her casually and said: "Name?"

"Fanny Brice. Mr. Cohan, I can . . ."

"I'm not Mr. Cohan. Eighteen dollars a week," he said. "Leave your name and address with the girl," pointing at the far end of the room.

Fanny didn't move. "Mr. Harris, I can sing," she said.

"I'm not Mr. Harris. They'll hear you at rehearsal. Leave your name with the girl."

"Mister, I've got my music right here," Fanny said, offering the sheets.

The young man took her arm and firmly pulled Fanny across the room to his assistant, where he left her.

Fanny was told that she would hear from them, and that night, reporting the day's glorious event to Carolyn, she could not understand why she had not been allowed to sing.

"I'll bet he would have given me twenty-five if he'd heard me," Fanny said.

In the two weeks that followed Fanny could not keep

food on her stomach. She could not sleep the night through without waking at least once, sitting up in bed, and staring for several minutes. She could not believe in the integrity of the United States postal service. She was furious when Lew suggested that she might have thought up the Cohan and Harris story while sweeping out the theater.

But she could work at the nickelodeon. There was the eight dollars to consider, and Fanny considered it.

When the postcard arrived summoning Fanny to rehearsal at the Amsterdam Roof on 42nd Street, Fanny quit her job immediately. There followed several days of song rehearsal. Fanny seemed to be getting along all right except for Mr. Cohan's repeated warnings that she must shut her mouth when the other girls shut their mouths and not linger over the last note like a lovesick coyote. Fanny had told her family that once Mr. Cohan heard her sing he would then and there assign her a solo and raise her salary to twenty-five dollars.

After the singing satisfied Mr. Cohan, he began directing the dances. For Fanny, who had never lifted a foot except to kick a can, and who, actually, didn't know her left from her right, this was something less than a lark. She soon devised her own method of distinguishing between her feet. She knew that she wrote with her right hand. By concentrating on her right arm, which she moved in a continuous circle, and remembering that she wrote with that hand, she could follow Mr. Cohan's orders. If he said right foot, she moved the limb below the swinging arm. If he said left, it was the one below the arm at her side.

George M. Cohan got one look at Miss Perpetual Motion up on the stage and stopped the rehearsal. "You," he said. "You with the St. Vitus's dance. Back to the kitchen."

What followed were not the phony tears of Coney Island, nor those of the wrapper who had a blind father. She wept with the heartbreak of all those thousands of unknown young men and young women who stand for their brief moment on a bare stage before the rehearsal lamp, looking out beyond the darkened footlights into the darkened theater, seeing neither director, nor producer, nor cast, but the seats full, the starched shirtfronts gleaming, the diamonds sparkling, the critics applauding, the audience rising to its feet in an uncontrolled passion for the new star born before their privileged eyes, bowing again and again in humble acknowledgment . . . until reality returns in the person of a stagehand who directs them to the stage door.

Alone in the dressing-room on the floor below, Fanny wept herself into exhaustion. She bathed her face with cold water and sat down. Many years later she wrote: "I had no place to go. At the nickelodeon they got another girl, and at home they think I'm the new Duse. I sit there, I don't know, maybe three hours, maybe four.

"Then I hear somebody coming. I spit on my eyes. I know they are all red from before, and I start crying quick. Well, in walks Cohan and I'm wailing like a funeral. 'Now, now, little girl,' he says, 'you've never been on the stage. You can't dance.'

" 'No,' I say, 'but I can sing.' I'm flooding the room with tears.

" 'Well,' Cohan tells me, 'we need dancers for this show. But there's another show in rehearsal and maybe they can use you there.'

"So he sends me to this other place and it's a saloon on Broadway, across the street from the Winter Garden. In the back they have all the tables piled on each other. Rose Green, Mitzi Green's mother, is in charge. When I compare what I see with the Amsterdam Roof, I think: 'Uh-uh, not me.'

"But I see the steps the dancers are doing and I think of

the steps Cohan is rehearsing. I decide I'll learn something about dancing. So I go home and tell my Mom that all the girls had to put on tights and Cohan said I was too thin. She buys that and I'm looking to learn dancing. So in a few days I hear about a woman putting a new show on tour and she'll take beginners and teach them to dance."

Fanny asked that Rosie accompany her. Carolyn, understandably envious of the attention her sister was getting in the house, decided she too would apply.

When the three presented themselves before the female impresario, Rosie launched into a rather overblown recital of Fanny's accomplishments. "Also," Rosie said, "she wants to learn how to dance."

The woman was in perfect accord with Rosie's wishes. While Carolyn tugged at Rosie's sleeve, reminding her mother that there were *two* daughters present, the woman said: "I can look at your daughter and see that she's very talented. I certainly will do all I can for you in making her a very great actress and it will cost you $250."

"Can you make her a good actress for twenty-five dollars?" Rosie asked.

"No, no, no, no, no," the woman answered.

Rosie gathered her darlings and made for the door, where the woman stopped her. "Fifty dollars," she said.

"Thirty," offered Rosie.

"Forty."

"Thirty-five."

"Come tomorrow," the woman said.

"How about me, Mom?" Carolyn asked.

"You shut up."

Upon arriving for her dancing lessons the next day, Fanny was surprised to find herself alone with the woman. The child had expected a studio full of actors and actresses. That day the woman had a splitting headache. The following day she left word that she was buying a song for Fanny. This went on for a week, until Fanny said: "My mother gave you thirty-five dollars and she wants to know when you are going to teach me?"

"I'm so glad you reminded me," the woman answered, and began to measure Fanny for a costume. This done, she dismissed her student until the next day, when Fanny found her drunk.

"Yeah?" said the woman, looking at her awkward student. "And whaddya want?"

"I came for my lesson," Fanny said.

"What lesson?" asked that amnesic alcoholic. She began to move on a bias, circling Fanny. "What lesson? What lesson?" she demanded.

"My acting lesson."

"Who says you're an actress? Tell me that," the woman said. "Tell me that, tell me that," she insisted as Fanny sprang forward to save her from collapse.

Leading the woman to a chair, Fanny said: "Don't you remember? My mother and sister were with me."

"Huh?"

"My mother and sister. You said you would teach me how to act."

The woman swayed in the chair with the regularity of a metronome. "Please teach me something," Fanny pleaded.

Suddenly Fanny's instructor sat bolt upright. She leveled a trembling finger at Fanny. "Thirty-five dollars," she said, her face contorting contemptuously before she spit on the bare floor.

"That's me," Fanny said hopefully.

The woman rose from the chair. "C'mon," she ordered, leading Fanny to a door across the room. Opening it and holding the doorknob as if it were a life preserver, she waved wildly at the interior of the closet she had exposed. "Bring it out," she said.

As Fanny stepped to the doorway, she saw two eyes looking up at her with such malevolence that she very nearly fainted dead away.

"Bring it out, bring it out," the woman said.

Fanny wanted to run. She wanted to escape. She wanted to give up the theater for life, but something . . . something made her reach inside. Her hand emerged with an alligator hide that, judging from its moldiness and odor, must have been stripped from the carcass of one of Noah's passengers. She stood before the woman, holding the gaping, toothless jaws of the hide at arms' length, the gleaming eyes on a level with hers.

"Now," the woman said, swaying like a sapling in the wind, "put it on, put it on, put it on."

Fanny, who was in a semihypnotic state induced by the inebriated instructor and the glowing eyes of the alligator, pulled the putrid pelt over her head and stood before the teacher, as upright as a pelican.

"Down!" the woman ordered. "You're an alligator! Get down, you alligator!"

Fanny fell to the floor.

"Swim!"

Fanny threshed wildly.

"Talk!"

Fanny growled.

"Louder!"

Fanny growled ferociously.

"Alligator! Alligator!" the woman commanded.

Fanny began to snarl.

"More!"

Fanny snarled louder, as the woman stepped over her

and made her own way to the chair, where she fell into a deep sleep.

After a time Fanny peered out from the jaws. The woman's snores filled the room. Fanny crawled slowly to the door, leaped out of the alligator skin, and ran from the building. Never, until the last months of her life, could she understand that day's events. It was a day of black magic for her always.

Fanny ran home to Rosie, to whom it was apparent that she should meet with the woman once more.

But as she and Fanny entered the studio on the following day, they saw it filled with people. Somehow the woman had sobered up, found a script and a cast. Fanny was given three lines to read. The show was to open a cross-country tour in Hazelton, Pennsylvania, the following week.

When the woman dismissed them, Rosie, holding Fanny's hand, began to edge toward the door across the room. She had been a victim of Fanny's imagination before. While the woman busied herself with other members of the cast, Rosie reached the closet, looked about her carefully, put her fingers on the doorknob, and opened the door.

The alligator's eyes glared at her.

Rosie slammed the door. Leaving Fanny to her art, she hurried home with bright plans for buying several buildings on the upper West Side of Manhattan with Fanny's enormous earnings in the theater.

Holding such schemes for the future, Rosie was hardly prepared for her daughter's homecoming within a month.

Fanny appeared at the apartment one Sunday night, gaunt, weary, very nearly famished. After watching Fanny eat steadily for more than an hour, Rosie made bold to ask for enlightenment.

Pausing briefly between long periods of chewing, Fanny explained that the show had indeed opened in Hazelton, where she was required to help clean the theater each day before the performance. She was also required to administer to the hunger and physiological functions of the leading lady's tiny dog, a mangy mutt, improbably named Sunday. Her hotel bill was paid and she received twenty-five cents a day for food. Since she had to share that sum with Sunday, and since that animal was apparently host to a tapeworm long enough to girdle the world, Fanny had not been eating very high on the hog. In fact, Fanny offered, she hadn't eaten a square meal since leaving home.

Yet she would have remained, even though the woman had introduced Fanny to a pawnbroker who relieved her of the diamond ring Rosie had given her, and even though the money went rapidly for the impresario's gin, had not that female Fagin decided to jump the show. It was only because the girl had followed the woman to the railroad station late one night, boarded the same train, and threatened to call a cop unless she paid Fanny's fare, that Rosie saw her daughter here.

"And now?" Rosie demanded.

"Now—I'll find another show," Fanny said.

She said it as casually and as matter-of-factly as the prizefighter who begins training once more a few days after having been knocked out.

The credulous kid had disappeared forever some time during those lonely, hungry days in Hazelton. The trembling little girl who had stood terrified on the stage of Keeney's Theatre was gone. The sister Lew Brice had called a "weeper," whom George M. Cohan had found sobbing in the dressing-room of the Amsterdam, had grown up.

Fanny Brice was in show business to stay.

✵ 4 ✵

TRIXIE WILSON: *"You Couldn't Use the Word 'Thanks.'"*

THERE is a tired, tiny diner that lies within the shadow of the Hollywood Bowl in the land of milk and madness. The waitress is tired. The cat on the counter is weary. The patrons resemble finalists in a walkathon.

Except for Trixie Wilson. She sat on a stool, both hands cooling on a glass of orange juice, smiling while she looked down into the liquid as though she could see within it all the days of her life with Fanny.

"She got me into the Follies," Trixie said. "Nobody but her, and not my talent, either. Ziegfeld was casting his '14 Follies and by then Fanny was a big star. She was the biggest. You could not have seen Fanny Brice on the stage and forgotten her, not as long as you lived.

"Well, she invited Flo to her apartment one night. He liked a home-cooked meal. Fanny could cook like nobody cooked. She made him a Hungarian goulash from her mother's recipe. There were just the three of us: Fanny, Flo, and me. I never saw a man eat like that. She fed him until he couldn't move, and then she said I was one of the best danc-

ers she'd ever seen. She'd never seen me work, but Flo
signed me for that year. I was in the '15 Follies, too.

"But you won't read that in her memoirs. Not a word
about what she did for people. I'm alone now. Since Fanny
died I'm all alone. These last years, I wouldn't see Fanny for
six months, nor talk to her on the phone more than once a
month. But I always knew, deep, deep inside of me that if I
ever was really up against it, Fanny would take care of me.
God knows she did it enough times.

"But you couldn't thank her. She'd say: 'None of that crap,
kid.' If you kept it up, she'd throw something at you. She
threw a glass of water at me once when I tried to thank her
for paying my dues in the Screen Extras Guild.

"You don't want to hear any of this, do you? You want to
hear about the early days."

At that time, Trixie explained, Hurtig & Seamon were to
burlesque what the House of Morgan was to banking. They
were burlesque. On the train coming home from Hazelton,
Fanny planned a frontal attack on Joe Hurtig, and the morning after she had eaten her first complete meal in a month
she was being shown into his office.

Reminding him that she had won an amateur night contest at his Harlem Opera House, she gave him a rapid run-
down on her theatrical past. It approximated the combined
activities of Sarah Bernhardt, Eleanora Duse, and Eva Tan-
guay. Joe Hurtig hired her for the chorus of his Transatlantic Burlesque, which was then in rehearsal preparing to take
to the road.

You must understand that in those years burlesque was as
daring as a church bingo party. The strip tease was as unknown as twilight sleep. In most cities the girls would not
wear tights, and in all cities they wore stockings.

Again Fanny was plagued by her inability to dance. The
director told Hurtig that either she left the chorus or he

left the show. But Hurtig had listened to Fanny sing. He gave her a song that she was to render from a box seat while a blue light played on her.

Another girl might have been grateful for being kept on with the show. Not Fanny. After every rehearsal she had gone home to regale Rosie with glowing accounts of a production that was being built entirely around Fanny.

While the director glared at her, she hold Hurtig that she wasn't satisfied with his decision. She wanted to be seen on the stage, not in a box in the theater. As she argued her anger mounted and, as her spleen rose, she looked about her for something to push into the director's face. Hurtig, perhaps blessed with a sixth sense that warned him his theater was about to be turned into a vacant lot, hurriedly ordered the director to shift Fanny to the back of the stage. She would be with the girls, Hurtig told Fanny, but in the last row. Taking her place in much the same spirit with which a relief pitcher occupies the bullpen, Fanny continued rehearsal.

The night before the Transatlantic Burlesque departed for its opening date in Birmingham, Alabama, Rosie packed her daughter's suitcase. Fanny stripped the closets of all the chemises, bloomers, and brassières in the Brice apartment. When Rosie asked if Fanny intended to establish an undergarment emporium in the Southern city, she explained that, since she was the star of the show, she was required to make several changes of costume during the performance. Certainly Fanny could not be expected to wear the same bloomers through an entire performance. Somewhat mystified, but dedicated to art and its financial returns, Rosie packed the unmentionables.

Arrived in Birmingham, Fanny looked about her for a means of breaking out from her beachhead in the last row. Selecting a front-line chorus girl whose bloomers and bras-

sière inventory was considerably less than her colleagues',
Fanny ostentatiously displayed her own swollen stock.

Trixie Wilson laughed aloud, startling the sleepy patrons
of the diner, as she remembered what followed. "Fanny
gave this girl one each—bloomers, chemise, brassière—as payment for a week's dancing lessons. After a couple of days,
the girl had enough. Then Fanny gave the girl most of her
salary for the week. The town was full of bananas, so Fanny
had bananas for breakfast, lunch, and dinner.

"But she picked up some steps. When the first girl wouldn't
teach her any more, Fanny picked another one. And she
started to make up to the dance director, who traveled with
the show, telling him he was the greatest thing since the
electric light.

"And she's winning Chorus Girls' night all the while.
That's an added attraction once a week after the regular
show. All the chorus girls do specialties for a ten-dollar
prize, and Fanny is the winner. She's buying the director
striped shirts and cigars the size of a baseball bat. Every
time she sees him, Fanny breaks out into a dance. Of course
she continues her lessons with whoever is hard up for a
chemise or a bra," Billie said, ordering another orange juice.

In St. Louis Fanny was moved forward into the second
row. When the show reached Chicago, she was kicking in
the first line. Although Fanny had exhausted her brassières,
she had only begun her campaign.

The soubrette, or leading lady, of the Transatlantic Burlesque was the stage manager's wife, a kind of Pauline Bun-
yan, with legs like barrel staves, and a bosom to which she
could have easily clasped the complete roster of the Notre
Dame football squad. For weeks the stringbean Fanny had
been oohing and aahing over this Amazon, inundating her
with compliments while carefully studying her role and se-
cretly praying for a mysterious disease to strike her.

In Chicago the soubrette appeared for a performance with a tiny boil behind her ear. Each night Fanny watched the bump as a farmer watches his crops. During the last show in the Windy City, it was the color of a beet and not much smaller. Fanny hovered about the soubrette's dressing-room, prepared to save the show, when the behemoth appeared at the door with a pink ribbon over her ear. Fanny, asking solicitously after her health, followed her as far as the wings.

From Chicago they moved to Cincinnati, Joe Hurtig's home town. The producer was in the city and had invited a great many of his friends to the opening-night show. Shortly before curtain time, the soubrette fainted in her husband's arms backstage. She was eased to the floor while the boil erupted.

In the midst of the confusion behind the curtain, Joe Hurtig appeared, demanding to know why the show hadn't started. Seeing him, Fanny bounced forward to announce that she knew the stricken soubrette's part as well as she knew her own name. By this time, Hurtig would have let the Siamese Twins play the lead in order to get the curtain up. He ordered Fanny to get with it, before returning to his guests.

"She got away with it," Trixie Wilson said. "You never saw a performance like it. Think of a one-man show with thirty people on stage. Fanny rolled her eyes, she winked, she kicked, she sang loud enough to wake the whole state of Ohio. She was all over that stage. They brought her back for seven encores. She would have given seventy but Hurtig kept the curtain down and told the stage manager to fit Fanny with the leading lady's costumes."

At the start of the following season, wanting to get out of burlesque, Fanny appeared at the casting office of Max Spiegel, who was producing what he termed a musical comedy, called *College Girls*.

Spiegel, who had heard her sing in Transatlantic Burlesque, asked Fanny if she did a specialty. Fanny assured him she had a specialty to end all specialties. When Spiegel asked Fanny what salary she expected, she replied that with her specialty she would work for twenty-five dollars a week. Spiegel hired her immediately.

After a week of rehearsals, Spiegel called the cast together. "I want all you specialty people to go on Friday night in a big benefit show in Arverne, Long Island. I'll be there watching so I'll know where to place you in the show."

As she listened to Spiegel, Fanny became faint with fear. "Well, here goes my job," she wrote long afterward. "I have no specialty. And I ran right to Irving Berlin. 'Oh, Irving,' I said, grabbing him, 'I've got a job in a show, and when Spiegel signed me up he asked me if I did a specialty. I told him yes, thinking that was the way I could get the job. I never thought he really wanted me to do one. And I have to sing something because I've got to do this benefit in Arverne or I'm finished.' Irving took me in the back room and he played 'Sadie Salome' and 'Grizzly Bear.' The first song was a Jewish comedy-song, and the second was a ragtime song. So of course Irving sang 'Sadie Salome' with a Jewish accent. I had never had any idea of doing a song with a Jewish accent. I didn't even understand Jewish, couldn't talk a word of it. But, I thought, if that's the way Irving sings it, that's the way I'll sing it. I learned them both in an hour, and the explanation for that is simple: youth and ambition.

"Of course," Fanny continued, "I came home and told my mother about the benefit—and what was I going to wear? She said: 'I better wash your white sailor suit.' It was linen. 'I'll put a little extra starch in it,' she said.

"At Arverne, every big star on Broadway was there. It was a big affair for some hospital. All the society girls were out

Fanny and Rosie when Fanny was a Ziegfeld star.

The Brices at the turn of the century.
LEFT TO RIGHT: Fanny, Lew, Phil, and Carolyn.

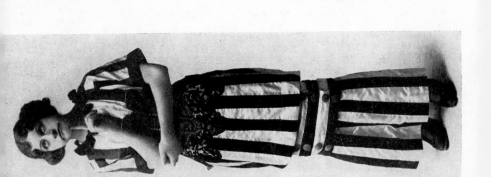

Fanny in burlesque.

front selling roses, getting money every which way they could for the benefit.

"Well, I came out and did 'Sadie Salome' for the first time ever doing a Jewish accent. And that starched sailor suit is killing me. And it's gathering you know where, and I'm trying to squirm it away, and singing and smiling, and the audience is loving it. They think it's an act I'm doing, so as long as they're laughing, I keep it up. They start to throw roses at me. I did 'Grizzly Bear' for them, and I'm still with that creeping sailor. More roses. I was a hit, I guess."

The following day, Spiegel called Fanny into his office and offered her an eight-year contract. The seventeen-year-old comedienne listened as Spiegel promised her a ten-dollar-a-week raise each year, reminding Fanny that in the last twelve months of her contract with him she would be making ninety-five dollars a week. Spiegel told her to take the contract home and have her mother sign it.

"My mother can't write," Fanny said, thinking of the ninety-five dollars each week, and worried lest Spiegel change his mind while he was waiting for the document. "I can write."

"Sign it," Spiegel said, extending a pen. Fanny signed.

It did not take Fanny long to learn that *College Girls* was just another burlesque show. But there was the contract she'd signed. Thinking of the almost-hundred-dollars-weekly she would soon be earning, the young woman plunged into rehearsals with her customary zeal.

The showed opened in Scranton. *College Girls* was a great hit, and Fanny Brice an even bigger hit. In New York, Spiegel read the notices and moved Fanny's contract from his desk to his office safe.

In the tiny diner below the Hollywood Bowl, the shadows had reached the mottled, flyspecked ceiling. Trixie Wilson slid off the stool, hugging her bare arms against the sudden, late-afternoon drop in temperature which is a southern California peculiarity.

"I haven't talked that much since the last time I saw Fanny," she said. She opened the screen door and stepped out to the sidewalk, watching the going-home traffic in the street. "Maybe all this talk will bring me luck. I think I'll go out to Gardena [a gambling suburb of Los Angeles] tonight for a little poker."

She turned away, and then turned back once more. "I suppose you know," Trixie said, "that it was while she was in *College Girls* that she married that barber. That Frank White."

5

FANNY: "*Nobody Ever Asked Me.*"

IN 1909, we were in Albany with *College Girls* and my roommate was Clara Hendricks," Fanny wrote in her notes. What followed actually began in Schenectady, but Fanny always believed it was Albany.

"One night after the show," Fanny continued, "Clara says: 'I want you to meet a man I was introduced to here in town. He's so good-looking and nice. He asked about you.'

" 'Me?' I said.

" 'Yes, silly,' Clara said. 'About you. He said that if you would come along, then he would take us both to supper.'

"So I said why not, after all he saves me the price of a meal. She introduced him. Frank White. He had a barbershop in the hotel there in Albany and he had one in Springfield, Mass. Well, he took us to a nice café. He was dressed in a checked suit and he smelled good of bay rum. He looked like William Farnum in pictures: brown, wavy hair, and long eyelashes, the kind I'd want to vomit if I saw them now. But then I thought he was worldly and smart, because he ordered our meals.

"Now comes the next night and he wants to take me to supper alone. And I go alone with him. It goes on like that.

After about a week we are back in the same café as the first night. And when we are through eating, he takes my hand. And he said: 'Let's get married.'

" 'Oh,' I said. 'Oh, I don't know,' because I don't know what else I should say.

" 'Would you like to be married?' he asks.

" 'Maybe I would,' I said, 'and maybe I wouldn't.'

" 'What kind of an answer is that?' he wants to know.

" 'Well, it's my answer.'

" 'Do you love me?' he asks.

" 'Do you love *me*?'

" 'I love you very much,' he said, and bends down to kiss my hand. And the mustache tickles my hand, and now he's mad because I'm laughing.

"So he says: 'You don't love me.'

" 'Sure I love you,' I say. Christ, I loved everybody in those days.

" 'Then that settles it,' he says. 'Let's get married.'

" 'I don't want to get married tonight,' I said.

" 'What do you want?' he asks me.

" 'I want some pie,' I said, because I didn't have a dessert and I wanted a dessert.

"So he orders the pie and while I'm eating it, he tells me to think it over about the marriage.

"When I get back to our room, I tell Clara: 'Frank White wants me to marry him.'

" 'I think he's nice,' Clara says. 'Why don't you marry him?'

"Well, the show moves to Springfield, Mass., and there is Frank White. Now he starts again with the marriage, and I say all right, I'll do it. It was as screwy as that. I know now that I wasn't stuck on him. I didn't think I was stuck on him then.

"So the next day he knocks on the door. 'Come on,' he said,

'we're going to get married.' He had the license and an open barouche waiting downstairs. We're walking down the steps of the hotel and I say: 'Why are we getting married now?'

" 'Because I ordered a big dinner for the whole company in the hotel. We are going to have a big wedding-dinner after the show,' he says.

" 'I ought to call my mother,' I said.

" 'You can call her later,' he said.

" 'Well, I don't feel so good,' I told him.

"He takes me out to the open barouche. 'What's the matter with you?' he wants to know.

" 'How dare you ask me such a question?' I tell him, and I drop my eyes.

" 'You will feel fine after the wedding, darling,' he says.

" 'Who are you calling darling?" I asked him.

" 'My own sweet wife,' he says.

" 'You be careful what you say,' I told him. 'I'm not your wife.'

" 'But you will be soon,' he says. 'We're on the way to the minister's house.'

"Holy Christ, now I am in it. I see the people on the street, and I'm thinking: 'Maybe one of them will help me. Maybe I'll yell something and make a big fight.' I'm thinking: 'My mother doesn't even know. I shouldn't be doing this.' But how can I back out? He's ordered dinner for the cast. If I don't get married, he'll cancel the dinner and the cast will never talk to me. Take away a meal from actors, they'll lynch you.

"So . . . I have to go through with it.

"Now we're married, and the dinner is over, but I won't let him in my room.

"He's standing in front of the door, and I'm standing in front of the door. 'Well, Frank,' I say, 'get a good night's sleep and I'll see you tomorrow.'

" 'We're sleeping together,' he says.

" 'Oh, no, we're not. You have to go somewhere else.'

" 'Where?' he asks me.

" 'I don't know where. You're a barber. You know those things, so good night.'

" 'I'm your husband,' he says.

" 'Now, Frank,' I say, 'it's been a hard day and tomorrow is a matinee, so go away.'

" 'Aren't you a virgin?' he wants to know.

"The only reason I'm a virgin is that nobody ever asked me.

" 'Of course I'm a virgin,' I say, 'but you can't have anything to do with me until the show ends its run.' And the reason I told him that is because I heard that you can't work afterward, and Frank White isn't going to interfere with my work.

"He says: 'Well, let me in the room and I'll sleep on a chair.'

"Well, I was dumb, but I wasn't that dumb. 'Now, Frank,' I said, 'you have to go away now, or I will call the manager. Do you want me to call the manager?'

" 'You have to kiss me good night,' he said.

" 'All right,' I said. 'Bend your head.'

" 'Bend my *head!*' he said.

" 'That's right,' I say. Because I am not going to let that mustache tickle me again, because I will start laughing and I know that will make him mad. So he bends his head, and I kissed him.

"So the show goes into New York and he goes back to Albany. I take Clara Hendricks home to stay with me and she tells my mother I married a barber.

"My mother asks me a lot of questions and she says: 'You had nothing to do with him, so I'm going to annul the marriage.' I said all right. I didn't care.

"Now we're playing Philadelphia. One night I come out of the stage door and Frank White is there. He grabs my wrist.

" 'You're my wife,' he says, 'and you have to come with me, or I'll call the police.'

"How did I know? I thought maybe you have to go with your husband. Maybe the police can do something to you if you don't. So he drags me to my hotel, makes me pack, and takes me to his hotel. On the way we pass a fruit stand and I see a pineapple.

" 'I want a pineapple,' I tell him. He buys it. The pineapple cost three cents.

"We get to his room and I put on my nightgown. It came from Siegel & Cooper on 14th Street and cost thirty cents.

"Now I got it on. I'm in bed and he's coming toward the bed.

" 'I want some pineapple,' I tell him.

"He cuts me a slice. It's good pineapple. I eat real slow and he takes off his bathrobe.

" 'I want another slice,' I tell him.

"He cuts me a real big piece. While I'm eating slow, he cuts himself a piece and begins to gobble it down. Now it's a race. He eats fast, and I eat slow, but he wins. Pretty soon there's no pineapple.

"I never saw Frank White again. I don't even know what happened to him. I went back to New York when the show closed. My mother tried to get it annulled, but I was three months over eighteen years old when I got married, so it couldn't be done.

"I forgot about Frank White altogether and a couple of years later I got a divorce in New York.

"I can't get it through my head. I can't understand it. It was like a dream. I knew so little. I was never even out looking for guys. I wasn't looking for romance or anything.

"Imagine . . . *Albany!*"

EDDIE CANTOR: *"They Were All There: the Whitneys, the Vanderbilts, the Goulds, the Harrimans, and the Astors."*

THERE isn't anybody like Florenz Ziegfeld around today, that's all. Nobody like him and nothing like his Follies. He was a combination of Louis B. Mayer, Sherman Billingsley, Jacques Fath, John Ringling North, Leo Durocher, Mr. John, and Grover Whalen.

He had the best of the talents of each.

He had showmanship, he had zest, he had courage, he had taste, he had flamboyance.

And the Follies!

There was not a dancer or singer, comic or juggler, dog-trainer or sword-swallower, from the Atlantic City Boardwalk to the San Francisco Barbary Coast; from the French Quarter of New Orleans through all the dusty, twisting, back roads leading to every county fair in America, who wouldn't have sold his—or her—soul for a chance at the Follies.

For the annual Follies were . . . they were the New York

Yankees of the theater. They were the best Broadway offered. To get into the Follies was like being knighted or tapped for the Supreme Court. You couldn't buy your way in. The dollar has never meant less to any man than it did to Flo Ziegfeld. The only way you got into the Follies was for Ziegfeld to put you there. It was the top of the mountain for show people. When you made the Follies, you were king of the hill, all right.

"Do you have any idea of what the Follies meant to a performer?" Eddie Cantor demanded. "Opening night in the New Amsterdam on 42nd Street, you played to the best people in the country. The Whitneys, the Vanderbilts, the Goulds, the Harrimans, the Astors, they were all there. Everybody from the Mayor down, or from the Mayor up, was there. We played thirteen weeks in New York and out we went.

"On the road," Cantor continued, "when we came into Pittsburgh to play the National Theatre, or Chicago at the Colonial Theatre, or wherever we played—Philadelphia, Detroit, Cincinnati, Kansas City—we knew as long as we were in that town we would never see an empty seat. We were sold out in advance. Tickets were harder to get than for a World Series. We stayed in the finest hotels, we were invited to the finest homes, people considered it a privilege if we *talked* to them."

Cantor stopped bouncing long enough to submit a rhetorical question. "Do you know what aristocrats are? We were aristocrats in the Follies, mister."

In his Beverly Hills office that day, Cantor looked as much like sixty as does Margaret O'Brien, and in the event of a foot race between the two, sensible betters would have gone with young Banjo Eyes. He was dressed like a University of California sophomore and he looked like one: hair as black, eyes as clear, enthusiasms as intense, and dislikes as passionate. He was young, he was earnest, and he was as zealously devoted to his profession as Thomas Dewey is to his.

"I came to the Follies in 1917," Cantor continued. "When I was with a juggling act, Fanny Brice was already a star. You see, Ziegfeld had the ability to engage the best in each particular field. The best roughhouse comic in the world, without a doubt, was W. C. Fields. The best comedienne, Fanny Brice. The best comedian, Bert Williams. And I guess I had the biggest eyes, so Flo hired me.

"Do you know how I felt to be in a show with Fanny Brice? She was not only the best comedienne of her time, but I will say that Fanny was among the first three funny women of the world at any time.

"There I am at the beginning of the season, my first Follies and Fanny Brice comes over to talk to me."

"Do you dance?" she asked.

"Of course I dance."

"We ought to get together," Fanny said.

"Fine," Eddie said. If she had told him to rob a bank with her, he would have gone out and bought a hammer and chisel.

During rehearsals Fanny said: "You can't dance a lick." But they kept the dance in the show until opening night.

"At last we came to our dance," Cantor said. "Remember, mister, it's my first opening and I'm knocking at the gates. Everything I was or hoped to be I was putting into that performance, and in the middle of it Fanny whispers to me: 'You sonofabitch, you still can't dance.'

"We had to hold each other up, we were laughing so hard. She did that, said what she said, to help me. And she did help me, because I relaxed and lost my fright and my tenseness."

As he went back in time, Cantor remembered Fanny's career as well as his own. She had told him about her bur-

lesque days, and now he recalled her first association with
Ziegfeld.

It seemed to Fanny then that she had never wanted anything except to work for the Great Glorifier. Once when
Helen Ziegfeld, a young woman employed by a song-pub-
lishing firm, saw her perform, she sent a card backstage to
Fanny.

On it was the name of the company and the words: "Please
see me. Miss Ziegfeld."

Fanny immediately wrote "Mr." over the "Miss," put her
thumb over the company's name, and showed it to everybody in the theater, shouting: "Ziegfeld sent me a card. See?
Ziegfeld! He wants to see me!"

Shortly afterward Ziegfeld did want to see Fanny. He had
watched her in *College Girls* at the Columbia Theatre on
Broadway, the first house built for burlesque on the Avenue
of Ambition. Like everybody in show business, Ziegfeld
knew that Max Spiegel had Fanny signed to an exclusive
eight-year contract. Discussing Fanny with Bert Cooper, a
successful agent of the time, Ziegfeld praised her abilities,
deploring the fact that Max Spiegel had her tied up. Cooper,
who knew Fanny well, told Ziegfeld that she was only seventeen, a minor, when she signed the contract.

When Fanny got to the Columbia Theatre the next day,
the stage-door attendant handed her a telegram. It read:
WILL YOU COME TO SEE ME AT YOUR EARLIEST CONVENIENCE.
FLORENZ ZIEGFELD.

Fanny was certain that somebody in the cast of *College
Girls* had sent her the telegram after listening to her story a
few weeks earlier. She telephoned Ziegfeld's office and asked
his secretary: "Did Mr. Ziegfeld send me a telegram? This
is Fanny Brice."

"He certainly did," was the answer. "He wants to see you
as soon as possible."

It was a warm autumn day, and the stage door was open. Fanny had called from a wall telephone just inside the door. She was almost nineteen years old, in perfect health, and possessed of a superb voice, with remarkable lung power. There are no available witnesses to what followed. To those who have heard Fanny speak in what she regarded as *sotto voce*, when, sitting in a movie, she could clear six rows fore and aft within the first reel, the thought of that set of pipes with all the stops out, its owner racing down Broadway to Ziegfeld's office, presents an alarming picture.

Pausing along the route and seizing the arm of anyone who was familiar and of several who were not, to let them in on her secret, Fanny finally reached her rendezvous.

There she immediately lost her voice completely. Having been ushered into Ziegfeld's office and greeted warmly, she could only stand staring at him while she bit her lip to keep from collapsing.

And who can blame her? There are people like Fanny now in all the cities and towns, the villages and farms of the country. Boys and girls who want to act, or sing, or paint, or dance, or write. Thousands upon thousands of them, each with his tiny bug that will not let him rest, that sets him apart from his fellows in the office, in the factory, in the classroom. That urges him on, gnawing at him, promising him that if only he will go to New York, go to Paris, go to Hollywood, go, go, go, he will become a star, paint a masterpiece, write a classic. They come like lemmings, always they come: to Greenwich Village, to Sunset Boulevard, to the Left Bank; and for every thousand, or ten thousand, each with his dreams to sustain him, each knowing one moment that he will make it, he *will*, and the next that he is doomed to failure, for every ten thousand, one stands at a Ziegfeld's desk and knows the race is run, the race is won, the prize is his.

It had come to Fanny at nineteen.

So Fanny remained speechless, trembling, until Ziegfeld rose and walked around his desk, and sat her down gently in a chair. Leaning against the desk, smiling at Fanny, he said: "I watched your work. You are very talented, Miss Brice."

Nobody had ever called her Miss Brice before. She locked her fingers and stared miserably at her hands, her feet together and her knees together, dressed in the white she always wore because: "I didn't want to look burlesquey."

"Would you like to work for me, Miss Brice?" Ziegfeld asked.

Fanny remembered later that she wanted to sneeze. To sneeze and to cry. To cry and to kiss him. To leap into the air. To tell Rosie. To tell Carolyn. To tell Clara Hendricks and her brother, Lew, and whomever she saw.

But she could only sit pulling her fingers.

"How old are you?" Ziegfeld asked.

Then, at last, she found voice. She could talk but she could not look up, and she said: "I was seventeen when I signed with Max Spiegel. Is that what you mean, Mr. Ziegfeld?"

"Yes," he said. "Then your contract isn't legal." He asked Fanny why her mother hadn't signed it. She told him. Rosie couldn't write.

"It's a good thing for both of us that she can't, isn't it?"

Ziegfeld produced a contract. It was, as Fanny later said, "on slick, shiny paper," and when she had signed the document, which provided that she receive seventy-five dollars weekly that year and one hundred dollars weekly the following year, Ziegfeld presented her with a copy of it.

Fanny would not have exchanged it for the Magna Charta. She thanked Ziegfeld and left his office slowly, as befits a lady who doesn't want to look burlesquey. She thanked his secretary and downstairs she thanked the doorman.

Then she set off for 47th Street and Broadway at a speed

that would have shamed a firehorse. Reaching that corner, the burlesque crossroads of the world, she pulled up and caught her breath and waited.

As soon as she saw a familiar face, she would shout: "Hey, Ziegfeld signed me. A hundred a week," quoting the following year's salary. Seizing the friend's arm, she would begin to read the contract word for word, from top to bottom.

As Fanny remembers it, "I'd stand there every day. I never went back to *College Girls*. In about four or five days the contract was torn to pieces. With that stiff paper, it cracked and nobody could make it out. If they couldn't make it out, they couldn't read it. They wouldn't believe me. So I went to Ziegfeld's office.

" 'My mother threw the contract out,' I hold him. 'You have to give me another one.'

"Which he did, and smiled. I wore *that* one out in a week too. I came for another contract. He gave me a fresh one. I think I wore out eight before the Follies even went into rehearsal.

"Not only a hundred dollars, but Ziegfeld! I couldn't stay home. I used to stand on Broadway with it, waiting for anyone I knew to show up."

The 1910 Follies, Fanny's first, was Ziegfeld's fourth. When rehearsals began, Fanny was forgotten in the crush of stars, beautiful women, sketch-writers, composers, set-designers, costume-designers, stagehands, all the hundreds of retainers that Ziegfeld, the monarch, kept at his court.

Here and there during rehearsals Fanny would be pressed into service for a moment or two, but most of the time she sat forgotten and unnoticed. It became quite apparent to her that while she might have a contract for the Follies, it contained no clause that guaranteed her appearance *in* the Follies.

She appealed to Ziegfeld. "Are you going to let me sing?" she asked.

"Of course, Fanny. Of course," he said. "Just talk to the music boys," he suggested, and was called away to another part of the theater.

Fanny looked over at Joe Jordan and Will Marion Cook, the two colored song-writers. Around them were two dozen performers, each fighting for a song, a lyric, anything to help their own status in the show.

Fanny went to the telephone and called Rosie. Then she waited until almost everyone had left the theater. Approaching Jordan and Cook, Fanny said: "How would you boys like a real, home-cooked meal? My Mom is the best cook in New York."

Jordan lowered the lid of the piano and reached for his jacket. Cook was buttoning his. Fanny led the pair uptown to Rosie's food.

She waited until they could eat no more. Then, leaning against the piano in the parlor, she asked if perhaps they didn't have a song she might sing in the Follies.

By this time, the pair *wanted* to give Fanny a song, but reluctantly admitted they had nothing for her. Jordan sat at the piano picking out a melody with one finger, and the frantic Fanny asked if that wouldn't do for her.

"That's nothing," Jordan replied. "That's just my tune. They call me Lovey Joe where I live, and I call this little old thing 'Lovey Joe.'"

"Sing me the words," Fanny pleaded. "Let's hear the lyrics."

"Haven't got lyrics," Jordan said. "This here ain't no song, Fanny."

"That's what you *say*, brother," Fanny thought. Signaling Rosie to bring fresh coffee and hot pastry, Fanny sat down next to Jordan at the piano. "Let's try together," said the young woman who could not have rhymed sky with fly. "Let's work on it," she suggested.

At rehearsal the following day Fanny followed Ziegfeld around until, in desperation, he agreed to listen while she sang "Lovey Joe." Jordan was waiting at the piano, and Ziegfeld took a seat near by. Winking at Jordan, Fanny scrambled onto the stage, found the exact center with the instincts of a homing pigeon, and burst into her song.

It's one thing to stop a show, it's quite another to wring applause from a cast in rehearsal. But the girl with the long legs did it. When she had finished, there was no polite hand-clapping from her colleagues, but a genuine, spontaneous acknowledgment to a superior performer.

Fanny had her song and a spot in "one" (alone on the stage before a lowered curtain) to sing it.

Ziegfeld's reputation as a reckless spender was one of the most deserved distinctions in history. He just never had enough money and he couldn't have been less concerned. He couldn't handle money any better than an infant can handle matches. He seemed to enjoy rather than suffer the burned fingers his profligacy brought him. When he needed, say, twenty-five thousand dollars, he had only to choose from a throng of money-men who considered it a privilege to let Ziegfeld spend it. For this, the 1910 Follies, he had allowed Abe Erlanger, of the theatrical firm of Klaw & Erlanger, to back the show.

Erlanger, a small man wearing a straw hat and a pink satin shirt that was immaculately tucked and pleated, was allowed to attend the dress rehearsal as a sop to his status as backer. There he sat beside Ziegfeld, straw hat atop his head, nodding knowingly as the performance progressed. He found no fault with the gorgeous production that unfolded before his cash-register eyes, and when he saw the skinny young woman appear before the dropped curtain, he was a particularly pleased little man.

Then Fanny began to sing:

> "*Lovey Joe, that ever-lovin' man*
> *From way down south in Birming-ham*
> *He can do some lovin', an' some lovin' sho',*
> *An' when he starts to love me*
> *I jest hollers for mo'.*"

At which point Erlanger was on his feet, waving his arms wildly to stop the music. "What?" he demanded. "What's that? What did you say? What's that last line?"

Fanny looked at Ziegfeld, who nodded. "I jest hollers for mo'," she repeated.

"Not for $2.50 a ticket you don't holler for *mo'*," Erlanger decided. "You're not in burlesque now, young woman. You holler for more. *More!*"

"This is a coon song, Mr. Erlanger," Fanny explained. "I can't do it any other way. I always say mo'."

"More!"

"I can't sing it that way. I have to sing it the way I feel it."

"Burlesque! Burlesque! Burlesque!" Erlanger screamed. "You're out! Get off the stage. You're out of the show!"

Fanny looked at Ziegfeld, but he only slid deeper into his seat, holding his chin in his hand. Erlanger waited, a bristling bantam with hands on hips, like an umpire who stands between the pitcher and the batter until the ejected ballplayer has left the field.

Fanny came down off the stage, walking up the aisle past Ziegfeld, who would not look at her, past Joe Jordan and Will Marion Cook, who shook their heads mournfully, until she had reached the last row of the theater. But she couldn't leave. She had waited so long, worked so hard, bribed, flattered, cajoled her way along such a tortuous road to reach this eminence, that now, two nights before the opening in Atlantic City, facing the doors to the lobby, she was unable to push them open. She fell into the aisle seat.

Here Ziegfeld found her when he slipped away from Erlanger. Motioning her to follow, he walked past Fanny and into the lobby, where she seized his arm. "What am I going to do, Mr. Ziegfeld? What's going to happen? I'm out. . . ."

"You're in," he said, and put his fingers to his lips, mindful of the Brice voice that could erupt throughout the theater.

"Why must you argue with him, my dear Fanny?" Ziegfeld asked softly. "Can't you sing 'more' now and 'mo' later? Must you *feel it* today, when Abe Erlanger is sitting with me?"

"I didn't mean to argue, Mr. Ziegfeld. I won't argue. I promise I won't argue."

"Good," Ziegfeld said. "Now you must listen to me, my dear. You must stay away from Erlanger until the opening in Atlantic City. Stay away from here, and on the train sit in the ladies' room. Do not let Abe Erlanger see you until you appear on the stage in Atlantic City. Do you understand now?"

Fanny nodded.

"All right, my dear. Change your clothes and go home. Remember, out of sight until Atlantic City."

A Ziegfeld road-opening usually ran until three a.m., for he used the days in Atlantic City to cut and prune the show until it fitted the Broadway theater-schedule. That first night Fanny appeared on stage at 9.30, walking past Abe Erlanger, who stood in the wings, as though he were not there. He wore the straw hat and he wore the pink shirt and Fanny would not have been surprised had he followed her to the footlights and dragged her off the stage.

She sang "Lovey Joe," and she sang it with the mo', and

she stopped the Follies as cold as any show has ever been stopped, before or since. She came back into the wings with the audience wild but she saw only Erlanger staring at her and she was so frightened that she had to be pushed back to take a bow.

But a bow was not enough for that audience. They wanted an encore and Fanny gave them an encore. They wanted another and she obliged. They brought her back twelve times before they would let the show continue.

Standing there in the wings as the curtain came up on the next number, feeling her mouth dry and her hands wet with perspiration, feeling the triumph all through her, hearing yet, over the sound of the orchestra, the applause that is like nothing in all the world to a performer, that nothing can approximate—not wealth and not fame, not husband and not children—hearing it still, Fanny had eyes only for Abe Erlanger.

And he took off his straw hat. He was smiling and he hit her on the head with the hat. "Good," he said, and hit her again. "Good, good, good," he said, and bang, once more. He slapped her with the hat until the crown broke, and he said: "You owe me a hat, Fanny," laughing at his joke.

"You owe me an apology, kid," she said to the little man who, with his partner, controlled more theaters in the United States than any ten theatrical firms in the country.

When the performance was over at last, ending at three o'clock in the morning, like all Ziegfeld's first-night Follies, Fanny went back to the hotel and asked the switchboard operator how much it would cost her to call New York.

Learning that she would be charged ninety cents for three minutes, Fanny sat on the bed in her room for two hours, unable to decide whether or not to phone and tell Rosie of her great success.

The sun was rising over the ocean when at last Fanny took

the receiver off the hook and gave the operator Rosie's number in New York. Rosie came down on the first available train.

Fanny, meanwhile, had made a quick but complete tour of the hotel.

Meeting her mother at the station, she took Rosie to the delivery entrance of the hotel and led her up the back stairs to her room. For the balance of their stay in Atlantic City, Rosie came and went through the rear of the hotel, sharing her daughter's single bed. So delicately attuned were the two on the same economic wavelength that Rosie boasted about the deception for years.

Opening night in New York was only a reprise of what had happened in Atlantic City, except that as Fanny waited to go on a bee stung her below the right ear. She carried the mark for the rest of her life, but that night the plague of locusts which stopped the Egyptians could not have held Fanny. A triumph before the vacationers on the New Jersey seashore was one thing. Tonight, two weeks later, to win the applause of the sophisticated audience that waited for her was another matter.

But win them she did. It was Fanny's Follies, all right, and you have to remember that the line-up of talent in a Ziegfeld revue was several light years removed from the cast of any current Broadway show.

They brought her back a dozen times, while the blotch behind her ear grew redder and redder. Fanny never knew whether the applause ended after her twelfth encore or whether she wanted to match the Atlantic City mark.

She *did* know what kept the audience clamoring for more. At a time when the taste in women's legs ran to gams resembling champagne bottles, Fanny's were as svelte, as shapely, as Grable's or Dietrich's. In any leg line-up during those years she was certain to finish last.

In her efforts to please the audience, Fanny lifted her skirts high as she began an imitation of the can-can. At its first glimpse of Fanny's legs, the audience howled. Whereupon Fanny, her dress high, looked down at her knees, put her hand to her head, shook it from side to side, and moaned: "Oy, oy, oy!"

Once she knew what the audience wanted, Fanny gave it to them. Always she maintained that between her and an audience there was a secret language, clearly understood, and always audible to her.

Writing of her work many years later, Fanny said, "I never worked out any business ahead of time. It would only happen when I hit that audience, because they speak so much louder than my mind. I could hear them much clearer. They would tell me what they wanted.

"You get your first laugh—boom! You're going. You lose yourself. You become whoever it is they're laughing at, but it isn't you. Any time I ever did any kind of dance, don't you think that in my heart, as I am making them laugh, that I don't want them to say: 'She's really so *graceful*'?

"Your audience gives you everything you need. They tell you. There is no director who can direct you like an audience. You step out on the stage and you can feel it is a nervous audience. So you calm them down. I come out before an audience and maybe my house burned down an hour ago, maybe my husband stayed out all night, but I stand there. I'm still. I don't move. I wait for the introduction. Maybe I cough. Maybe I touch myself. But before I do anything, I got them with me, right there in my hand and comfortable. That's my job, to make them comfortable, because if they wanted to be nervous they could have stayed home and added up their bills.

"If you're a comic you have to be nice. The audience has to like you. You have to have a softness about you, because if you do comedy and you are harsh, there is something offensive about it. Also you must set up your audience for the laugh you are working for. So you go along and everything is fine, like any other act, and then—boom! You give it to them. Like there is a beautiful painting of a woman and you paint a mustache on her."

When Fanny left the stage that opening night of the 1910 Follies a star had been born. When she came down from her dressing-room wearing a blue foulard with white polka dots, she was engulfed by admirers. Recognizing George M. Cohan among the group, she shouted: "How do you like the kitchen you sent me to?"

She was introduced to Ethel Barrymore, to Diamond Jim Brady, to Mrs. J. Borden Harriman, who was later to become ambassador to Denmark. She was hugged by women whose pictures she had seen in the society sections of the newspapers. Her hand was kissed by men whose names she had heard spoken only with awe.

After a time, Diamond Jim Brady said: "I'm giving a party, little girl. Wouldn't you like to come to my party?"

"Sure," Fanny said.

Diamond Jim escorted her to a private room at Sherry's. There she noticed that most of the girls immediately lifted their plates. Fanny lifted hers, saw a dollar bill, and wondered if it was for the waiter. She set the plate down and was watching the festivities when the girl beside her said: "Did you get your hundred?"

"Hundred what?"

"Your hundred dollars. Look under your plate." Fanny lifted the plate once more.

And saw that the buck had multiplied with astonishing rapidity, for there, below the crockery, was a bill whose four corners bore the figure *100*.

This was too much for *any* waiter, Fanny decided, depositing the century in her bag while platters of food, the variety and amount of which she had never seen in her life, were set upon the table. Fanny fell to with gusto, noticing that one of the chorus girls got up to offer a short dance for her host. When the girl finished, Diamond Jim passed her a hundred dollars, whereupon Fanny swallowed her food, cleared her throat, rose to her feet and burst into song, shuffling toward the head of the table as she sang, until, finishing the tune, she bowed before the money-man.

Clutching her second hundred, Fanny returned to her chair. But she had scored her second hit of the evening, and the guests clamored for more. She immediately obliged. At that price, she would have continued singing until the following night's Follies, but for the venomous glances of her colleagues, who waited more than a little impatiently to offer their specialties before Diamond Jim's provident eyes.

When Fanny resumed eating, the purse she clutched to her bosom contained four one-hundred-dollar bills. She could not wait to get home, wake Rosie, and thrust the money at her mother. She was not certain at that moment whether Rosie would even believe her.

For Fanny had never seen a hundred-dollar bill before. She had never heard of Diamond Jim Brady. She had never set foot inside Sherry's. She had never been told of these parties, but Fanny was never prone to look a gift horse in the mouth. When Diamond Jim told Fanny that he would take her home, she looked at the twenty sparklers in his shirt, and said thank you. When he also told Vera Maxwell, a chorus girl and a great beauty, that he would take her home, Fanny felt the familiar envy that always possessed her in the company of lovely women. When Diamond Jim dropped Miss Maxwell first, Fanny clutched her purse and pushed herself into a corner of the carriage. He wasn't getting his four hundred dollars back, she decided, but he wasn't getting anything else either.

Arriving at Fanny's flat, Diamond Jim helped her from the carriage, bowed to kiss her hand, and thanked her for a delightful evening.

Fanny only stared as he turned away, and then she fled to wake her mother.

Once, talking of the early Follies, Fanny said: "The funny part about burlesque is, the people were so nice. They were always paying off some little house in Long Island. Circus people the same way, also vaudeville people. I noticed the difference when I got into the Follies. My last season in burlesque, there were twenty chorus girls and eighteen were virgins. There were hardly any virgins in the Follies. If there was one around, I didn't know about it."

When Fanny walked into her kitchen the next morning, the room was full of neighbors, each holding a newspaper, and all reading simultaneously to Rosie. Fanny heard her name spoken again and again until a woman saw her and thrust a morning paper before her eyes, pointing at the review of the Follies.

Fanny had never known there were such things as reviews, or individual notices for performers. Quickly gathering up the papers, she emptied the room of neighbors, and sat down to read. Rosie, bored with such profitless activity, began to badger Fanny about the millionaire who had brought her home. When was he coming to call? Had Fanny been a lady? Did he like her? Why hadn't Fanny brought home a few diamonds? Why hadn't Fanny asked him to dinner? She, Rosie, would cook that millionaire a dinner he would never forget.

Ziegfeld meanwhile had a new star in the Follies firmament, and the master showman made the most of it. When he had exhausted run-of-the-mill publicity concerning Fanny, he informed the press that he had discovered her singing on a corner below the Brooklyn Bridge while she peddled her papers. Fanny, who had done everything to earn money *except* sell newspapers, enthusiastically fell in with his deception, weeping daily for the reporters and photographers as she told them of the bitter years of privation when, summer and winter, she had stood below the bridge, trying to eke out enough money to keep life in her undernourished body.

To Rosie, who had once bought a vacant lot in downtown Newark and paid taxes patiently for three years until an insurance company decided to build there, her daughter's name and pictures in the public press meant only one thing: larger receipts for Ziegfeld.

When Rosie's pleas that Fanny ask for more money fell on deaf ears, she put on her finest one afternoon and announced that they were going to see this Mr. Ziegfeld.

Within an hour, mother and daughter were ushered into his office, where Rosie said: "Hello, Mr. Ziegfeld. Fanny is so good for your business, you couldn't give her a little more money?"

"All right," said Ziegfeld. "Bring in the contract and we'll draw up a new one."

Rosie opened her purse, extracted the contract, and set it before him. Ziegfeld promptly tore it up and wrote a new agreement in which Fanny would receive $100 weekly from that day forward, and $150 the following year. Rosie solemnly thanked him, as solemnly shook his hand, pocketed the new contract, and left her daughter to face the day's interviewers.

"You know," said Eddie Cantor, pacing the floor of his Beverly Hills office that day, "you are taking me a long way back. I am sixty years old. One of the compensating factors of being my age is that you haven't got too much of a future, and so everything is velvet. This is exciting for me, to go back to those times. All of us who were in the Follies, from the biggest star to the extra chorus-girl, we brag about it. This is the high point of our lives. But I will say this: of all his stars Fanny was really in everything with Ziegfeld. Take Will Rogers, Bert Williams, Bill Fields, any of them; when you say Fanny, you have to say Ziegfeld.

"Except for one year Fanny was in every Follies from 1910 to 1923. When the Ziegfeld Midnight Frolic started on the Amsterdam Roof, Fanny was in that. She would play the regular Follies, then go upstairs with other selected members of the cast to do the Frolic. There was a radio program long ago: Ziegfeld Follies of the Air. Fanny was a star in that. They made *The Great Ziegfeld* out here in Hollywood. Fanny was in it. They made *The Ziegfeld Follies* as a picture, and they called for Fanny. The Shuberts revived the Follies for two years after Ziegfeld died. Fanny headed the cast.

"A few years ago Ziegfeld's daughter got married, and Billie Burke, his widow, asked Fanny to attend the wedding with her, because she wanted someone there close to Flo.

"Finally," Cantor said, "Fanny's ex-husband, Billy Rose, *buys* the Ziegfeld Theatre.

"There was a Ziegfeld thread in Fanny's whole life," Cantor continued. "He changed everything for her. One day she is a soubrette in a burlesque show and the next day she is the biggest star in New York."

Immediately after the signing of the new contract, Fanny took a flat in the Albany apartments at Broadway and 52nd Street, moving in with her mother. It was a huge place for which she paid $130 a month. Many of the rooms had red damask walls.

One night a few weeks later, Rosie went to the door in answer to an insistent, loud knocking. Opening it, she was confronted by three drunken middle-aged men. Pushing their way past her, they staggered into the living-room.

"Come on, mother," one said, "where are the girls? We've been here before."

"My Fanny is by the Follies," Rosie answered, trembling with fright, "and my Carolyn is married."

While the trio searched the apartment, calling for the dames, Rosie ran downstairs to the manager's office. He summoned the building's male employees and ejected the drunks, imploring Rosie to be quiet about the incident.

Rosie was afraid to remain in the apartment. She waited for Fanny at the Amsterdam. After the show, she told her daughter what had happened.

The next day Fanny had an audience with the landlord, who reduced the rent to one hundred dollars and promised to decorate the apartment within a week in return for a pledge of silence from Fanny.

"That was one of the main characteristics of Fanny," Cantor said, "that the worst thing that could happen to her was to be mistaken for a sucker. The truth was that she was probably the biggest sucker the world has ever known. She had the acclaim of all of America: here was a woman who was up in the money; here was a woman who had jewels, fine clothes, furs, beautiful homes, everything she could want. But she always had some guy around to break her heart."

✬ 7 ✬

NICK ARNSTEIN: *"Not Only to Women But to Men."*

===

J ULES ARNSTEIN strolled into my sanctum leisurely, and sat down opposite in the club-chair, facing me across the walnut desk; his blue eyes twinkled as he brushed, nonchalantly, the bit of down that adorned the upper lip of his small but well molded mouth. 'Twas a gesture that I knew well, and the smile, an indulgent smile, asked volumes."

So begins the unpublished *autobiography* of Jules W. Arndstein, otherwise known as John Wilson Adair, James Wilford Adair, and J. W. Arnold, but best known as Nick Arnstein, second husband of Fanny Brice.

The italics are used with good reason: let's have no doubt concerning the author of those worshipful words. That's Nick writing about Nick.

He continues:

"Jules Arnstein nodded graciously. He's a fine-looking man, tall, slender, broad of shoulder and slim of waist, a perfectly groomed gentleman, distingué. At ease, always! His past hasn't hindered, nor disillusioned; on the contrary,

I'd venture to say, he has weathered the fray, the victor! In the past, Jules sought everywhere for Maeterlinck's elusive bluebird o' happiness.

"Jules has met strange, interesting people, in strange, exotic places, under strange and unaccountable conditions. He has met people in all walks of life, from the high to the low, characters never portrayed before and with it all, he has ever had a yearning, burning desire for more.

"It is a tale of palace and prison, of love and intrigue, success and disappointment, of happiness and much sorrow; of the circus, the theatre and gambling with high-rolling gamblers on land and sea."

Eddie Cantor said of Nick:

"He was a far better actor than anyone Fanny had ever known. Nick gave her a wonderful performance, morning, noon, and night. The curtain never fell. There was no intermission. He was the best-dressed man I ever saw. When he took his shoes off, he would put them in shoe trees that he had made from a cast of his feet. He knew about food and wines, and flowers, and furniture, and sterling silver, and cars. Nick was a fascinating guy, not only to women but to men. W. C. Fields used to follow him around. That language Fields used later in the movies, the high-blown talk—he heard Nick talking that way. Nick was very suave, gentlemanly. He was all the time the perfect gentleman."

And Nick himself last summer, at seventy-three, in the three-room apartment on Olympic Boulevard in Beverly Hills, opening the door as though it led to Hyde Park. He bowed slightly, and smiled faintly, and offered a firm handshake.

"Jules Arnold," he said, introducing himself, and he could have been a long-ago Secretary of State living quietly with his memories. He could have been an exiled premier receiv-

ing a student of government. He could have been a banker
whose bank had failed but who had paid every depositor
every penny, selling house and securities and cars and
horses, refusing, against the counsel of old friends, to submit
to bankruptcy, standing erect and looking squarely at you
with self-respect, with dignity, with honor.

His hair was gray and his mustache was gray. His stomach was as flat as a featherweight's. He wore pince-nez. His
nose was long, thin, and distinguished. He wore gray slacks
and above them a matching, plaid jacket and vest. His tie
clasp was an unobtrusive gold pin, worn low on the shirt,
and his French cuffs were as white as Pullman sheets and as
soft as silk.

Across the street, in Beverly Hills High School, the kids
were studying atomic energy and jet-aircraft design, and you
came in out of the sun into Nick's apartment, and you were
looking at a set for a Clara Bow movie.

There was a huge Buddha staring obscenely at you. There
were thick, maroon drapes hanging from spears. There were
Chinese chests and red-lacquered tables and old, tarnished,
sterling cups; lamps with shades as big as beach umbrellas,
each with its border of foot-long fringe.

There was Nick in a Queen Anne chair, legs crossed, right
hand caressing an ornate table-model radio.

"I had this set made to my specifications," Nick said. "It
cost me $230, you know. There aren't any made like that
any more. I get all the ships at sea. I'm in the shipping business and I have to know what's going on everywhere. But
you're not interested in my current affairs, young man. It's
my past you want, I take it. Things happened in my life and
I am not ashamed of anything, for I was unjustly accused
and convicted. But . . . fire away, and don't pull any
punches with me. Nick Arnstein can take it, as has been
proven many times."

The name Nick, he explained, was a diminutive of "Nickelplate." In his youth he had been a bike rider, and his machine had nickelplated spokes in the wheels.

A great favorite of the crowd always, he was cheered on by their cries of, "Nickelplate! Go it, you Nickelplate!" Within the riding fraternity this was soon shortened to Nick.

"I became Nick when I was sixteen years old," he announced. "Lords of England, princes of Morocco, and powerful men the world over have called me Nick. I've known good luck and bad luck, and . . ."

"What?" he asked, in response to a question, and paused. Then: "Just say I'm over sixty."

He uncrossed his legs and after a moment crossed them again, carefully arranging the crease in his trousers as he listened.

"The first time I saw Fanny," Nick said, "was in my suite at the Canon Hotel in Baltimore. She came in with another woman. I had a friend sharing my suite. He brought them. I paid no attention to either Fanny or her companion. They were just show people, and I was there racing my stable of horses."

In Fanny's account of their first meeting she said: "We went up to their suite for supper. After all, it was a free meal. We always ordered a club sandwich or chicken à la king after the show. That was real elegance for us. So we go up there. I'm sitting and talking to them. We had our supper and after we finished, I said: 'Where's the lady's room?' Nick said: 'Use mine,' pointing at his bedroom. There was a sitting room in the middle and the two bedrooms. I've been upstairs an hour, eating and talking, and I didn't notice him or anything. So I got to his bathroom and I look, and I see he's got seven toothbrushes. *Seven!* I see gold-backed brushes.

I see everything in leather cases. I see a big, wooden bowl
and it has soap in it. England, it says on the bowl. I see all
that.

"I look at the back of the door. There is a Scotch plaid
robe hanging up and also his pajamas with a monogram *that*
small on the pocket. Gee, class, because the monogram was
small. I see the pajamas are twill silk, it's like a serge, but
it's silk. And not that shiny pimp silk, this is dull finish.

"I came out of that bathroom full of personality! Did I
get born in that can! Honey! Boy, I was all over the place. I
really got stuck on him in there. Well, I had him dying, he
was laughing so much. We were up until five or six o'clock.
He didn't go anywhere, he stayed in Baltimore.

"It always left a question in my mind. What did I get
stuck on, the toothbrushes or Nick?"

You have to remember that this was an actress talking;
an actress and a comedienne. You have to remember that
she was swearing nobody to secrecy and that what she said
was printed time after time after time.

Because you don't fall in love with seven toothbushes, no
matter how funny it sounds, or how many laughs you get,
or how well it looks in the newspapers. Not with toothbrushes, and not with twill silk. Nor with soap in a wooden
bowl. At thirty-three, Nick Arnstein was as handsome a
man as Fanny had ever seen and there are pictures to prove
it.

When did she fall in love with Nick? Who knows? Who
can tell, and what's the gain from wondering? There is the
kind of falling in love that happens after you've known the
man all your life. He lives on the block and he played with
your brothers. You went to kindergarten together, and on
through high school. Maybe he danced with you once at the
junior prom because his mother made him promise. Then
one day, one summer day, he saw you wearing a silk print

I'm an Indian," Fanny's famous Follies
outine in the Warner Brothers movie, My Man.

BELOW, LEFT TO RIGHT:
The comedienne in two numbers
she made famous in the Follies.
Fanny at the height of her career in
New York.

ith her two children

dress. For an instant he was standing at just the right angle, and that night he took you for a ride. All that summer you went for rides. You went swimming together. You went to the movies. And you didn't come straight home from the movies. Until the evening he didn't appear, and you were suddenly host to the shakes. You prayed then he would ask you to marry him soon, and not put you through any more nights without him.

There is that kind of falling in love, and there is the falling in love with a stranger: when you meet a man wherever and he takes you home and shakes your hand at the door, and you either wanted him to kiss you, or hoped he wouldn't try. If the former, you wait for him to telephone, and if he never calls, you can't even remember his face in a month. But if he calls, you buy a new dress. That night, sitting with him wherever, you watch your grammar, and you're thinking from the start: Will he kiss me good night?

And there is the way Fanny said she fell in love: in a moment, in the man's suite, having come for a midnight supper to kill a few hours and save the price of a club sandwich, and, as she said: "I never left him until the day I divorced him."

For Nick Arnstein had no horses that he was racing in Baltimore. The only silks he owned were the pajamas in the bathroom. When Fanny went back to New York and the Albany apartments, Nick went with her and Rosie.

There he promptly objected to the décor. He thought it tasteless, vulgar, and depressing. He went to Gimbels, where he ordered ten thousand dollars' worth of furnishings. As the clerk wrote the order, Nick asked that everything be sent C.O.D. When he got home and told Fanny what he had done, she paled and said she had nothing like that amount of money. Nick only shook his head. He told her that when the furnishings were delivered Fanny was to explain that she wanted to pay in monthly installments. That way, Nick told her, she would save the extra cost for credit which he said they would have added to the price of the furniture.

With the coming of spring Nick began to get the itchy foot. Through the months of April and May, Fanny pleaded with him to remain at the Albany, but Nick, faced with Rosie's disapproving eyes, professed a longing for the shores of England. He seemed preoccupied and Fanny found him cool and distant. There was an evening when he was silent throughout dinner. When Fanny prepared to leave for the theater, Nick said: "Have you any plans for tonight, my dear?"

"Nothing I can't get out of, Nick. Why, Nick? Do you want to do something?"

"I thought perhaps we could have supper together after the show, Fanny."

"That's wonderful, Nick! Where should I meet you?"

"I'll pick you up at the theater, my dear, if that meets with your approval."

Fanny leaped at him, flinging her arms about his neck.

Nick chuckled and disengaged himself. "I'll be there, old girl," he promised. "Now run along."

When Fanny was gone, Nick sat with his brandy for a time before leaving the dinner table. In his bathroom he shaved carefully, trimming his mustache with skill and patience. He dressed with as much attention to detail as though he were being presented at Court: boiled shirt, black tie, dinner jacket, diamond studs, and soft-brimmed black hat. He arrived backstage at the Follies a few minutes after the performance had ended.

"I have something to tell you and I'd like to get out of here," Nick said.

"I'm with you, Nick. Let's go."

He said nothing as they left the theater. He said nothing

as they walked to Broadway where he paused and Fanny waited.

"Where do you want to eat, Nick?"

"Oh, I don't care, Fanny. I . . . would you mind walking with me?"

"That's just what I wanted to do, honey," Fanny said.

They started up Broadway: the tall, handsome gambler, and the tall, striking, Follies star. They walked in silence for several blocks until Nick said: "Fanny, I'm married."

He said: "I haven't lived with her as man and wife for three years."

He said: "I want a divorce but she won't give me a divorce."

Fanny held his arm. She smiled at someone she knew and a moment later Nick nodded at an acquaintance. Walking, Fanny turned on her ankle, and Nick's arm tensed as he held her.

"She has a daughter by a previous husband." Nick said. "I adopted the daughter when we were married. I don't love my wife, Fanny."

"I love you," Fanny said. That was the first thing she said.

"She's hounded me across the length and breadth of this country, Fanny," Nick continued. "I have no argument with her demands for support. Nick Arnstein never welshed on a promise in his life. But she wants me to return, and I won't do that. Nobody can tell Nick Arnstein what to do, or where to live."

They passed the Albany apartments. Fanny saw the doorman at the entrance, who raised his cap in greeting and reached for the door, but she turned her head and held Nick's arm and walked past the building.

"I wanted you to know that, my dear Fanny," Nick said. "I should have told you sooner, as would any gentleman of honor, but . . . somehow . . . I didn't have the courage.

My wife knows I've been living in your apartment. She's had detectives watching me. I've got to leave the country, you see. Besides," he continued, "I have many important deals waiting on the Continent. I'll spend several weeks in and around London. There is a young Lord, I'm not at liberty to divulge his name, but he and I have spent many a pleasant evening together. He has a plan that needs my supervision and I've committed myself to helping him."

They had reached Central Park and Nick paused, turning to Fanny. "I wanted you to know about me, my dear," he said, looking at her.

"Now I know about you," she said. That was the second thing she said.

"Well, old girl," he said. "We've had our laughs, haven't we? It's been a lot of fun, Fanny, and I think you're a swell pal. I'll always think so."

"Come on home," she said, and that was the third thing she said.

When they got to the apartment, Fanny led Nick to the kitchen and sat him down. "I'm going to make you a Welsh rarebit like you never ate," she said happily. "Are you hungry, honey?"

"Why, I could stand a little food, my dear."

"You get out of those soup and fish," she ordered, "and when you get back, I'll have you a supper you couldn't get anywhere. I'm the best cook in this town."

Fanny learned through her own sources that Nick's wife was Carrie Greenthal Arnstein, whom he had married on May 5, 1906, in Jersey City, but she said nothing of this to him. She learned that her apartment and her coming and going, as well as Nick's, were under constant surveillance, but she said nothing. Long afterward she remembered that Nick's wife tried to see her, but Fanny would not dignify the floundering marriage with a meeting.

One day, after Nick had left the apartment, Rosie burst into Fanny's room. "Your Nick is married," she announced.

Fanny was brushing her hair.

"He has a wife and a daughter," Rosie declared.

"It's not his daughter," Fanny said.

"Whose?" Rosie asked. "President Wilson's? And whose wife? Emperor Franz Josef's?"

"She won't give him a divorce." Fanny said. "He hasn't lived with her for three years."

Rosie advanced on the dressing-table. "Maybe she hasn't got a maid for Prince Nicholas."

"Mom!" Fanny said.

"Maybe she hasn't got champagne for the gentleman," Rosie said.

"Stop it, Mom!" she said. And Mom stopped.

In the days that followed Fanny tried unsuccessfully to persuade Nick that Asbury Park was as safe from his wife's private eyes as London, but he was adamant. Soon afterward Nick booked passage for England, and was relieved to hear Fanny's stolid acceptance when he announced he was sailing. She bought him a matched set of luggage, helped him pack, and explained that she would not see him off because of a previous engagement. Leaving Nick, Fanny carried some jewelry to a pawnshop. She waited until Nick had left the apartment before she returned. Her face aglow, she kissed Rosie several times as she told her that a girl friend had asked Fanny to spend the summer at the family's mountain retreat.

But she must leave immediately, Fanny explained. Locking the door to her bedroom, she pulled her packed suitcases out of the closet, lifted the mattress to extract an envelope, and examined her tickets to be certain for the hundredth time that she was on the same deck as Nick.

Nick unpacked as soon as he came aboard ship. Later he

went up on the promenade deck for a preliminary survey of the passengers, cataloguing those whom he believed might not be reluctant to take a whirl at a gentleman's game of poker. He went into the saloon for a brandy and soda, toasting the Statue of Liberty as the ship passed her, after which he settled himself comfortably in a deck chair. He pulled the blanket up to his chest, pulled his cap down over his eyes, and was very nearly asleep when Fanny threw herself down on his chair, wrapped her arms around his neck, and kissed him soundly.

Nick disengaged himself, pushed his cap back, held Fanny at arms' length, and said no more nor less than could be expected from any man in such circumstances: "Well, for Christ's sake!"

For Fanny, the voyage was "wonderful and heavenly and enchanting and I was never happier in my life. I didn't know what the word happy meant until I saw Nicky in that deck chair."

Waking with Nick, breakfasting with him, walking with him on the promenade deck and holding his arm all the tighter because of the admiring glances he received from other women, dining with him and sitting speechless while he ordered food and wine, Fanny was in an ecstasy that she wanted never to end. She listened to Nick's plans for making money when they got to England, and wanted only to help him. Her salary for the past season had been five hundred dollars weekly, but show business was another world, an old world that meant moving from city to city, living in hotels, eating chicken à la king after each night's performance, sharing a room with a girl, working when she didn't feel like it, and making people laugh when her feet ached and her head throbbed.

Over and over she told herself how lucky she was, not to have signed a contract for the coming year. Nothing could

take her from Nick now: not Rosie, not his wife, not Ziegfeld. He would work at his schemes to make money and
Fanny would be at his side.

While he talked, Fanny would only look adoringly at him.
"All my life," she said once, "I was afraid I was going to
get stuck on some little guy who played the piano in a joint
filled with smoke. That's what I thought. And if he ever got
up and sang 'Melancholy Baby,' I would have been a goner.
But when I met this tall handsome guy with the beautiful
hands and thin ankles, I said: 'Oh, oh, this is the guy. I want
to have children with this guy.'

"When you're young," she continued, "you make pictures
in your head, you have ideas. You pick the type guy you
want. But if I went to a party, and there was one no-good
bastard in the room, I'd go for him right away. It's so funny:
for my friends I must have admiration and I must respect
them. In fact, I never liked the men I loved, and never
loved the men I liked.

"Because I never really loved but once. I could never understand when people say they have been in love two or
three times. That first love, that's the last one, it takes everything in. I think love is like a card trick. After you know how
it works, it's no fun any more."

Upon their arrival in London, Nick immediately took a
flat for them on Jermyn Street. After a few weeks of living
in what Nick felt were cramped quarters, they moved to a
huge apartment at No. 1 Marble Arch. Fanny happily went
to work in the kitchen, but Nick disapproved, installing both
a cook and a butler, and asked Fanny to advance him a few
dollars until his plans for making money were realized. During the incubation period, Fanny paid the domestics, the
rent, and the cost of two racehorses that Nick assured her
would make them rich.

Owning a stable, however, quickly drained Fanny's cash.

She soon became aware that Nick's nags couldn't outrun the brewery horses that had pulled the beer to Pinochle Charlie's Newark saloon. Nick insisted they would win the Grand National. While she was as much in love with him as ever, she felt their love would not suffer if she looked about her for work.

Gaby Deslys and Harry Pilcer, the French music-hall favorites, were playing in London. Fanny had met them in New York. She went to Gaby, who introduced her to Alfred Butt, the English producer. Butt had a notebook in which he kept one-line evaluations of all American performers. After Fanny's name he had written: "Very good dancer." He agreed to let Fanny go on at the Victoria Palace, a vaudeville theater, for one performance, as a try-out.

Fanny saw no need to tell Butt what George M. Cohan had said about her dancing, particularly at that moment when her cook might soon be unemployed for lack of food to cook. Fanny was an instant hit at the Victoria Palace, and Butt moved her to another of his theaters, the biggest vaudeville house in London.

A few months earlier, at this same theater, Grace La Rue, an English star, had been a great success singing "You Made Me Love You," straight. The same song had been one of Fanny's numbers in America. Her own manner of presentation was to sing the verse and first chorus straight and then deliver the second chorus in comedy form.

Fanny knew nothing of Grace La Rue, and as she began to sing the verse, she heard a kind of buzz go through the audience, and saw the people begin to fidget in their seats.

Grabbing the curtains, Fanny began to swing on them while she sang. Swinging, she kicked her long legs, she winked at the orchestra leader, she leered, she rolled her eyes, she beckoned to the men in the audience to join her upstairs. She didn't stop grimacing or kicking or clowning until the audience was hers. Then, with the sixth sense that she always had, she left the stage, returning when she was satisfied that she and not the people beyond the footlights was in command.

Nick was not altogether happy with the situation at the Palace. He had become a friend of Clifford Fischer, another producer, who needed a replacement for Anna Held in his revue, *Come Over Here.* Doubling Fanny's last salary to one thousand dollars, Nick told Fischer that he might persuade Miss Fanny Brice, the darling of America, to join the show for that weekly figure. Fischer offered $750, Nick demanded $900, whereupon they closed for $800.

Nick told Fanny about her new job when she came home from the Palace that night. A week later she went into *Come Over Here.*

Of the months that followed Fanny wrote: "Nick and I were living in a style I never knew existed in this world. What did I know about such things? I knew how to dress, because I always loved good clothes, but what else did I know? What I learned, I learned from watching and listening. I remember once when I was in burlesque somebody gave a party after the show. A man came up to me. He was complimenting me on my talent. He said: 'You're going to get there, little girl, but you ought to pay attention to your nails. You ought to have a manicure.'

"I said: 'What's that?' He said: 'Oh, they cut your nails and polish them.' So the next day I had forgotten the word, but I knew I wanted it, because he was a nice clean-looking man. So I asked everybody in the show: 'What do they call it when they fool around with your fingernails?' Nobody could tell me, so I asked the hotel manager. 'Manicure,' he said. I walked along the street looking for a manicure sign. How should I know that manicures are given in hairdressing parlors? But I asked people on the street, and finally some-

body sent me to one. I ask how much, and the girl says: 'A
quarter.' So I said: 'Okay.' I'm sitting there, watching her,
and I ask: 'Will they stay like that always?' She said: 'Oh,
no, you have to do them every week.'

" 'A quarter every *week*?' I said. 'Oh, no,' I said, 'not
Fanny. Where can I buy those things you're using?' She
told me they sold them in the shop. She told me what they
were: a file, an orange stick, a buffer, polish. 'Wrap them up,
kid,' I tell her, and from that time on I never had ugly nails.

"I always watched and I always listened. Another time,
at a party, when I was in the Follies, I sat next to Charlie
Schwab. I didn't know Charlie Schwab from John McGraw.
If they weren't in show business, they meant nothing to me
then. And Charlie Schwab says: 'Save your money and buy
U. S. Steel.' I came home and I told my mother about him.
'Imagine that real rich man asking me to buy his goods.' It
was like somebody saying: 'You must come down to my
store, we got some nice clothes on sale.'

"Nick knew all those things. He knew everything and he
was always talking about the big people who were his
friends. But I never met any of them."

Sitting there in his Clara Bow apartment, Nick listened
to what Fanny had said, and smiled indulgently. He shook
his head as though a naughty child had come to him and
confessed a misdeed.

"She was a fine woman. I want you to remember that. A
fine woman, but a short memory. Why at that time I was,
let me see . . . yes, I was running around with young Lord
Stanley, of one of the wealthy, aristocratic families in England. I was chummy with him and Clem Hopkins, who
owned Ciro's in Paris, and Ben Sulky and Cliff Fischer, both
producers and in our group, though on the edges of it.
Fischer induced Lord Stanley to put up some money for a

show. It was at the London Opera House that Hammerstein
built, one of the most beautiful in the world. In the first
week of the show Fischer knew he was in trouble and came
to me for help. I told him he needed comedy, and he gave
me an advance of five hundred pounds to send for Fanny.
I cabled her to drop everything in New York and take the
first ship over."

When he was reminded that Fanny had accompanied him
to England, Nick was annoyed. "This was another time,
quite another time," he insisted. However, he and Fanny
were together in England only once.

He rose and walked across the room, moving very slowly,
holding his hand against his chest. Watching him, you had
to tell yourself that he was seventy-three years old. He
looked his age, and he *didn't* look his age, and maybe you'll
understand if you think of Cary Grant or Gregory Peck,
made up to look old. You watch them on the screen with
the gray hair, and the lines the make-up men have put in
their skin. They act old, they walk old, they talk old, and
all the time you know they are young people.

Nick returned holding a pack of cigarettes, which he
opened as dramatically as though it held diamonds. He was
a long time tapping the cigarette against his thumbnail, and
he waited patiently for a light.

"Well, to get Fanny more publicity," he continued, "I gave
her two horses. I had her name on every bus in London. We
remained in England until war was declared. I got rid of my
horses, sublet the apartment, and we came back to the
States. Fanny went into the Palace on Broadway."

Fanny's appearance at the Palace occasioned this story in
the *New York Mail:*

*From nothing theatrically to a vaudeville headliner in
the brief period of four years is a record for stage celeb-*

*rities to shoot at. As an example of this high-leaping
stunt, go to the Palace this week and see the performance of Fanny Brice, who is making her first New York
appearance after an eight months' engagement in
London.*

*It was during an engagement at Broadway's burlesque
palace, the Columbia Theatre, that Fanny Brice was
really discovered and forthwith became a popular comedienne.*

*The Columbia shows are gone over with a fine-tooth
comb every week by theatrical managers and agents in
the hope of 'discovering' a to-be Broadway star. Miss
Brice, unheralded and unsung, was the fourth girl from
the end in the second row of the chorus.*

*But her ability and promise did not escape the alert
and crafty eye of Flo Ziegfeld who happened to be
looking for good material for his 'Follies of 1910.' Op-
portunity arrived and at the close of that week at the
Columbia, Miss Brice was under contract with Mr. Ziegfeld. From a little street urchin and a burlesque chorus
girl to one of the principal parts in the 'Follies of 1910,'
was her destiny.*

*Miss Brice's yearly income is said to be in excess of
that of the President of the United States.*

A large part of Fanny's income, when she returned from
abroad, went into the furnishing of a duplex apartment on
West 58th Street, across from the Plaza Hotel. A branch of
the Vanderbilt family lived on the corner, in a home facing
Fifth Avenue. Beyond, where Bergdorf Goodman now stands,
were the socially prominent Alexanders, and next door to
them the building in which Fanny and Nick lived.

Fanny, whose notion of a big time before she met Nick
was to buy a dress at half price, hurrying home after her

night's performance to work on the garment, now began to
entertain and be entertained in a constant whirl of parties.
This was not, you understand, Nick's idea. He liked a small
group over which he could preside at a graciously served
dinner. He liked an evening in one or another of the best res-
taurants in New York. The open house was Fanny's wish.

"The big thing I wanted to do in my life was live well,"
she said, referring to those years. "I wanted a nice home and
good food and I wanted to serve good food. That I got from
my mother. She liked to feed people. She liked good food
better than anything in the world, and maybe I did too."

While it was true that Fanny never took to the road in a
show without her cooking equipment—a trunk filled with
pots, pans, a portable stove, spices, herbs, and other condi-
ments, most of her friends of that period attribute her sudden social life to her love for Nick. The Fanny who would
let none of her gang sing in Brooklyn back yards, the Fanny
who had asked a thousand questions of anyone from whom
she might learn something, the Fanny who had stood on a
Broadway street-corner proclaiming to the world that she
was now with Ziegfeld, that Fanny took to sitting quietly at
her own parties while Nick talked.

"He would be surrounded by people ten minutes after
he entered a room," Fanny said. "He was a wonderful
speaker. Of course half the things he would be telling them
were lies. He was a man who couldn't face the truth in his
life. He never worried about anything, and I knew all those
things from the time we left Baltimore together. Nick would
make himself out to be such a daring guy. Inside he was
really a child, Nick."

But Fanny was in love, and if she could not display Nick
on a Broadway corner as she had once displayed her Ziegfeld contract, she could share her happiness with as many
people as could be brought into her apartment. Will Rogers

came, and Nick says he taught the famous humorist how to play the violin. Eddie Cantor came and was enchanted with Nick's stories. Bert Williams came on occasion, standing quietly in a corner and talking of books with Nick. John Wanamaker, the department-store heir, was a nightly visitor and one of Fanny's great admirers. Ann Pennington, of the dimpled knees, Lillian Lorraine, Vera Maxwell—all the Follies beauties—were frequent guests.

Long afterward, Nick complained of those years with Fanny. "Her life was the night life, the life of the theater," he said. "Should I wish to rise at seven in the morning and go to work after a good night's sleep, I was confronted with the fact that she did not reach home until midnight, and then usually with a bevy of stage friends who gaily turned the night into day, because with the day they must sleep."

Nick doesn't mention the thousands upon thousands of dollars that Fanny pressed upon him, or the patience with which she listened to his endless schemes for making money.

"Nick's disease," Fanny said, "was dreams of glory. In 1918 he would say: 'In 1919 I'm going to have a million dollars.' In 1919 he would say: 'In 1920 I'm going to have a million dollars.' He was always going to have it, but he never got around to making it. He tried a hundred different businesses, and after he would tell me about each new one, I would reach for the checkbook. One business was manufacturing advertising signs which would shine all night. He furnished his office with big mahogany desks, big leather chairs, thick carpets, expensive drapes. I said: 'Nick, why do you have to spend so much on the office?' He said: 'Fanny, my dear, if you start small, you finish small. Start big and you'll be big.'

"He was also the first one to start a shirt hospital. Do you think he would get four or five machines? No, he had thirty-five machines right away.

"Whenever he started a new business, he would be all raring to go at it. For a week or two he would be at his office at eight o'clock, and if it didn't start going right away, he would start losing interest, and show up at noon or one o'clock, and pretty soon I was selling the equipment."

Often, during those years, Nick's wife would begin to make things uncomfortable for the husband she never saw, and he would disappear for a time. And Fanny continually had to pacify Rosie, who early recognized Nick's peculiar talents for extracting money from her daughter, and who, according to Carolyn, "hated Nick from the beginning."

For her part, Fanny could have faced down the opposition of the combined military forces of the United States. She was not at all concerned with his past, with his wife, with his friends. She entertained them, she accompanied Nick to gambling-rooms, she waited dutifully while he had his try at the craps tables or the roulette wheel. She wanted only to be with him, to look at him, to touch him, to feel his hand on her arm, to see him smile, to see him eat and drink and shave and sleep.

On a night when Nick was out on "business" Fanny waited for him to come home until long after midnight. When she could no longer stay awake, she took her lipstick and scrawled "I love you, darling" on the mirror, before going to sleep.

On a warm spring day, when they were walking along upper Fifth Avenue, Nick led Fanny into Central Park, hired a boat, and rowed her around the tiny lake.

On an evening when they were having a late supper after her show they were joined by a gentleman whom Nick introduced as "the whitest of them all, Arnold Rothstein." Turning to Fanny, he said: "Arnold, may I present Fanny Brice, the finest little girl in the world."

She remembered nothing else for days. She would come

off the stage of the Follies, the audience pleading for an encore, and hear only: ". . . the finest little girl in the world."

She would be standing for one of her endless fittings while a squad of dressmakers surrounded her, asking her endless questions, and she would answer, agree or disagree, hearing not their voices but Nick's: ". . . in the world."

Always, in speaking of those first years with Nick, Fanny would forget details. She could remember neither weeks, nor months, nor years, only that her life was: ". . . heaven. I didn't know I could be that happy. I didn't know there was that much happiness in the world."

She was happy even during the early months of 1915, when Nick was arrested on a wire-tapping charge and stood trial for grand larceny in New York's General Sessions court.

One day Rosie arrived at the apartment on 58th Street for a visit, entering Fanny's bedroom unannounced as her daughter was filling a purse with jewels.

Greeting her mother, Fanny continued to empty her jewel case. When Rosie asked if Fanny had taken a safe-deposit box and was transferring the valuables to it, she was told that the jewels were being sold that afternoon.

"I have to pay Nick's lawyers," Fanny said, as matter-of-factly as though she were telling Rosie of a new dress she had bought. She had used most of her money to raise Nick's bail bond, and now she had to assure Nick of adequate counsel.

Rosie, to whom a dollar was as sacred as her soul, staged a scene that would have compared with the performance of any tragedienne of the time, but Fanny calmly finished packing her diamonds. Followed through the apartment by Rosie, who cursed Nick with every epithet she had heard in several years of managing Newark saloons, Fanny went out to get the money for Nick's defense.

Nick warned Fanny against appearing in court, since his wife hounded him for support with the dogged persistence of a salesman who works on commission. She might, upon seeing her husband's inamorata, provoke enough trouble in the courtroom to harm Nick's case.

Any doubts that Fanny may have had concerning Nick's absolute love and devotion were dismissed by him in a strong denunciation of his wife and of her refusal to grant him a divorce so that he might marry Fanny. It was all Fanny needed to hear from Nick. On June 28, 1915, when he was sentenced to from two years and ten months to three years in Sing Sing, Fanny knew that she must do everything she could to make his stay in Ossining easier. She sent weekly food-packages. She made weekly and semiweekly journeys to the prison. In their short visits together she made him laugh, and she made the guards laugh. She went away from those brief interludes knowing that she was his only love, for hadn't he told her so?

But he didn't tell her that he also enjoyed visits from his wife.

Nick served two years in Sing Sing, and all through her life Fanny remembered nothing of that time. Not of his Sing Sing days, nor of the more than twenty thousand dollars she received for her jewels and gave to Nick; nor of the friends who tried desperately to break her love for Nick; nor of the reputation for loyalty and integrity and utter honesty that she was to enjoy through all her years in the courts at Arnstein's side.

Even her marriage to Nick was difficult for her to recall. Two friends of Nick's accompanied them to Brooklyn. For Fanny, the ceremony was only a legal rider to a relationship she had considered sacred for more than six years. Therefore when the witnesses began to talk of an elaborate wedding-dinner at a Manhattan café, Fanny cut them short. "We'll eat at home," she decided. "I bought the most beautiful black bass this morning and I'll broil it for us."

Within three months, when Fanny learned that Nick's divorce had not been final, they had to cross the Hudson River and stand together for another wedding ceremony.

As a newly married man, Nick felt that their home on West 58th Street was too small. Soon he found a ten-room apartment on Central Park West at 83rd Street, for which Fanny obligingly paid the rent. She had for a long time felt ashamed of her ignorance of furnishings. She had become one of the best-dressed women in New York through a combination of inherent taste and unbounded determination. Now she set about learning the fundamentals of interior decoration by attending every auction on Manhattan Island.

"When I started out," she said once, "I'd buy anything that was carved, because I figured that all the work that had gone into it made it valuable. The biggest thing would come up, all carved, and I'd get it for $50. Then up would come a very wonderful table, say, a plain, simple Pembroke dropleaf, and that would go for maybe $350. I'd look at the person and think: 'Christ, they're crazy. Didn't they just see what I got all *carved*, and for only fifty bucks? What kind of jerks come here?' Once a big Moorish bedroom set came up, the biggest damned thing. The biggest bed you ever saw and a chest of drawers as big as a swimming pool. I had this extra guestroom. I thought it would be nice to put the set in there. I got the whole set for $175. Ten or fifteen pieces. About a week later the auction-room owner called me up. He wanted to know when I would take the set out. I wanted to leave it there while they're doing the remodeling. He said they needed the space. So I got some storage people down to look at it and now they told me I had to pay a hundred dol-

lars a month to store it. Oh, no, that's no good. A hundred
bucks a month and I'm not even using it yet. Next I got a
mover and he looked it over, looked at my apartment. 'We'll
have to take it apart and put it together inside your house,'
he told me. All the time I'm beginning to hate that set. One
day I had lunch with a friend of mine, a playwright. I asked
him if he ever thought of doing a Moorish play. 'I've got a
hell of a set for you,' I told him. He didn't want to do a
Moorish play. Well, I finally had to pay a guy forty dollars to
take it. It was a gift, but the forty bucks went for moving it.

"So now it's costing me money. I think: 'If you're going to
do it right, then you better learn it right.' So the next thing,
I'm going to antique shops. I tell them: 'I don't know a
damned thing about any of this, but I want to learn.' That's
all they have to hear. I'm refreshing, they tell me. Most people come in and they want to impress you with how much
they know, and they don't know a goddam thing. Antiques
are the blindest racket in the world. Next I buy books on
antiques and study them. While I'm studying, I keep looking
at the stuff around town. And no matter how right it is in
the book, if I don't feel it inside, I don't want it. It's like when
I'm working. I *feel* what's right to do and what isn't."

When Fanny learned that she was to have Nick's child,
she was probably the happiest woman in the Western Hemi-
sphere. Nick could not bring himself to share her enthusiasm
for the coming blessed event. "He hated to see me big,"
Fanny said. "I'd get out of bed and he'd go like a shot out of
hell for my robe to cover me up. He didn't like anything that
wasn't nice to look at. And that made me sad, because I had
waited so long to have this baby. I wanted him to say: 'Let
me feel it,' or: 'It's jumping, honey,' or anything to make me
feel he wanted the baby too. Every morning I was sick as a
dog. It was murder."

Fanny worked until she was seven months pregnant. When she left the show, Ziegfeld sent her this telegram:

YOU SHOULD HAVE MORE RESPECT FOR YOUR CONTRACT THAN TO ALLOW YOURSELF TO GET IN A POSITION WHERE YOU ARE FORCED TO QUIT ANY TIME YOU SEE FIT.

"My baby was born in Huntington, Long Island," Fanny said. "I had a house down there. That was the one thing Nick ever bought. He made some money gambling and he paid fourteen thousand dollars for it. And I paid twenty-five thousand dollars to have it remodeled. Nick had to have stables for his horses. So he lines the stables with mahogany. 'If we can't have it good, we won't have it at all,' he tells me. Well, he builds the mahogany stables, and I never saw a horse in them. Not even horse-blank."

Fanny's first child, Frances Brice Arnstein, was born on August 12, 1919. Fanny said the infant was the ugliest baby she ever saw, "all wrinkled up and old, like a rabbi who just lost his synagogue. I was going to name her Hope. All I could do was hope. But at six months she was beautiful."

A few days after Frances was born, Irene Castle, who was expecting a baby within a few weeks, called Fanny at the hospital on Long Island. "How does it feel, Fanny?" she asked anxiously.

"Like pushing a piano through a transom," Fanny replied.

✿ 8 ✿

POLLY MORAN: *"Wait, Maybe He'll Pinch the Other Leg."*

Laguna Beach is what all of us mean when we say: "Where the rich people go." It lies fifty miles south of Los Angeles along the Pacific. Its water seems bluer, its homes handsomer, its flowers more fragrant, its people better dressed, its boats bigger, its streets cleaner. It is a small jewel of a town that starts in the hills ringing the Pacific and comes down to the water's edge. Far up a sloping street, standing on the small front porch of a modest wooden bungalow, Polly Moran waited for her guests on a Sunday afternoon a few months before she died last year.

She was wearing a print apron, soiled and wrinkled. Her stockings were knotted below the knees. Her hair, gathered in curlers, was half covered with a red bandanna. She wore white sneakers, and she waved her callers forward.

"Got some new girls for you," Polly said. "You'll love these, young stuff, all of them. We got raided down below, you know. Yeah, had to move, but I'm running a real nice, clean house now."

Polly waited to see if her guests had been warned of this, her standard greeting to all visitors from the city. When she saw them grinning, she said: "Come in, come in. I've had five heart attacks since eleven o'clock (it was now three in the afternoon). I'm not supposed to smoke, but give me a cigarette for Christ's sake, I'm dying for a drag."

When she talked, you could hear her dentures clicking rhythmically, like castanets keeping the beat.

When she took the cigarette, she transferred the tiny bottle of nitroglycerin she always carried for her heart from her right hand to her left. "I speak of Fanny as though she's still here. Me supposed to be dead and she the healthy one. Well, figure it out, I can't."

Polly was mortally ill. The doctors had told her she had long since rounded the clubhouse turn, but that afternoon, sitting on the chintz-covered sofa, she was as indifferent to the expected visitor who would lead her to the deep sleep as you might be to a pimple on your finger. She talked about her own death as though she were waiting for a fourth at bridge, and never, not once, did she abandon the gaiety, the warmth, the friendliness that began with the greeting.

"Christ, I knew Fanny," she said, "since the *College Girls* in 1909. We were in New York together once and we went to a burlesque show and sat in a box. Some guy leans over and pinches my leg. 'Let's blow the joint,' Fanny says. 'Are you crazy, girl? Maybe he'll pinch the other leg,' I tell her.

"Nobody was too big for Fanny, that she couldn't set them down, let me tell you. She knew the biggest of them, and they never meant anything to her. She couldn't even remember their names. She would just be herself with all those society folks, and if she wanted to take off her shoes, off they came, and the next thing Fanny would be stretched out on the couch. One time John Wanamaker called . . ."

Fanny had promised to meet Eddie Cantor at the theater

for an impromptu rehearsal of a number they were doing in the Midnight Frolic, since this was Sunday and no performance was scheduled. Fanny was in her kitchen frying smelts, for which she had been yearning all week, and Nick was in the library with the Sunday papers, when John Wanamaker telephoned Fanny. He was in the neighborhood, he told her, he had an English friend with him who wanted to meet her, and could he bring the fellow up?

"Come on," Fanny said, and returned to the stove.

When Fanny heard Wanamaker's voice, she shouted: "In here, John, come on in the kitchen." She looked up from the stove as Nick, Wanamaker, and a slender, blond young man entered. "Take a load off your feet," Fanny said. "I'll be through here in a little while. We'll all eat smelts."

The Englishman sat down in a kitchen chair, and Fanny turned the fish carefully in the pan. The men chatted until the English butler appeared to ask how many would be having lunch.

"Four of us," Fanny said, and saw the butler stiffen as if he had just been accused of perpetrating the Boston Tea Party.

"Your Highness," he said. "I beg . . ."

"Your what?" Fanny asked.

Wanamaker and Nick were convulsed with laughter. The Englishman smiled uneasily. The butler, his face drained of color, was in danger of being taken with a fit.

"What the hell's going on here?" Fanny asked putting a lid on the smelts.

The butler backed slowly out of the room.

Fanny jabbed Wanamaker's chest with her forefinger. "Come on, John, come on, what's up?"

Wanamaker wiped the tears from his eyes. "Fanny, I'd like to present Edward, Prince of Wales."

"Yeah?" Fanny said. She set her spatula on the table, and

gave the young man her hand. "How are you, Prince? Say, I bet I'll get a thousand bucks for my chair now that you sat in it."

There followed a fine luncheon. The Prince complimented Fanny on her smelts. "Thanks," Fanny said. "Will Rogers loves my smelts," intimating that if the humorist, whom she considered the greatest man alive, enjoyed them, it was small surprise to her that the world's favorite royal personage should find them pleasing to his palate.

They lingered at the luncheon table, until the butler appeared, carrying a telephone, to announce that Mr. Cantor was calling. He plugged in the instrument and Fanny heard Cantor explode at his end.

"Tell me you're not coming," Cantor said, "but don't keep me waiting around here all day Sunday."

"Eddie, I swear I forgot. The Prince of Wales is here."

"Fanny, stop with the excuses."

"Honest, Eddie, he's sitting here. I'll put him on." Handing the receiver to the heir to England's throne, she said: "It's Eddie Cantor, Prince. He don't believe me."

"Hello," the Prince said. "Hello, this is Edward."

"Edward who?"

"Edward of England."

"Why don't you free Ireland?" Cantor demanded, and hung up.

Polly remembers that Nick seemed embarrassed at being a father. Once Fanny walked into the nursery as Nick was bending over Frances's crib. Fanny saw him talking to the child, and touching its body as though amazed at its perfection. He took his daughter's tiny hand in his and touched it with his lips. Fanny stood behind him, watching this scene for which she had waited and fought and defied Rosie, defied Ziegfeld, turned her back on friends, indeed on all of

society. She had wanted children with Nick, and now she
had his daughter. Let them talk. Let them whisper when
they saw her with Nick. What did they know of Fanny's
happiness? She said: "Nick, darling," putting out her hand
to touch him, but he avoided her, springing away from the
crib and hastily leaving the room.

In the past Nick had answered her love with lies that she
had responded to by offering her heart. He had made a thousand broken promises that she was able to forget. He had
hurt her, and Fanny had only come back for more. But this:
walking away from his daughter and from his daughter's
mother, she could not understand; for this she had no excuses to make for him, no smile to offer him, no arms to welcome him.

Polly paused in her story to cadge another cigarette, lighting it from the butt in her fingers. "Just a year ago I says to
Fanny, we're sitting upstairs in that big house of hers, and I
says: 'Why don't you quit? What are you working for,
Fanny?' And she tells me: 'I'm working for the kids.'

"Well, she left it for them. She worked for those two kids
from the day they were born, and what's better than that?"

Fanny herself, talking of her children, said: "Before they
were born, I made up my mind to one thing: when I had
children, they were going to know me as I was. My kids always got the truth. They knew I lived with their father six
years before I married him. If I wanted to swear, I would
swear in front of them. If they walked into the room and I
was telling a dirty story, when they were seven, eight, or
nine years old, I didn't stop. I think it's the most awful thing
when a mother or a father is telling a dirty story or talking
about sex, and a child walks in, and they say: 'Sh-h-h-h-h,
the children. Yes, darling, you want something?' The kid
knows you have stopped saying something that he isn't supposed to hear, that has an effect on a child. I could always

talk to my kids and say the things I wanted to say. I've told
them all about the things that happened to me. Everything.
I always wanted my kids to like me, not to love me as a
mother. You *have* to love your mother. I never wanted that.
One time the nurse said: 'Kiss your mother,' and I said to the
nurse: 'If you ever say that again, you'll be looking for a
job.'

"You know, that has a bad effect on the child, if you tell
the child he must love his mother. When that child gets to a
certain age, he says: 'Why must I love my mother? I like to
be with this person better than I like to be with her. Does
that mean I don't love her?' It's bad, that's all.

"Another thing. I didn't open a toy factory when my kids
were growing up. I put twenty-five dollars a month in the
bank for each of them, from the day they were born. You
see, when I knew I was going to have children, I had a terrible worry of them being brought up in a theatrical world,
where the parents are too busy for the kids, so they give them
a dollar a day to eat on, and when the boy is eight years
old he knows to look for dames already. I saw all those theatrical punks whom I could have killed, every one of them.
And I made up my mind that wasn't going to happen to me.
And I stuck to it."

While Fanny had no intention of forsaking the theater
for the joys of motherhood, she turned a deaf ear to Ziegfeld's persistent pleas that she rejoin the Follies. She might
have taken a sabbatical leave from the stage during the first
year of Frances's life, had it not been necessary that she earn
money to maintain her household. She compromised with
Ziegfeld by signing contracts to star again in his Midnight
Frolic on the Amsterdam Roof. Here, in a digest version of
the Follies being presented in the theater below, she appeared once nightly, together with Eddie Cantor, Bert Williams, Will Rogers, and W. C. Fields.

She saw little of Nick during those first months after
Frances was born on August 12, 1919. When she woke in
midmorning, Nick would be gone from the apartment, occupied with one deal or another. Sometimes he would return
during the late afternoon to change clothes and go out again.
Sometimes he would have dinner with Fanny in the apartment. Sometimes he would occupy a table at the Midnight
Frolic, playing host to a party of male friends, signing the
check for their liquor and food, which was deducted from
Fanny's salary. Sometimes he would escort Fanny home after
her performance, but more often she would take a cab back
to the apartment, because Nick had appropriated her big
green foreign limousine and her chauffeur. Sometimes Nick
would be sleeping when she returned from the night's work,
and one time, on Washington's Birthday in 1920, he was
packing. She had let herself into the apartment quietly, as
usual, not to waken Frances. She had taken off her shoes in
the foyer, as usual, and walked noiselessly into the nursery
to stand beside the baby's crib for a moment. She had leaned
over to kiss the child, as usual, before going to her bedroom,
when she saw the glow of lights, and Nick in shirtsleeves
putting clothes in a suitcase, which was not at all usual.

She said: "Where are you going?"

"Were you followed?" Nick asked.

"Followed where?"

"Did anyone follow you?" Nick asked.

"Who?" She came to his side. "Who's supposed to follow
me? What are you talking about? Nick, what's the matter?
What did you do? What did you do?" She was rapidly approaching hysteria as she begged him to tell her what had
happened, walking beside him from closet to suitcase, and
from suitcase to chest of drawers.

"You're sure nobody followed you?" Nick demanded as
he closed the suitcase.

"Tell me what's happening, Nick. Please, please tell me what's happening. Where are you going?"

"I have to get out of town for a few days, Fanny."

"What's a few days? Nick, what do you mean, a few days?" she asked, and sat down on her bed, her coat dragging on the floor, her hands limp in her lap, and her purse opening, the contents spilling and scattering like a broken bag of marbles. Long afterward she remembered that her feet were cold, and that she suddenly saw a run in her stocking and looked at it for a long time, unable to take her eyes from it, as Nick got into his jacket and his coat, and adjusted a black fedora carefully on his head.

"Where's your mustache?" Fanny asked.

"I was tired of it."

"You're lying," Fanny said. She noticed then that the coat was an old coat he had not worn for years; that the hat was one she had bought for him in England and that he had never liked. Nick turned from the mirror and reached for the suitcase.

"I'll keep in touch with you, Fanny," he said.

"Yes." She looked up at him. She could not get up. She held one hand in the other hand.

"I didn't do anything, Fanny."

"No," she said.

"You must believe me. I'm innocent of all this, and when the time comes I'll prove it."

"Yes, Nick." She had no idea what he was talking about.

"I'll keep in touch with you, dear," he said.

"All right."

He leaned over to brush her lips with his lips. "Don't worry, old girl," he said.

"Tell me how," Fanny said. She heard his quick steps. "How should I stop worrying, Nick?" she asked loudly. She heard him moving down the hall. "How?" she said, louder still. "How?" she asked, but the door had shut behind him then, and she sat there on the bed with her hands in her lap and the purse on the floor with its contents spilled around her feet, until she could no longer hear the echo of his voice in her mind, or the sound of the door closing behind her husband who was gone for an unknown reason to an unknown place for an unknown time, leaving her alone.

9

FANNY: *"He Couldn't Master Mind an Electric Bulb into a Socket."*

FOR nine days Fanny knew no more about Nick's disappearance than did six-month-old Frances. Then, on February 21, 1920, the *New York Times* printed a front-page story that told, as completely as it has ever been told, the details of the bond thefts that were to plague Fanny for so many years.

This three-bank headline topped the story:

NAME MASTER MIND IN GREAT BOND PLOT

Court Petition Calls "Nicky" Arnstein Head of Plot to Steal $5,000,000 in Wall Street

One of the Gondorf Gang

Surety Co. Seeks to Seize Money Gained by Thefts of $1,500,000 from Messengers

Then:

Through the filing of an involuntary petition in bankruptcy yesterday the identity of the man the police allege to be the "Master Mind" in the recent plot to steal

$5,000,000 worth of securities from brokerage houses and banks in the financial district was revealed.

According to the petition, which was filed . . . for the National Surety Co. at 115 Broadway, the man is Nicholas Arnstein, better known in the "white light" district as "Nicky" Arnstein.

The petition of the surety company also says that Arnstein, who also is identified under half a dozen aliases, is the man who received securities valued at $1,500,000 from criminals who robbed messengers in the financial district.

Wm. A. Thompson, a vice president of the surety company, declared . . . that the assertion that the bankrupt was "Nicky" Arnstein was based on a confession recently made to Richard C. Murphy, Asst. District Attorney, by Joseph Gluck, one of seven men arrested ten days ago . . . in connection with the plot to steal $5,000,000 worth of securities.

When the detective recently arrested Gluck and "Big Bill" Furey, also well known in the "white light" region, on the charge of stealing $2500 worth of securities from Murray Abramovitch, a messenger employed by Parrish & Co. brokers at 115 Broadway, they revealed that they had uncovered a plot to steal $5,000,000 in securities from brokerage houses. Furey and Gluck were arrested in front of the Woolworth Building at Broadway and Park Place just after Joseph Gluck had taken the securities owned by Parrish & Co. from young Abramovitch's pocket.

Several messengers in the financial district who were approached by Gluck with the proposal informed the detectives of having accompanied Joseph Gluck to the Claridge Hotel (in Times Square) where they met Furey, who later, guiding them around Tenderloin re-

sorts, introduced them to several alleged politicians who, Furey explained would aid the plotters to escape with the $5,000,000 worth of securities without interference from the local police.

Within the last four days detectives have escorted Gluck and the messengers through the "white light" district in quest of the "Master Mind" in the plot. It is now believed that the detectives sought "Nicky" Arnstein who is known to the police of this country as a member of the notorious Gondorf band of fake wire tappers, who several years ago fleeced scores of men in this city for sums aggregating upward of $1,000,000.

It was in a campaign inaugurated by the police against the band that "Nicky" Arnstein, on June 28, 1915, was sentenced . . . to three years in Sing Sing on his conviction in a "wire tapping" swindle.

Fanny was still asleep that morning, having seen no newspapers and heard nothing from Nick, when the maid woke her to announce two gentlemen callers. Two *police* gentlemen, the maid added. Fanny, who all her life would not be seen when she was not faultlessly groomed, threw a dressing-gown about her and rushed into the library barefoot, forgetting even her mules.

Where one of the cops displayed a morning paper with the story of Nick's alleged implication in the stolen-bonds case. Fanny read the headlines and gave the cop back his newspaper, refusing even to read the story.

Fanny never believed for a moment that Nick was involved in the bond robbery. Writing of the case many years later, she said: "This is what actually happened: there were a couple of messenger boys, runners in Wall Street, who used to deliver bonds to peoples' houses. The bonds were in different names and some guy in the gang that Nick hung

around with, some stupid guy somehow got the idea that he
could get rid of them. He got to the messenger boys and
told them he knew a banker in Washington who could get
rid of the bonds for them. The boys told the man they would
like to meet the banker and talk to him, but the guy said
that this was impossible; they could see him, but he was too
important a guy to talk to punks like them. So the fellow
arranges for them to be in a restaurant on 86th Street and
Broadway. He then called Nick and said: 'How about a
drink? I want to talk to you.' So Nick meets him for a drink
in this restaurant, the two messenger boys see the guy with
this tall, handsome, well-dressed man, and they go in on the
deal. In those days Nick looked more like a banker than
J. P. Morgan.

"After the kids got caught, they told all about the banker
from Washington. They were asked: 'Did you meet the
banker?' They said: 'No, but we saw him.' So they were
shown a lot of pictures, and when they saw Nick's picture,
they said: 'That's the banker.' "

Fanny's story of Nick's involvement in the case is substantially the same as Nick's explanation as recorded in his own
unpublished autobiography. However, the facts in the case
pointed to something more.

"Master Mind," she told the law. "He couldn't Master
Mind an electric bulb into a socket."

The two detectives disagreed. First graciously, then po-
litely, then bluntly, then rudely, then insultingly, they ques-
tioned her about Nick, about the securities, about Gluck.
To all their questions she gave the same answer, "I don't
know," but the police were neither satisfied with her reply
nor bored with repeating their queries. Her relief at discovering to her own satisfaction that Nick was innocent soon
gave way to annoyance, which later grew to complete, en-
veloping fear.

Which was precisely the effect that the two detectives had been working for.

You have to understand something about police in whatever city and country in the world: they're tough. Reporters have a word for it: copper-hard. It's not a cause so much as an effect. You walk a beat for eight hours, with kids jeering at you, drunks clawing at you, women screaming at you, men insulting you, and nobody, not the shopkeeper, the cab driver, the bartender, the pedestrian, none of them with even a smile for you, and you get tough awful fast. You read and hear now about fingerprints, and lie detectors, and laboratories, and college-trained criminologists, all of them busy as bees outsmarting the thief, but more crimes are solved daily in any detective squad-room by two cops who can punch than by all the microscopes and machines at headquarters. Question a thief and he'll laugh at you. Put a light on him, take his cigarettes away, and hit him a blow just above the kidneys where it won't leave a sign, and he'll stop laughing. Hit him enough blows and pretty soon he'll be pleading to answer questions. This isn't telling secrets and it isn't breaking a scandal. It's a fact of life. Doctors use stethoscopes and cops use force. And remember this is not a defense of cops, it's an explanation of how they operate. Get tough with a thief, and he talks. Get tough with a private law-abiding citizen, and he talks even quicker.

Except that Fanny had nothing to tell them. Nine days ago she had been certain Nick had done something outside the law. Now she was as certain that he hadn't. That first day she stayed the entire ten rounds with the cops and you had to call it a draw. When they left at last, she played with Frances, took a hot bath, tried to eat something and couldn't. She tried to sleep and couldn't. She stayed in the apartment, refused to answer the telephone, gave orders to admit no one. When the time came for her to dress for her night's work, she rang for her maid, thinking no more about it than the true soldier who obeys the order to advance.

There was none of "the show must go on" business in Fanny with which to dramatize the situation. Katharine Hepburn said of her: "Fanny had a kind of peasant quality in her honesty to her work. The theater was what she did, as the butcher cuts meat, and the tailor mends clothes. One didn't talk or think about one's work. One did it."

Any qualms Fanny had about going to the theater that night were of an entirely different nature. She told the stage manager when she arrived at the New Amsterdam to spread the word: Don't talk to Fanny about Nick. Just forget the whole thing. "I was afraid," she said, "that somebody would put an arm around me and say: 'I'm sorry, Fanny.' If anybody had done that, I would have slugged them: I just can't stand anything like that."

"I just hate for anyone to cry in front of anybody," she wrote once. "I don't want anybody to cry in front of me, and I don't cry in front of anybody. You should be alone if you want to cry. I could only cry in front of the man I was in love with.

"Being a funny person does an awful lot of things to you. You feel that you mustn't get serious with people. They don't expect it from you, and they don't want to see it. You're not entitled to be serious, you're a clown, and they only want you to make them laugh.

"When my mother died, I called my sister up the day of the funeral. 'Carrie,' I said, 'I don't want one tear out of you. If you let out one yell, you are going to force me to walk out of the undertaking parlor.' You see, Carrie had no way to express herself, and if there was any situation came up where she could go dramatic, she loved that."

That night at the Midnight Frolic, the cast and the stage-hands stayed away from Fanny. She remained in her dress-

ing-room, alone with her maid, and she didn't know that
W. C. Fields and Will Rogers took turns standing guard before her door. She didn't know that Eddie Cantor had gone
to Ziegfeld with a proposal that Fanny's part in the Frolic
be shortened temporarily. She didn't know, it just didn't occur to her, that the Amsterdam Roof would be jammed,
hours before she was to appear, with the Broadway habitués
who are never so happy as when they are sadistically wit-
nessing heartbreak while they remain safely wrapped in the
false cloak of friendship and loyalty.

When she appeared before her audience that night, Fanny
saw the two detectives at a ringside table. She was making
her entrance. Watching them and abandoning her usual routine and tripping purposely all in one instant, she had the
audience helpless with laughter by the time she had righted
herself, clapping her hand to her forehead in the gesture
that had now become her very own.

That was the start. She stayed out there alone for nearly
an hour. She was not content with winning an audience. Tonight she had to own them, and own them she did, con-
vulsing even the cops who had been assigned to go wherever
she went, to keep her under twenty-four-hour "tail." She
worked that night out of a repertoire that had its beginnings
on Forsythe Street on the Lower East Side, that had roots
in a Newark saloon and on a Brooklyn street-corner, that
had flowered in burlesque and bloomed on Broadway. She
performed as she had never performed, and watching her
with no trace of envy were such workmen as Will Rogers,
and Eddie Cantor, and W. C. Fields, whose applause, when
she had finished, matched the audience's.

Who would not let the show continue. They stopped it
for twenty minutes, but Fanny was finished for the night.
They were still applauding when she walked out of the
stage door, walked past the two detectives, not looking at

them, to the chauffeur who waited beside the open door of
her limousine.

In the days that followed, Fanny lost twenty pounds, until, at 110, she was gaunt and drawn. She could keep nothing
on her stomach except liquids. She slept now only with the
help of pills. She was greeted daily by the morning newspapers, which she read carefully, and by Frances's nurse,
who brought the baby to her bedroom. One morning as
Fanny held her child the nurse said: "Such a pack of reporters and photographers outside, ma'am, as you wouldn't imagine. I hope you won't think I'm complaining, but going
past them every day is getting to be more and more difficult."

"Yeah?" Fanny said.

"They are so rude, ma'am."

"They are, eh?"

"When I take the child to the park, they ask me so many
questions as to drive me daft."

"You're not going to the park," Fanny decided.

"But the child must have the air, ma'am."

"She'll have the air," Fanny said, and shouted for her maid.
"You take Frances and get her ready," she told the nurse.
"I'm taking her to the park."

"But you can't," the nurse protested. "You do need your
rest, ma'am."

"Don't worry so much about my goddam rest," Fanny
told her. "I'll get my rest. How long do you keep the baby out
every day?"

"Two hours, ma'am. But you shouldn't . . ."

"Shut up, and get the baby dressed." Fanny held up
Frances and, when the nurse had taken her, left the bed. In a
moment Rosie hurried into the bedroom.

"Fanny, all those reporters," she began. "Fanny, please,
for your own sake don't do it."

"Mom, don't start with me," Fanny warned. "If those bastards think I'm ducking them, they're crazy. Now don't tell me what to do, for Christ's sake."

Within thirty minutes Fanny emerged from the building, pushing the baby carriage. The cordon of newsmen followed her into the park, where the photographers, walking backward, began to adjust their cameras, preparing to take their pictures on the move.

"Just a minute," Fanny said. She stopped, raised the lid of the buggy so they could see Frances, and stood beside the carriage.

Standing there, she looked at all of them and each of them until they had taken their pictures and dispersed. Then she pushed down the lid of the buggy and resumed her walk.

She would accept no aid. She wanted no arms to help her and no shoulders to weep on. There was an evening when she returned to her bedroom after feeding Frances, and lay down on the chaise longue, hoping to rest for a time before dressing for the Midnight Frolic. Fanny's maid found her there, lying on her side, unable to get up. Alarmed, the maid telephoned Rosie, who appeared quickly with an osteopath in tow. While Rosie paced the room, first threatening, then pleading to be allowed to call Ziegfeld and cancel Fanny's performance, the osteopath massaged, pounded, and cracked bones. After working on Fanny for some time, he told her to get up. She rose, felt her body as though counting her limbs to make certain that the osteopath had not removed a leg or an arm, slapped that gentleman on the back, and hired him on the spot.

"You're with me, Doc," she said. "You're going to the theater with me, and you'll be here every night at six o'clock, okay?" The osteopath agreed, and Rosie led him into the library while Fanny changed clothes. Later, in her dressing-room, he massaged her once more just before she went on stage. When she had finished her performance, one of the girls in the chorus stopped Fanny in the wings to tell her Arnold Rothstein was out front.

"Tell Flo to watch the knives and forks," Fanny said, and went to her dressing-room.

On the night of February 26, two weeks after Nick had walked out of the bedroom, W. C. Fields came into Fanny's dressing-room, trembling as with ague. At a sign from Fields, Fanny told the osteopath to take a walk. As the door closed behind him, Fields locked it, leaned against it, and handed Fanny an envelope. It was from Akron, Ohio, and it was addressed to Fields.

> *How are you old Pal* [Nick had written]. *Just sitting here thinking about our old friends, the trips we had, and thinking about that little girl. I believe her name was Fanny. If you see her, give her my regards. Tell her I am all right and will get in touch with her.*

He did. The following day, as she entered a dressmaking shop where she had an appointment for a fitting, a man who was leaving whispered: "Go to the Opera Café." This establishment, across the street from the Metropolitan Opera House, was a sporting men's favorite, and that afternoon she talked to Nick on the telephone. He would not tell her where he was, he could not tell her when he would return; but he ordered her to retain William Fallon as his counsel.

Fallon, the subject of Gene Fowler's biography, *The Great Mouthpiece*, was then New York's most brilliant criminal lawyer. A flamboyant figure with orange-colored hair he was reputed to cut himself, Fallon, with his partner, Eugene F. McGee, was on a Roman holiday in the courts of New York. At the moment Fallon was in a Bronx courtroom defending one Ernest Fritz, a cab driver accused of the murder of his mistress while both were engaged in particularly vehement dalliance in the back seat of his taxi.

After the luncheon recess, while Fallon was cross-examining a state's witness, he heard a murmur sweep the courtroom. Turning, he saw Fanny Brice take a seat beyond the rail. Fallon, normally a tiger at the bar, outdid even himself that afternoon. When court was adjourned for the day, Fanny asked Fallon if he would represent Nick. Fallon, who would have defended the Mafia if a woman had asked him, bowed before Fanny and told her gallantly that he was her humble servant.

Before the week was out, Nick had been adjudged an involuntary bankrupt and Fanny had been ordered to turn over all bankbooks and safety-deposit-box keys. Within twelve hours, sixteen thousand dollars in the Pacific bank, as well as Fanny's funds, were held by the court, and Fanny was summoned to appear before a United States Commissioner in the Federal Building downtown. With Fallon at her side she walked the gantlet of Manhattan's newspapermen and photographers. She answered no questions, she paused for no pictures, she walked up the steps as though she had been summoned to be decorated by her government, and if the federal attorney expected a sobbing, hysterical woman, he was disappointed that day.

When Fallon objected to the government lawyer's repeated insinuations that Fanny was hand in glove with Nick, that she had been in on the bond thefts from the start, that she was now shielding her husband, and could, indeed, tell the court where he could be found, she paused to tell the Commissioner: "Let him ask me anything he wants. I'll answer whatever I can."

"How much money did you give him [Nick]?" she was asked.

"Oh, I don't know," she replied. "He'd say: 'Fanny, lend me five hundred dollars,' and I'd give him the money, and he'd go out and gamble it. Sometimes he'd come back and hand me twenty dollars or fifty dollars."

Once, as the attorney paused to marshal his attack, Fanny said: "I'm used to standing up while others sit. Here things are reversed. I'm sitting and the audience is standing."

"Would you rather stand?" asked the attorney in a rare moment of courtesy.

"No," Fanny said, "I'd rather sing a song."

She sang as usual that night and saw Fallon sitting at a table with Arnold Rothstein. Fallon sent a note to Fanny's dressing-room asking her to join them. When Fanny appeared, Fallon introduced Rothstein, who said he wanted to help her. Nick had informed Fallon that he would not surrender himself until a reasonable bail bond was guaranteed. Fallon gave this information to the reporters, who hurried to Assistant District Attorney John T. Dooling, in charge of the case. While the newspapers announced bail in amounts ranging from seventy-five thousand to two hundred thousand dollars, Nick remained in hiding, although his picture was posted in every precinct station and post-office lobby in the country.

"I don't need any help from anybody," Fanny told Rothstein.

"I understand," Rothstein said. "If you ever do, I am ready to post any amount up to one hundred thousand dollars as bail for a certain fellow."

"Why?" Fanny demanded.

"Because I like guts," Rothstein said, "and you've got guts."

Fanny became worried that the police would tap the telephone at the Opera Café, and arranged to take Nick's calls in the apartment of a woman friend who was enjoying the Florida sun. One afternoon, as she waited in the apartment for Nick's call, rereading the latest letter Fields had given her, there was a knock at the door. "This is the janitor," a man said. "There's a leaking faucet in there I've got to fix."

Fanny put the letter in her purse and opened the door. Three detectives whom she had never seen pushed their way past her. This time there was no period of courteous questioning. They knew, Fanny was told, that she had been hearing from Nick.

"You're crazy," Fanny told them.

"He's written you," one detective said.

"You're crazy," Fanny said.

"We know you get letters from Nick," another said.

"That's more than I know."

"What are you doing in this apartment?"

"It's my friend's place. You cops won't let me alone in my place. I've got to rest somewhere."

While two detectives made a thorough search of the flat, the third continued to question Fanny.

"When did you hear from him last?"

"I told you," Fanny said. "Washington's Birthday."

"You're lying!"

"You're nuts!" Fanny replied, as loudly.

"What's in that pocketbook?"

"White mice," Fanny said, not daring to look at the purse beside her.

"You've got a letter from Nick."

"That's what you say," Fanny replied, reaching for the purse. "Here," she said, offering it to him. "Do you expect me to carry letters around in my pocketbook? Go on, cop, open it and see for yourself, and stop asking me all these goddam stupid questions."

For a moment Fanny and the detective stared at each

other, the purse in her hand between them. Then the detective turned his head. "Got anything?" he asked his colleagues. They returned empty-handed, and the questioning began again as the telephone rang.

A detective took a step toward it, but his confederate held his arm. "You," he said to Fanny. "You answer it."

"This isn't my apartment," she said. "I was just using it . . ."

And a third ring echoed through the flat.

". . . to get away from you. I'm not . . ."

"Answer it!" the detective ordered.

". . . going to answer it," Fanny continued, "and you're not going to make me answer it."

It rang again.

And the leader released the other man's arm, nodding to him.

When Nick, telephoning from Pittsburgh, heard a man's voice, he hung up immediately. The detective at once ordered the operator to trace the call, and while they waited, one of them offered Fanny a cigarette.

"I wouldn't take the time of day from you," Fanny replied. She got up from the sofa. "Now, if it's all right with you jerks, I'm going to take a nap," she said, leaving them as she went into the bedroom.

But she forgot her purse.

She lay on the bed, with the purse in the other room. She would not move, lest the bed creak and drown out the noise of the pocketbook opening. She breathed carefully, she lay stiff, she held the pillow with both hands, gripping the percale with all her strength, until she heard their steps as they crossed the other room, and the door opening and closing. She waited for ten minutes more before rising and going into the other room, locking the door, and rushing to the purse.

Where she found her letter from Nick, untouched.

Within two days a new rendezvous was chosen where Fanny could get her calls from Nick; this time a brassière factory in downtown Manhattan, owned by one of Nick's friends.

"I would spend two hours between my apartment and the factory," Fanny wrote later. "One trick I used was to go to Macy's, head for the ladies' room, and leave there by a special doorway for employees which led to a back stairway. I remembered it from years before, when a girl I knew worked there."

Six weeks had passed since Nick had walked out of their bedroom. Fanny's weight had dropped to something over eighty pounds. She would not see a physician, and she would not miss a performance of the Frolic. The osteopath, alarmed at her condition, refused to continue the massages. Rosie was frantic with worry. Ziegfeld pleaded with Fanny to rest. Newspapermen and detectives dogged her, yet not once did Fanny ask Nick to come home. Not once did she reply to Nick's questions concerning her welfare, except to say: "I'm fine, darling. Don't worry about me."

The newspapers began to demand Nick's arrest, and their columns were filled with derision and scorn for New York's police and for the District Attorney's office. Now Fallon came to John T. Dooling and offered a deal: he would produce Nick if bail were set at fifty thousand dollars and a letter were given him promising Nick safe conduct to the Criminal Courts building. When that was refused, he proposed that three detectives accompany his partner, McGee, to Nick's hiding-place. Arnstein would return with them. Dooling dispatched the cops and McGee led them to Pittsburgh, but Nick sent word that he would meet them in Rochester, New York. From Rochester the quartet was told to go to Utica, thence to Niagara Falls, back to Utica, over to Syracuse, and, after two weeks of sleeper jumps, once more to

Pittsburgh. Here McGee told Arnstein that the latter could stay away for the rest of his days as far as he was concerned, and boarded a train for New York with the detectives.

Then, on the night of May 15, two months and three days after Nick had disappeared, Fallon received a telephone call. He was told to go to Fanny's apartment the following morning, pick up Fanny's car, and drive it to 90th Street and Columbus Avenue, where Nick would be waiting on the southwest corner.

The next day, with Fanny in the back seat, Fallon began to drive down Columbus Avenue toward 90th Street. Fanny sat first in one corner of the car and then in the other. She leaned forward, she lay back, and finally sat on the edge of the seat, her right hand holding the door handle.

"Jesus, Bill," she said, "I'm nervous. Are you nervous, Bill?"

"Fanny," said that gallant, "I was born nervous."

"What time is it, Bill?"

"Plenty of time, Fanny."

"He'll be there, won't he, Bill?"

"Of course he will."

"I hope nothing's gone wrong. Jesus, I *hope* nothing's gone wrong. *Bill—a cop!*"

"Protecting the citizens' property, Fanny," Fallon said, waving gaily at the policeman.

As they passed 93rd Street, Fanny said: "Do you see him, Bill?"

"We're quite a distance, Fanny."

"Look for him, Bill. Be careful. You'd better drive close to the curb," Fanny said. "Look at that stupid sonofabitch," pointing at a truck for whom Fallon had to swing out. She lowered the window rapidly. "Blank-head!" she roared as they crossed 92nd Street.

And Fallon slammed on the brakes while a dog unhurriedly crossed the street. Fanny leaned forward until her chin was resting on the front seat. "I don't see him," she said.

Fallon was close to the curb.

"Bill, I don't see anybody."

Fallon searched the intersection as they approached 90th Street.

"Bill, where is he? Where is he?" she asked again. Then: "He won't be here, Bill. He couldn't make it," she decided. "Bill, something is wrong, I know it," she cried, as Fallon stopped the car and Nick came out of a doorway, smiling confidently at his wife.

He climbed into the car and into the arms of Fanny, who held him, pushing him back against the seat. She held him and looked at him, examined him carefully, and she said: "You're thin, darling."

"I'm innocent, Fanny."

"I know you are, darling."

"Hello, Bill," Nick said.

"Hello, Nick," Fallon replied.

"You haven't been eating, Nick," Fanny said.

"I'm okay, my dear."

"Won't you ever grow your mustache?" she asked. She touched his lip with her forefinger. "I like your mustache," she said.

"Back it goes, Fanny," he promised.

"You're not hurt?" Fanny asked.

"They can't hurt Nick Arnstein, old girl."

"You're sure you're all right?"

"Don't worry about me," Nick said, while Fallon started the trip downtown. The irrepressible Irishman, knowing that a police parade was scheduled to begin within the hour, drove east to Fifth Avenue and swung the large limousine into the parade route. As they passed the reviewing stand on lower Fifth Avenue, Nick leaned out of the window to salute most of the city's ranking police-officials, who were gathered to watch the parade.

Arriving at the Criminal Courts buildings, Nick alighted first, and turned to help Fanny out of the car. Fallon suggested that Nick go alone to Dooling's office. Fanny took her husband's arm, holding it tightly, saying nothing to Fallon, or to Nick, until the lawyer shrugged and the three entered the building. Nick surrendered and was immediately taken before the United States Commissioner. On Fallon's advice, he would not answer any questions, offering the now standard explanation: "I refuse to answer on the ground that to do so might tend to incriminate me." The Commissioner held Nick in contempt of court, without bail. A Sunday-morning newspaper account of the proceedings read, in part: "Fanny Brice was with her husband from the time he met her and his lawyer at 9 o'clock in the morning until the door of his cell in the Ludlow Street jail was slammed shut for the night."

It neglected to add that Fanny went from the jail to the Amsterdam Roof for her performance in the Midnight Frolic.

✵ 10 ✵

THE NEW YORK GRAPHIC: "'*My Man' Killed Our Love!*"

Wᴛᴛʜ Nick behind bars, held without bail, Fallon tried desperately to obtain a writ of habeas corpus. No federal judge in New York would sign it. While Fallon took the necessary legal steps to sue for the writ before the United States Supreme Court, Fanny took on another chore: the daily preparation of Nick's meals. She would not let Nick eat the food served prisoners at the Ludlow Street jail. She would not let Rosie do the cooking. She would not give up her walks in the park with Frances, and a friend remembers that she never appeared in the visitors' room for her daily visit with Nick in the same dress twice. It was as if Nick had just returned from the wars and Fanny wanted him to fall in love all over again.

Fallon finally was ordered to appear before the Supreme Court. The United States Marshal in New York was directed to bring Nick to Washington, where he immediately took a suite at the Willard Hotel. Fanny sent her butler to the capital to wait on her husband. She made the journey two and

three times a week, taking the last train from New York after
her performance, and staying with Nick until after lunch.
On those nights when she remained in New York, the suite
at the Willard was filled with more women than Washington
was to see until Franklin Delano Roosevelt ordered the
WAC activated, twenty-two years later. You have to remember also that while Nick was waiting in Washington for the
Supreme Court's decision, and staying in the Willard Hotel,
and pouring wine for a large number of the District of Columbia's female population, he could not have raised the
price of a bottle of beer.

After several weeks the Supreme Court ordered the United
States District Court in New York to issue the writ of habeas
corpus. Fallon had won, but he was not satisfied. He appealed the contempt conviction before the nine black-robed
men, and won again when the tribunal ruled that no man
need give any answer that he felt would incriminate him.

A few days later Fallon produced Nick in New York's General Sessions Court, where the counselor announced that his
client was ready to stand trial and prove his innocence. Fallon asked that bail be set, and the judge named seventy-five
thousand dollars as the price for Nick's temporary freedom.

A newspaperman who covered the court that day remembers Fanny rushing to Nick as the judge left the bench: she
hurrying to Nick and the uniformed attendants walking toward their prisoner: she holding Nick, promising him he
would sleep at home tonight, and the attendants pausing,
standing a few feet from husband and wife while they embraced.

"I'll be back here this afternoon, darling," she promised
Nick.

"Don't worry about me, my dear."

"Who else is there to worry about? I have to worry about
you. I love you, Nick."

"They're waiting, Fanny," Nick said.

"Let them wait." She didn't turn to look at them. "I waited longer than they did. Eat a small lunch, Nick, and we'll have a big dinner tonight."

"All right, my dear."

"What do you want for dinner, Nick?" she asked, while Fallon stood by, and the attendants stood by, and the reporters for once, this one time, waited. "I'll make it myself. Gee, I'll give you a dinner you'll never forget."

"I think we ought to worry about the bail first, Fanny," Nick said.

"I'll get the bail," she said again, and turned to Fallon. "Bill, I want to talk with you." And to the court attendants: "All right, kids, you can have him for an hour or two."

When Nick was gone, she said: "Where can I find Arnold Rothstein?"

"Fanny, there may have been an easier question to answer since the dawn of time, but I doubt it," Fallon said.

"I haven't got much time, Bill. You're his lawyer, aren't you?"

"He prefers to think I am," Fallon said, as they crossed the lobby to the street. "I have his telephone number, Fanny, but I warn you, Rothstein is not an easy man to find."

"I'll find him," Fanny said. "Give me that number."

Fallon wrote it on a newspaper he was carrying. They parted and Fanny hurried to a phone booth. When there was no answer, she left the building and directed her chauffeur to take her uptown, naming a well-known gambling-house to which Nick had once taken her.

Where a man looked through a hole in the front door and said they were closed.

"I'm Fanny Brice. Rothstein sent me here. Do you want to let me in, or do you want me to get Rothstein?" she asked.

The door opened and Fanny hurried past the plug-ugly to

the card room, where she accosted a man in shirtsleeves.
"I'm Fanny Brice," she repeated. "I want Arnold Rothstein.
You get him for me, or get someone who will get him for me.
Tell him I'm waiting here for him. And hurry."

The jacketless man disappeared and Fanny leaned back
against a card table, surveying the empty room. In a moment
a door opened, another man stared at her, and the door
closed.

Within five minutes the shirtsleeved man returned. "Broadway and 45th Street," he said. "Northwest corner. Thirty
minutes."

"Thanks, kid," she said, and hurried out.

She told the chauffeur to drop her at the appointed intersection and had just reached the curb when a taxi drew up
behind her limousine. "Miss Brice," someone said in the cab,
as the door opened.

Fanny got in beside a young, fair-haired man who looked
as if he were down from Yale on a holiday. "Mr. Rothstein is
waiting, Miss Brice," he said, as the cab left the curb.

Fanny studied him. "What's a nice-looking kid like you
doing with these guys?" she asked.

The man flushed.

"You're a sucker, kid," she said, as the cab sped west toward the Hudson River.

And stopped behind a huge, black car, a block from the
waterfront. "Mr. Rothstein is in there," the man said, nodding at the car.

He opened the door for her and Fanny walked the few feet
to the other vehicle. As she approached, the door opened,
and in a moment she was sitting beside Rothstein.

"Fanny, this is a distinct honor and a great privilege,"
Rothstein said, removing his hat.

"Yeah, sure," Fanny said. "Listen, Arnold, you said that
you . . ."

Rothstein put an envelope in her hand.

"It's seventy-five thousand dollars, I believe," he said.

Fanny just stared at the envelope.

"You'd better count it, Fanny," he said.

"Gee, Arnold. Gee, thanks," she said, as she reached for the door handle.

"Count it, Fanny," he said quietly.

"I'll never forget you for this, Arnold," she said, pressing down on the handle, but Rothstein pulled the door shut.

"Fanny," he said. "Fanny," he repeated, waiting for her complete attention. "Count it, Fanny. We wouldn't want you to be short."

Fanny opened the envelope. She counted seventy-five thousand dollars in Liberty Bonds, counting slowly, and then Rothstein nodded.

"Give Nick my very, very best," he said.

"I will, Arnold, I will," she said, reaching for the handle again, but Rothstein was already out of the door on his side of the car. He stood beside the car, his hat in his hand, smiling at Fanny, until he turned to the chauffeur. "Take Miss Brice downtown," he ordered, and waited until the limousine had pulled away.

She got Nick home for dinner that night, and for many nights following, while Fallon stalled, waiting for the case to lose its front-page importance. But Joseph Gluck and his brother, Irving, who had also been arrested in the case, turned state's evidence and named Nick as the seller of the bonds in Boston and Washington, D.C. Knowing that Nick faced up to twenty-five years in prison if convicted in New York, against a maximum sentence of two years if found guilty in the District of Columbia, Fallon succeeded in having Nick tried in Washington. When Fanny went to Rothstein for another five thousand dollars to be used as bail in

Washington, the gambler asked her why she stuck with
Nick.

"Because I love him," Fanny replied.

"But how can you love a man like that?" Rothstein asked.

"With my heart," Fanny answered.

To others who continually brought her unsolicited stories
of Nick's infidelity, she replied always with the same question: "Did you see it?" and for the increasing number who
advised her to leave Nick, there was another answer. When
her husband's trial opened in Washington, she was carrying
his second child.

Fallon elected to keep Nick off the stand, since any testimony he gave might be used against him if he were later
forced to stand trial in New York. In cross-examination Fallon so confused the government's witnesses that the jury disagreed and a new trial was ordered.

"I think Nick enjoyed all the publicity," Fanny wrote later.
"When he was out on bail, everyone would want to meet
him. When someone sat down at our table in a restaurant
and I would tell them Nick had nothing to do with it, he
would shut me up. He enjoyed all that stuff and the headlines. He wanted people to think of him as the Master
Mind."

The "Master Mind" was in Washington waiting for his second trial when his son was born. Remembering that morning, Fanny said that her doctor had been calling on another
patient in the same building, and decided to have a cup of
coffee with her. "After breakfast," Fanny said, "the doctor
figures he might as well examine me while he's there. So he
examines me.

" 'Come on,' he says, 'you're going to the hospital.'

" 'You're crazy,' I tell him. 'What's the matter with you?
I feel wonderful.'

" 'I don't care how you feel,' the doc says. 'You're in labor.'

" 'I got no pain,' I tell him.

" 'You will have,' the doc says and gets my coat.

" 'Will you for Christ's sake let me get dressed?' I ask him.

"He throws a coat over my robe. 'For what you're going to be doing, you won't need any clothes,' he says, and hustles me downstairs to his car and drives me up to the hospital. Now the nurse puts me in bed, and he goes away to make some arrangements, but I feel nothing. Absolutely nothing. Now, Lillian Lorraine [a Follies girl] is in the hospital, so I get out of bed, and take a walk to visit with her. So I'm up in Lill's room with her, eating some of her candy, and the phone rings. The doc says to come right down, I'm going to have a baby. I say to Lill: 'You know that guy's nuts. Do I look like I'm going to have a baby?'

" 'No,' Lill says.

"But the baby isn't even moving. I sit down and get another piece of candy. All of a sudden the door opens, three nurses come shooting in, they grab me, hustle me out to the hall, and flop me down on one of those tables, you know, with wheels on it. They wheel me into the delivery room, put my feet in the stirrups, and—*zing*—there's the baby. Now I've been praying nine months for a boy, so the first thing I look to see what I got. Holy Christ, it's a boy! I let out a yell and the doc says: 'Get her out of here, she's making too much noise.' "

She named her son William, after Fallon, and three weeks after his birth she was rehearsing for the new Follies. When she was asked why she returned to work so soon after leaving the hospital, she replied: "Somebody has to pay the rent."

One day during rehearsal Ziegfeld asked her to listen to a song. It was a French tune, *"Mon Homme,"* or "My Man," for which an English-language lyric had been written by

Channing Pollock. As the pianist pounded out the melody, Ziegfeld handed her a copy of the lyric.

Which Pollock might have taken from the newspaper accounts of Fanny's courtship of Nick. Which he could have written only for Fanny. Which detailed, with keyhole clarity, what went on behind the closed doors of her life. It was a maudlin, weeping, melodramatic lyric, and Fanny could no more have handed it back to Ziegfeld than she could have given up the stage for field work in the Women's Christian Temperance Union. Fanny made Ziegfeld *give* her the song then and there.

Except that nobody else could have sung it. It was Fanny's own from the day it was written. It became her trademark, as "Some of These Days" became Sophie Tucker's, and "Mammy" became Al Jolson's.

With one important difference: Tucker and Jolson made a song theirs by repeated renditions of it. "My Man" was Fanny's song before she sang it.

And before she would sing it that afternoon at rehearsal, she hurried to her dressing-room. Somewhere she borrowed a red wig and a shawl, and she got into a black dress, around which she draped a red scarf, tying it in a bow behind her. She came back to the empty stage thinking she looked as French as Colette. Ziegfeld very nearly took a fit.

"Who do you think you are?" he demanded, as he raced to the stage. "You're not Bert Savoy" (a female impersonator). He leaped up on the stage and reached for the wig. He flung it from him, hurling it far back into the darkened corners of the stage. He tore the red scarf from her dress and threw it into the orchestra pit. He seized the black dress with both hands and ripped it. He ripped it again and again, and when it hung in shreds on the frightened Fanny, he kneeled and rubbed the palms of his hands in the dusty floor. Then he wiped them on Fanny's dress. Then he rubbed his hands again, and wiped them on the dress again; and when, finally, he stepped back from the trembling Fanny, he nodded with satisfaction. He was about to return to his seat in the theater when he was struck with still another thought. He draped the scarf over her head and around her shoulders so that she looked like the errant daughter returning to her home in a blizzard.

"Now," Ziegfeld said, "now, sing it."

She sang it without looking at the lyric. She, who was such a bad study that in a Baby Snooks broadcast many years later she once began to read the commercial in that rasping, raucous child's voice, sang it from memory. She stood on the bare stage with the lights low and the piano softly leading her on. She stood without moving once, holding her bare left arm with her right hand. She sang it straight, with no frills and no flounces and no invention and no tricks.

> *"It's cost me a lot*
> *But there's one thing that I've got—*
> *It's my man."* *

She sang it soft, and the fingers that caressed her skin were not her fingers but Nick's fingers. His fingers and his hands touching her, his arms holding her.

> *"I—don't know why I should,*
> *He isn't good.*
> *He isn't true,*
> *He beats me too,*
> *What can I do?"*

She sang it gently, her eyes closed and Nick beside her. She sang it ten thousand times after that afternoon when only Ziegfeld heard her, but she never sang it without caressing her arm and closing her eyes, so that she was alone

* *From* MY MAN (MON HOMME). *Published by Leo Feist, Inc. for North America. Used by permission.*

with Nick, with no orchestra supporting her, and no audience watching her, only the Nick she loved—who was never the Nick she knew.

> *"What's the difference if I say*
> *I'll go away,*
> *When I know I'll come back on*
> *My knees some day?*
> *For whatever my man is*
> *I am his forever more!"*

She left no one dry-eyed on the opening night of the 1921 Follies . . . not that night, and not any night or any day, on any stage, in any town in which she sang "My Man." She touched the heart of whoever heard her, man or woman. They were never too old or too young, too much in love, or too far past for love, that she could not make them remember, and make them see, and make them weep.

Except Fanny. Because she was never sad while she sang her song. It was a true, happy time for her.

"Once," Fanny said, "I remember Frances standing in the wings when I was singing 'My Man.' And when I came off the stage, she was crying. And I wondered why she cried—she was so young, and what could the words mean to her?

"I picked her up and I carried her to the dressing-room, and I wiped her tears. 'Why are you crying?' I asked her.

" 'Because you looked so sad,' Frances said."

Of her appearance in the Follies that year, the critic for the *New York American* said:

> *Underneath the flickering glare of a street light, Miss Brice sings of her love for the dock walloper who beats and chokes her and thunders his abuse whenever he comes around. Slushy, mushy hedgetalk. And yet the sheer artistry of Fanny Brice lifts it out of the muck of the commonplace.*

That was for "My Man." A few days later the *New York World* said:

> There was . . . only brief reference the other day to the glow of positive genius which Fanny Brice imparts to the interludes in which she appears. Miss Brice is a consummate artist. Each year she achieves her effects by more subtle and delicate means. There is humorous suggestion now in the slightest movement of her hands, in the merest glance of her eyes. Her sense of the comic is unfailing.

Seven years later, in a series of articles he sold to the *New York Graphic*, Nick claimed that the song had caused the first serious rift between him and his wife.

Under the headline: "MY MAN" KILLED OUR LOVE! SAYS NICKY OF FANNY'S SONG, there appeared the story:

> Just a few years ago when my liberty was at stake, when I had been falsely and unjustly accused of complicity in the $5,000,000 bond plot, Flo Ziegfeld, astute showman, got hold of the song.
>
> "Don't sing it. Please don't sing it," I pleaded with Fanny. "Can't you see that it will hurt me?"
>
> "I must sing it," she replied.
>
> So she sang that song. She was always adamant where her ambition and success were concerned. How often I have wished that Fanny were but a little housewife, taking care of the kids and keeping me company, instead of the brilliant comedienne, the girl who can make 'em cry or laugh as she pleases.
>
> I feel only sorrow, and not anger in my heart when I think of how our ship of romance struck the rocks of ambition and went down.

*A career! There you have it. And if one has already
carved out successfully a niche in one corner of the hall
of histrionic fame then there is the ambition to excel in
yet another line.*

*They are all alike. Every comedienne on Broadway or
Main Street wants to play heavy parts. Fanny was no
exception to this rule. She wanted to make her audience
weep . . . to send them out of the theatre wiping their
eyes.*

*And . . . I blame that song for the greatest misfor-
tune of my life.*

When Fanny was asked about Nick's story, she replied
succinctly: "He's nuts."

During the New York run of the Follies, Nick and Fallon
quarreled over the latter's attentions to Gertrude Vanderbilt,
a young actress with whom the lawyer had become infatu-
ated. Nick, who had introduced the two during the appeal
to the Supreme Court, now charged Fallon with neglecting
his defense while the lawyer pursued Miss Vanderbilt. Nick
added a few choice epithets to a rather earthy description
of Fallon's beloved, whereupon Fallon quit the case completely. Fallon's partner, Eugene McGee, represented Nick
at the second trial, where he was found guilty and sentenced
to two years in a federal penitentiary.

Nick changed lawyers again and immediately appealed
the verdict. Fanny was back from her Follies tour and she
took Nick and her children to Atlantic City. There she met
Dr. Henry J. Schireson, a plastic surgeon, who convinced
Fanny that he could remodel her nose painlessly and quickly
if she would submit to an operation. The surgery occasioned
more newspaper stories than any other medical event until
the birth of the Dionne quintuplets.

Here is the *New York American* quoting Fanny:

"I owe it to my public. I must look my best to repay my admirers for their confidence and respect."

Here is Fanny:
"I was the beginning of this guy's career. I posed for him for 'before and after' pictures. He made a big nose on the 'before' picture. He was crazy."

Here is the *New York Times* quoting Fanny:

"No woman of the stage today can afford to have a nose that is likely to keep growing. I have all kinds of faith in Dr. Schireson, and I am coming out with a nose which I hope will not detract from if it does not add to my stage appearance."

Here is Fanny again:
"What got me is that he said it would only take ten minutes. He novocained it and what he did was to put a stitch up there on each side. When I got off the table, I sneezed, and one stitch came out. He said: 'Get right back on the table.' I said: 'Nothing doing, Doc.' This is my own nose on the left and his nose on the right."

And the *New York American* the day after the operation:

"It has been said that we all practice some harmless form of pretense," Miss Brice announced. "Plato remarks how we customarily gloss over the defects of our friends."

And Fanny, talking about the operation:
"He just wanted to get that knife into me. He'd cut you if you had dandruff."

☼ 11 ☼

ANN PENNINGTON: *"I Started with Nothing and I've Got Nothing."*

Ann Pennington is tiny, cheerful, round-faced, enthusiastic, warm, friendly, healthy, optimistic, loyal, discreet, and very proud. She smiles all the time and laughs most of the time. And if the lobby of the Eighth Avenue hotel in New York is a trifle shabby, and less than absolutely modern; if the patrons are less than successful, and the service less than first-rate, you would not have known it from Ann Pennington, who was receiving that day as though she sat in the morning room of her home in Oyster Bay, or in Grosse Point, or on the peninsula below San Francisco.

For Ann Pennington is a lady. You could think that it was a long way from star billing in the Follies to this hotel. Or you could think that it was a short way, really, for it was no more than a hundred yards from this lobby to the lobby of the New Amsterdam on 42nd Street. But that theater is now a second-run motion-picture house, and Ann Pennington is thirty years older than when she was the dimpled-knees darling of the Broadway Bills. You did not have to think that: the facts struck you under the heart, but you could not say it, nor hint it.

Ann Pennington is not a woman who looks behind her, and she does not accept sympathy. No sympathy, no help, and no crying-towel for Miss Ann.

"She's the most wonderful person I ever knew," Fanny wrote of Ann Pennington. "At one time she was making $3,500 a week. And when that was gone, and she wasn't working any more, and getting nothing, she was just the same. She's the only performer I ever knew who went down in the business and never said: 'I . . . I . . . I . . . I,' all the time. So I said: 'I think you're a wonderful person, Penny.' And she said: 'Well, this is how I figure it out: I came to New York with nothing and now I feel I am even.'

"She doesn't feel that anyone owes her anything. Nothing at all. I think the reason Penny never married was because she wouldn't take anything from anybody. I never heard her knock anybody, not one person. I never heard her say: 'He isn't nice,' or: 'She isn't nice.' She never saw any part of anybody that was wrong.

"And she couldn't take the thought of somebody doing her a favor. She was out here in California staying with me one time and she went to the races. While she was gone, a telegram came from Billy Rose. He had the Diamond Horseshoe then. He wants her for the Horseshoe, and he will pay her so much. I forgot how much, but for Penny it was like a Godsend. It was during the war and they weren't delivering telegrams then, so they read it to me over the telephone. Well, I'm wild. I'm crazy. I go all the way out to the track to look for her; go into the main entrance, into the club-house—and I look all around—and I can't find her. So I come back. So she stays downtown after the races and has her dinner alone, although I don't know this. And I'm dying. I can't stand it. Just can't wait until she gets back. I'm so excited I call the William Morris office [Fanny's agents] and I get a ticket on the train and a lower.

"Well, it's late that night and still no Penny. I'm in the bathtub and she comes in. I said: 'You got a telegram from Billy Rose!' I tell her all about it, that Billy Rose wants to pay her so much, and that she has to be there by this date; that I had gotten her ticket, called the William Morris office, and all that happened I tell her.

"She said: 'Where's the telegram?'

" 'At the telegraph office.'

" 'Why isn't it here?' Penny asked me.

" 'Because there's a war, that's why. They don't deliver telegrams during a war.'

"So then here's the picture she makes in her head: 'The William Morris office. They know Fanny's buying me the ticket. They are all so excited about a job for little Penny.'

"And it made her feel little. She said: 'I don't think it's from Billy Rose at all.'

"Well, I just died. I just went mad. I said: 'You know, Penny, I think you're right. I don't think it's from Billy Rose. I think it's from President Roosevelt and he wants you to take over the WAVES!'

"And the way Penny plays the races. I only bet two dollars now since I got mine at Saratoga. I lost ninety thousand dollars at Saratoga, and that was my lesson. But I like the horses. So Penny and I are at the races. She whispers to me: 'This race is fixed.'

" 'What do you mean fixed?' I asked her. 'How do you know it's fixed?'

" 'I just know.'

" 'You can't just know.'

"Well, she looks all around her like she was a spy and then she whispers: 'The jockeys are happy.'

"I look at her. I know I'm not crazy. So she must be crazy. 'The jockeys are *happy*?' I say.

"She nods. She says: 'Look at the jockeys. See the boy touching his nose?'

" 'Yeah, I see him.'

" 'He's giving them the office.'

" 'Giving who the office?'

" 'Them. The fixers. He's got the race in his pocket.'

"So we bet on him. Do I have to tell you where he finished?

"The next race, she's with the fixing again. I told her: 'Penny, do me a favor. Give me no more tips.' But her, she believes it."

That winter morning in New York, sitting in the imitation-leather chair, Ann Pennington suddenly dropped the *Morning Telegraph*, the daily horseracing newspaper, on the floor, and shook her head vehemently.

"I did not buy that, you know," she said. "I just found it in the lobby here. I almost never play the horses. Oh, no, no, no, no!" shaking her head furiously.

"I go for my walk every morning, and I drink only milk. I never smoke. Poor Fanny, eating all those pickles and mustard and hot dogs any hour of the night. She never took careful care of herself, you know. She was just careless that way. Oh, yes, we were very close. Like sisters."

Ann Pennington's feet did not touch the floor. She sat with her ankles crossed, her purse in her lap, her fingers twisting the straps.

"Fanny never went looking for anybody," Ann Pennington said. "She'd stay home and they all came to her. That was in the big house on West 76th Street."

While Nick's new lawyers appealed his conviction in the bond case, Fanny bought a five-story, twenty-room town house from the Colgate soap family, taking three floors for herself and renting the top two floors to theatrical friends. She hired a staff of five servants, including a nurse for her children, a butler, a cook, and a chauffeur.

On the day she moved into the new house, she received a visit from Arnold Rothstein. She had not seen the gambler since their meeting near the Hudson River.

"Fanny," he said, "I want to congratulate you on the purchase of this lovely home. I hope your life here is happy, healthy, and prosperous."

"Gee, thanks, Arnold."

As the draymen moved in and out of the house, Rothstein said: "Is there any place we can talk, Fanny?"

"We can talk right here."

"I mean a private talk, Fanny," Rothstein said.

"What's private about my life?" she asked. "I got no secrets."

Rothstein waved his arm at the confusion. "All this noise makes me nervous," said the gambler who could bet ten thousand dollars on the turn of a card with no more acceleration of heartbeat than you would have in betting two cents on a pair of aces.

"How about the kitchen?" Fanny asked.

"The kitchen sounds fine."

Fanny led him downstairs to the first floor, where Rothstein carefully closed the door. Fanny leaned against the sink while Rothstein sat in the only chair. "What's on your mind, Arnold?" Fanny asked.

Rothstein frowned as though in pain. "I've been worrying about you, Fanny," he announced.

"I'm okay, Arnold. You don't have to worry about me."

He frowned again, before lighting a cigarette. "No, you've

been bothering me. You're moving into this lovely home and you've got to furnish it. All that trouble ahead of you, besides Nick to look after."

"I *want* to furnish the house," Fanny replied. "That's one reason I moved in here. I like furnishing. It's a kind of hobby of mine."

"But you won't have time, Fanny," Rothstein said. "Now I like you. You know that. I have a great deal of respect for you, Fanny. Whether you know it or not, I'm interested in furnishings myself."

"*You?*"

Rothstein played small-boy-digging-foot-in-hot-sand in a manner that would have done credit to Baby Leroy. "Oh, yes," he said, and he was telling the absolute truth, "I've probably got as good a collection of Oriental rugs as you'll find anywhere."

"Well, that's wonderful, Arnold. I think one of my kids is crying," Fanny said, and as she started to leave, Rothstein took her wrist. Held her wrist not firmly and not gently, but held it.

"So maybe I could save you the trouble of decorating your house, Fanny," Rothstein said.

"I don't get you."

"I know exactly what you need here, Fanny, and what you ought to do is forget it and leave everything to me."

"You think that's a good idea?"

"I think it's a wonderful idea, Fanny. You can just pay me the cost of the furniture, and save the price of an interior decorator," he said.

"That's what you think, eh?"

"Yes, I do, Fanny. As a matter of fact," Rothstein said, "I'll have the furniture in here tomorrow."

"Okay, Arnold," she said, as he looked at her.

"It's all settled then, isn't it, Fanny?" he asked, watching her.

"Yeah, sure."

Rothstein released her wrist then. He rose, held his cigarette carefully, and dumped the ashes in the sink. "I'll just let myself out, Fanny," he said, and left her there in the kitchen.

He sent the furniture the following day, and with it an envelope containing a slip of paper on which was written: "$50,000."

Fanny called in an expert appraiser, who told her Rothstein's stuff was worth thirteen thousand dollars at the most.

She paid the fifty thousand. "It took me a while," she wrote later, "but I paid it, and I paid it without saying a word. I knew, and Rothstein knew I knew, that the thirty-seven thousand dollars was his price for interest on Nick's bail money. That was the way he worked. Rothstein never said no when you asked a favor, but sooner or later you had to pay for it."

Her home became the scene of nightly parties that began after the Follies performance and continued until she could no longer keep her guests awake. Fanny seemed intent on laughing more, telling more stories, entertaining more guests, pouring more wine than anybody in New York, and, from the reports of those people who were her intimates, she evidently succeeded.

She was then the favorite of the social set, and the top hundred of New York's four hundred were always represented in her home. The late Tommy Hitchcock was a frequent guest. Averell Harriman was a long-time friend. Once when he and his wife were in Fanny's home she admired a diamond bracelet set with emeralds which Mrs. Harriman was wearing. Two weeks later she received a package from one of the most expensive jewelry shops in the world, containing an exact duplicate of the bracelet she had admired.

Mrs. Borden Harriman, who was to become America's first woman ambassador when President Roosevelt appointed her his minister to Denmark, was as familiar with Fanny's home as she was with the drawing-rooms of Newport. Their friendship had begun during World War I when Fanny was still living on West 58th Street. At that time Fanny bought her bras, slips, panties, and all her undergarments from a woman named Mrs. Frieda Hammerman, who called on her customers in their homes.

"One day I am in the bathtub," Fanny wrote of her second meeting with Mrs. Borden Harriman, to whom she had been introduced at her first Follies opening in New York. "My maid comes in and says: 'Miss Brice, Mrs. Harriman is downstairs to see you.'

"So I say: 'Well, send her up and I'll look at the stuff.'

"I really bought from the underwear woman because I liked her so much; a nice little woman and she made me laugh. Well, the maid goes away, and I'm soaping myself, and the door opens and in walks this beautiful woman with the white hair, the most *beautiful* white hair I ever saw.

"I said: 'Oh, I'm sorry. I'm very sorry.'

"Because I didn't know this woman from the Statue of Liberty, but I know she's got class.

"'Pardon me,' I said, 'I thought it was my underwear woman.'

"And Mrs. Harriman said: 'I love it, I love it. Just go on with your bawth.'

"So I'm scrubbing and she sits down and tells me why she is here. She wants me to sell doughnuts on the steps of the Public Library on Fifth Avenue, for Liberty Bonds. So, of course, I went to sell doughnuts. I would have sold gold bricks if she told me."

There were others. "I was very fond of John Wanamaker,"
Fanny wrote. "When I lived at this same apartment on 58th
Street, my mother used to have a poker game every Thursday. One week it was at one woman's house, and so on. Well,
this week it is at my house, and my mother has all her
friends up there playing. Who walks in but John Wanamaker. I introduce him around and he loves all those old
dames. He sits down and plays with them, for nickels and
dimes. He loses maybe three or four dollars. When he leaves,
my mother and her friends are so worried. Such a young
fellow to lose that money.

" 'Don't worry, he'll get by,' I told Mom.

"With all these society people I knew in New York, I
knew they liked me because I was natural. And they enjoyed me, because I didn't give a damn if they were society
or pimps. They liked me for what I was, and I liked them
for what they were. I think the most deadly thing that can
happen to anybody is when the chi-chi bug hits them. When
I first met Grace Moore she had this natural hair, and was
so beautiful. And she was just a good kid, working at her
career. Then, when she came out here, she was different.
She was impressed with people. One night she is visiting me
and she's talking about all the royalty in Europe who are
her friends. Going on and on, so and so was there, and then
the king comes in, she says.

" 'What king are you talking about?' I ask her.

"She quit with the royalty then.

"She quit with me too.

"But I couldn't get excited about anybody because they
had money or a title. I never got stuck on myself, so why
should I be stuck on anybody else? I can't stand compliments. If I was in another room and heard somebody talking and saying something nice about me, that would be all
right. But if I was there, I wouldn't like it. Once Sir Charles

Mendl came to see me and he said: 'You're a very lovely woman, Miss Fanny.'

" 'Don't give me that blank, Charles,' I said.

" 'No, no, Miss Fanny. You are, you are. You have beautiful bones.'

" 'Maybe that's why I've been attracting such dogs all my life,' I told him."

If she included Nick in that category, she certainly showed him more than canine concern. By word and deed, she proved her devotion to him while he fought to stay out of prison. To a newspaperman she said: "I think Nick is just perfect and the only man I would have wanted for the father of my children. I think the greatest joy in the world is having children with the man you love."

There seemed to be no limit to her patience with Nick, to her indulgence, to the amount of money she gave him. In the midst of his troubles with the law, while he was still free on bail, he came to the theater one night in her big car. A traffic policeman suggested that he park beyond the entrance to the theater. Nick told the cop he was there to pick up Fanny Brice, that she was the star of the Follies, that he wasn't moving an inch, and that the cop had better move on before he found himself patrolling the cow pastures of Staten Island. The cop insisted and Nick was adamant in his refusal.

When Fanny appeared after the performance, the doorman told her that Nick had been taken to the precinct station. She took a taxi home and waited until Nick had returned from Night Court, where he had unsuccessfully challenged the traffic regulations of New York.

There was another night when he didn't appear at all: not at the theater, not at home, not by dawn, and not by mid-afternoon of the next day, when Fanny left her house to keep an appointment. When she returned, in time for dinner, she heard Nick whistling while he shaved. As she changed her clothes, Nick called: "Fanny?"

She didn't answer.

"Is that you, old girl?" Nick called from the bathroom.

"Who'd you expect?" Fanny answered.

"Why, I've been waiting for you, my dear," Nick said, as he came into their bedroom.

"And I've been waiting for you, my dear," Fanny said, walking away from him.

She took her place at the dinner table and in a moment Nick sat down opposite her. When the maid appeared with the soup, Fanny said: "Where were you last night?"

"I didn't want to wake you, darling," Nick said, as he reached for his spoon. "I would have called, but it was quite late."

He explained that he had been talked into a poker game far out on Long Island. He had been a heavy winner and didn't want to quit while his luck was running so well. He thought of telephoning, but it was too late, he knew Fanny was tired and needed rest.

"Sure, sure," Fanny said. Her soup was untouched. "So how much did you win? Let me see the money."

Nick sipped his soup. "Oddly enough, my dear, my luck changed in the last hour," he replied. "I was fortunate to break even."

"Liar!"

She rose from the chair as Nick dipped the spoon in his soup.

"You're a liar!" Fanny said again, but Nick gave no sign that he heard her.

"You were out with some dame!"

Nick didn't look up.

"LIAR!" Fanny screamed, reaching for the tablecloth, seiz-

ing a corner of it, as furious with Nick's indifference as with
his real or imagined philandering. She seized the tablecloth
with both hands, pulling it high above her head, so that
soup, salad, bread, knives, forks, spoons, candles, cigarettes,
glasses, all fell and spilled on Nick: on his face, on his hands,
on his clothes.

As Fanny stood glaring at him, still holding the tablecloth,
her face white with anger, Nick reached for a napkin, wiped
his lips slowly and carefully, and went to their bedroom.

In a moment Fanny followed, screaming imprecations at
him. Neither that night nor any night, before or after, did
she mention the money he had taken and would take, the
things of which he was accused, his gambling, or his failure
to provide so much as an electric bulb for their homes. He
had hit her, at last, where he could hurt her, and he had
hurt her badly.

When she got to the bedroom, Nick was once more in the
bathroom. She fell on the chaise longue, empty of epithets,
drained of anger, finished with jealousy, only wanting him
to put his arms around her and tell her she was his true and
only love, anxious to believe whatever story he offered for
his absence, needing him, needing him.

But Nick got out of his clothes, arranged the suit carefully for removal to the cleaners, slipped trees into his shoes,
ran himself a tub, and laid out pajamas, dressing-gown, and
cordovan slippers.

And the maid stood in the doorway, and knocked on the
open door.

"Miss Fanny?" the maid said hesitantly.

And in a moment: "Miss Fanny?" once again.

"What d'you want?" Fanny asked, listening to the splash-
ing in the tub.

"Would you like some strawberry shortcake, Miss Fanny?"
the maid asked, poking her head into the room.

"No!" Fanny exploded, but as the maid backed away, Fanny began to think of it. She saw the snow-white whipped cream. She saw the layer cake that was her cook's specialty. She saw the deep-red strawberries, and she felt the juice running from the fruit as she bit it. Her salivary glands were flowing like the Mississippi at flood time. She turned to the maid.

"Two pieces," Fanny ordered. "Big pieces with a pot of coffee. Mr. Arnstein and I will have our dessert here."

In the bathroom Nick began to whistle.

But there were other nights when he felt no song in his heart. Fanny took to clocking his homecoming with the diligence and efficiency of an Olympic-games official. What is it in a man that makes him want to get caught? What is it that makes him lie so badly, smile so wickedly, talk so softly before the wife to whom he has come from the perfumed boudoir? What is it that makes no amatory adventure complete unless by insinuation, by innuendo, by the thousand and one giveaways that a woman classifies as surely as fingerprints, he somehow makes certain that his wife knows, knows absolutely, of his journeys to the bedrooms of forbidden fun?

Nick made certain now. He was always "on business," or "in a big game," or "talking a deal with several high-placed gentlemen," as though daring Fanny to think otherwise.

To get Nick away from his endless conferences with lawyers, his constant worry over the conviction he faced, the never-withdrawn curtain of newspapermen which covered the sidewalk before their house, Fanny took him one weekend to a hotel in Long Beach, on the ocean in Long Island. She left the children with their nurse. She and Nick rode in her car to their garage, sent the chauffeur out for a taxi,

which he was ordered to bring into the building, and there
boarded the cab. Within minutes they were free of newspapermen, of courts, of lawyers, and photographers, and riding happily over the Queensboro Bridge to the Long Beach
hotel where Fanny had reserved a suite in the chauffeur's
name.

"So we're having a good time," she wrote, "so what happens: the second night there is a fire in the hotel. I wake up,
I smell smoke, and I'm moving like a bat out of hell. 'Nick,
the joint's burning!' I yell, and I've got my robe around me
then. 'Hurry, Nick!' I yell at him.

" 'Plenty of time, my dear,' he says, and he's sitting on the
bed, fixing his garters.

" 'Nick, for God's sake, come on!' I say.

" 'No hurry, Fanny,' he says. Now he's standing in front of
the mirror. He's got his shoes and stockings on, his shirt on,
and he's knotting his tie.

"I grab his robe and throw it around him, but he shakes it
off. 'We'll make it, old girl,' he tells me. I look at him, getting his tie pin adjusted just right, and I think of my kids at
home. What good will the money do them if they're or-
phans? I look at Nick again. He's pulling his belt through his
pants, and I think: 'The hell with you, Jack, I got kids who
need me,' and I make for the door.

"We're all out on the lawn, everybody in robes and pajamas, and the smoke is pouring out of the windows already.
The firemen push us back away from the hotel, and all of a
sudden there is Nick.

"He walks out of the door like he's going for his morning walk. He's not only dressed, he's wearing his goddam
hat!"

Nick's self-control and presence amazed all those who
knew him. To combat the straying of his eyes, Fanny persuaded Nick to accompany her on the Follies tour that year.

They traveled from city to city with Eddie Cantor and W. C. Fields, in the latter's limousine, which was as well stocked as the best cellar in the country. One night, after a performance in Pittsburgh, they decided to drive directly to Cleveland, their next date. As they stopped at a red light on the outskirts of Pittsburgh, a particularly unfriendly-looking young man leaped on the running-board of the limousine, thrust his hands through the open windows so that he could hold the door on the inside, and demanded a ride to the next town.

Fields, who had not yet had time to fortify himself against the dangers of the world with his customary quart of courage, was terrified. Cantor, sitting nearest the unwelcome guest, thought only of his growing family, and slunk far back in the seat. Fanny, who had been happily enjoying the company of three men, now looked happier at the prospect of being the only female in the midst of four.

She beamed at their unshaven hitch-hiker. "Wait'll I move my jewel box," she told him, lifting the case full of high-priced pretties from the seat beside her to make room for the fourth, menacing male.

Upon hearing her, Fields's face drained of color and his nose shone like the rising sun on a Japanese flag. Cantor hoped that the child Ida carried would be a boy, and that she would have the decency to name the lad after his dead father.

But Nick said: "Get going, Bill," seized Fanny's jewel case, dropped it to the floor and, as he straightened up, suddenly lunged forward, pushing the unsuspecting running-board rider off the moving car.

Cantor bowed his head in thankful prayer, and Fields made for Cleveland as though the feds were following. Whereupon Nick said to Fanny: "I don't think you would have enjoyed that fellow's company, my pet."

Even the danger of disfigurement could not ruffle Nick. When they returned from tour, Nick once more began systematic absences from their home. Since their only common meeting-time was the dinner hour, the dining-room was usually the scene of their scenes, or, strictly speaking, Fanny's scenes, for while Nick may have been the cause, he was never the effect.

On this night, when Nick, accustomed to interrogation, "assumed," in the words of a reporter who had covered his trials, "a bored air during the proceedings," Fanny picked up the plate on which lay her entree, and hurled it at Nick's head.

Nick moved his head. The plate, whirling horizontally, went through the second-floor window laterally. Fanny, who had watched the plate's voyage as a bowler watches his ball, rose excitedly from her chair—and Nick reached for the salt to season his steak.

As he cut the filet, Fanny ran past him to the window. She was amazed at the narrow opening in the glass made by the plate.

"Nick, Nick," she said, forgetting the cause of her anger, and past anger itself now, "come look here. It's no thicker than a dime."

"Yes, my dear," Nick said, as he touched the wineglass to his lips.

"Nick, look," Fanny said. "There's the plate on the sidewalk and a dog is eating the food."

"Yes, my dear."

"*Nick!*"

Hoping to avert a renewal of Fanny's pitching activities, and thinking that she might next time throw a strike instead of a ball, Nick reluctantly left his steak and joined Fanny at the window.

"Look at that dog," Fanny exclaimed. "He's starved."

Nick looked. "Any man who lets his dog run loose in the city should be flogged," he said. "Come, my dear," he said, "I'll have Cook bring you another steak."

Fanny's throwing arm got a rest, however, when Nick's efforts to keep out of prison came to an end. On May 9, 1924, with Fanny beside him, Nick surrendered to Washington, D.C., authorities and was put in jail to await transfer to a federal penitentiary.

While he remained in the Washington jail, Fanny stayed in the capital. Nick asked her to arrange that he be sent to Atlanta, which he believed to be an "easier" prison, and she scurried around the city, hiring more lawyers, seeing more officials, asking help from those she knew were her friends among the Congressmen on Capitol Hill. Had Woodrow Wilson still been the tenant at the White House, Fanny would have gone to him, for, as she wrote once, "I loved that guy."

"He [Wilson] always used to come backstage when we played Washington," she wrote. "I thought he was just the most wonderful man. He was interested in the individual human being. He was the only man besides Frank Murphy (the late Supreme Court Justice) who I really felt liked you as you and not because you were in show business and a star. The last time I saw Wilson, he came backstage, and two men were holding him up under the arms, and the whole cast gathered around him. I couldn't face him that time. I ran to my dressing-room and cried. I just loved him. I know Wilson liked the girls. He wasn't a dried-up old thing and didn't live by a pattern: 'I won't do this because I'm not supposed to. It wouldn't look nice.' He was a man who gave in to his feelings."

But Wilson was no longer living at 1600 Pennsylvania Avenue. Fanny could find no help. Lawyers told her it was hopeless. Nick must serve his sentence. She could not arrange his removal to Atlanta. He was marked for Leavenworth in Kansas.

On the day he was to be taken to the train for the long ride to the Middle West, Fanny appeared at the Washington jail again. She asked for—and was granted—ten minutes with her husband. When she left the building, reporters asked her what she and Nick had said to each other. She disregarded the newsmen. In her notes she makes no mention of that visit with Nick. Neither her children nor her friends nor anyone in the world was ever to learn what those two, whose married life was as private as page one, talked about during those few moments alone together in the jail.

When she arrived in New York, she was met by a throng of reporters and photographers at Pennsylvania Station.

If you've never been in the soup yourself, if you've never had to buck a big city's press, if your days have never been spent in the company of a flying squadron of newspapermen, you might think enviously of those who have. You might, in fantasy, imagine yourself going from home to car, from car to office, from office to taxi, from taxi to dentist, from dentist to tailor, from tailor to restaurant, flanked from start to finish by reporters, pencils poised, pads clean, to be filled with your every word, your every gesture, the description of your clothes, your hair, your eyes. You might, in continued fantasy, think it exciting, and glamorous and important, and fun.

It's as much fun as the gas chamber, and don't ever forget it. We're not talking now of the current movie-favorite, who gets on the Super Chief in Pasadena, who travels with a G-2 of public-relations advisers, whose schedule is relayed ahead to every daily, semiweekly, and weekly newspaper in the republic; who counts the press when she gets off the Twen-

tieth Century Limited at Grand Central, as the owner of a
country carnival counts the house on Saturday night.

We're talking about someone in trouble; whose son has
robbed a bank; or whose daughter has eloped with a thug;
or whose child lies dead beneath the wheels of a truck there
in the middle of the street; or whose husband is on his way
to Leavenworth.

Then the endless flash of photographers' bulbs becomes a
thousand needles pressing into your eyes. The endless questions of reporters who must feed five editions a day become
a thousand knives piercing your skin.

For it's: "Hey, Fanny, did you kiss him good-bye?"

And: "Here, Fanny, give us a smile."

And: "One more, Fanny; wave like you were waving at
Nick."

And: "How about that divorce, Fanny?"

And: "You gonna stick with him, Fanny?"

And: "What's this about some woman on Long Island,
Fanny?"

And: "Fanny, give us a statement."

And: "Fanny, say something."

While from the left a photographer shouts: "Fanny, here!"
Startling her so that she turns, and then the bulb flashes.

And from the right: *"Fanny!"*

So that she turns again, blinking with pain and nausea and
throbbing head, while another camera clicks.

"FANNY!" from directly ahead of her, where another photographer crouches in her path, the camera raised like the
mouth of a cannon as he shoots her.

But you can't blame them: they have an edition to make;
they have engravers to feed. You can't blame the city editor:
he has the competition to meet. You can't blame the pub-
lisher: he has newspapers to sell, and he won't sell them with

stories about 4-H Club conventions, or a dry day in Congress. He needs heartbreak in his paper, so that tonight, and tomorrow morning, and tomorrow night you have something on the front page to keep you from television.

So don't envy Fanny that day, feed no fantasies of being in her place that day as she made the long walk alone from the train to the taxi stand, the reporters barking at her heels.

She answered none of them until, as she waited beside the taxi starter, one said: "What are you going to do now, Fanny?"

She looked at that one. Turned and looked at him carefully. Spoke carefully so that he might not misquote her.

"I'm going to wait," Fanny said.

Now, in the lobby of the Eighth Avenue inn that Ann Pennington currently called home, the sharpshooters and the zoot-suiters had arrived. The fight managers were there with the prizefighters they managed. The tinhorns and the crapshooters and the horseplayers were present. The lobby traffic was at its height. Ann Pennington's soft, asking-for-candy voice could hardly be heard.

"It's getting late and I really have to go."

Ann Pennington rose to her feet. The *Morning Telegraph* she insisted she had not bought was folded under her arm. Post time for the first race was approaching. She stood brushing imaginary specks of lint from her coat. She looked about her, smiling shyly.

"I suppose you might say she was devoted," Ann Pennington decided. "Yes, Fanny was very devoted to Nick."

✻ 12 ✻

GEORGE CUKOR: *"I Believe in Talking One Language Good."*

===

S HE had this extraordinary smile," George Cukor said of Fanny, "so that if you were in the audience you knew the smile was directed at you and at you only and that she had never smiled at anyone before. She would come out, smile, and wait until she had *willed* the audience to be hers; the programs put aside and the theater dead silent. She would get a fix on the first row of the first balcony and only when the theater was absolutely still would she begin.

"She was like a liontamer when she walked on stage," Cukor continued, "and the audience were the beasts to be subdued.

"She had discretion in her comedy: a 'healthy vulgarity'; so that when *she* belched, it was all right. And she was terribly fastidious. Fanny was one of the great, great clowns of all time. Later, when she had become a star, she never gave an encore, never took more than one bow. When she was through, she was through.

"Of her own work she was as confident as all the greats of

the theater. She always felt herself in the class of Chaplin, or Olivier, or Barrymore."

Fanny herself could always explain her abilities to her satisfaction. "Of course," she wrote, "I think there is no energy like thought energy. I think with *real* concentration, if you really want to do something—I don't care what it is—you will do it. If I get up and I want to take a cigarette, well, I know I'm going to get that cigarette. Now if I could be so sure that I could take a piano bench up with my one arm and lift it up—I'd lift it.

"Well, why don't I lift it? Because I am not positive. Right away I go over there and I think: 'Gee, I *hope* I can lift it.'

"See? You're through before you start. Well, I think that everybody who's gotten anywhere got there because he wanted to. You have to *do* something, of course, you can't sit back and say: 'I want to, I want to, I want to.' Because there is no push like ambition. And confidence, which you get in experience. Every time you do something that comes out all right and there is somebody there to say: 'You're all right, kid. You're going to make it,' then you got it beat. And you have to be bigger than your mistakes. Because if you make two or three mistakes and you don't hold on to your *will* to be something—boy, does it take the confidence away from you. And when you start to lose confidence in yourself, you are done."

George Cukor sat in his house very early on a Sunday morning, having finished directing Judy Holliday in a movie the day before. He is the women's director in Hollywood. He has worked with Holliday, with Hepburn, with Greta Garbo, with Ethel Barrymore, with Claudette Colbert, but his heart that day belonged to Fanny Brice, whom he had never directed. He had seen her for the first time from far,

far up in a Broadway balcony, when his name was not known beyond the New York block in which he lived.

He is known now wherever movies are shown, and his house lies high in the Hollywood hills, surrounded by a cement wall, and protected by the most tortuous and circuitous route in Southern California. It is a rambling house, built at angles, of varying heights and in rolling ground. There is a formal garden off to the right of the house, with walks and stone benches, and birdbaths. There is a swimming-pool in which dead leaves float on the water. There is a telephone at the gate, from which you must call to gain admittance, and there is Cukor himself, finally, to welcome you, tall, broad, but not heavy; eager, enthusiastic, gracious, charming, and proud of his friendship with Fanny.

"Fanny was really intimate with me," Cukor said confidentially. He was maybe the twentieth person to admit it, and it seems curious that she could so enlist the hearts of such large numbers of people, each of whom believed that he—or she—was *really* the one, the only one, with whom Fanny could be honest, hiding nothing and keeping nothing secret, letting her hair down before this trusted intimate.

"Once I told Fanny about a contract I was thinking of signing," Cukor said. "I asked her what she thought of it."

" 'You know me, kid,' she said, 'I don't know anything about business.'

"Her idea of not knowing anything was to name the highest possible fee she could think of for her services. That was it: no haggling, no arguments, no discussions, no meetings. You paid or you didn't get her.

"Once Moss Hart and George Kaufman sent her a wire telling her that, if she would take one thousand dollars a week to star in it, they would write a play for her.

"She answered: 'If I take $1,000 a week, everybody in America will be writing plays for me.' "

Always Fanny refused to talk business, claiming she had
no head for it, but during the time Nick was in Leavenworth, Fanny was taken to a rehearsal of a show called
Is Zat So?

"I was then being handled—that is, my agent was Jenny
Wagner, a wonderful, wonderful person," Fanny wrote in
her notes. She said: 'Fanny, there is a show in rehearsal.
Some man is loaning them the theater, and they are so poor
they can only have one light bulb burning. And they have
no money to produce the show. Let's go over and see the
rehearsal.'

"So Jenny and I went over there. 'How do you like it?'
Jenny asked me after I saw the rehearsal.

" 'I like it,' I said.

" 'How would you like to produce it?'

" 'I don't know,' I said. 'How much do you think it would
cost?'

"Jenny said: 'I think you can swing it for nine thousand
dollars, if you're careful.'

" 'If I was careful,' I said, 'I'd run the hell out of here as
fast as I could.'

"But I wasn't careful. I said okay to them, I'd produce the
show, *Is Zat So?*

"Now I'm going to produce this show, and I figure that it
has to be handled by somebody who knows how to book it
and all that stuff. So I told Sam Harris, who was producing
the Music Box Revue, that I saw the rehearsal and I liked it
very much, and that I had said I would produce it. And
would he come over and see it? So be came one night. They
did the show for him, and he liked it very much. He said he
would take half of it, if they would rewrite some of the show.
But they didn't want to rewrite; they thought it was all right
the way it stood. They wanted it produced, they didn't want
to stop for rewrites. So Sam Harris said: 'Count me out.' I

came two and three times a week for rehearsal. And the more I see it, the more it don't look so good. I begin to think maybe this *isn't* so good. So I went to Lee Shubert. I sold him forty per cent. Then I let somebody else have five per cent, and so on. Well, I kept twenty-five per cent for myself but now I got my money back; I have the nine thousand dollars in the bank. When the show opens, it opens on velvet as far as I'm concerned. Well, the show opens, in Worcester, Massachusetts, and it is a big hit. So now I like it a little better. Then it plays another town, and I like it more. And some guy calls me and he says: 'Hey, my wife is crazy about the show.'

" 'That's great,' I say.

"And he's trying to laugh me out of it. 'What do you need with a show?' he says. 'Why don't you sell the other twenty-five per cent? You're a performer, what do you want with it? My wife likes it. I want to make her happy. I'll give her the twenty-five per cent. I want to let her play around with it.'

" 'I'll play around with it,' I told him. 'It stands me nothing, why should I give you gifts?'

"Well, the show comes into New York. *Is Zat So?* is a big smash hit, sensational. And we sell the moving-picture rights for a big pile of money. I got checks from that show for years and years. I made a hundred and some thousand. If I had any brains, I would have owned one hundred per cent instead of twenty-five per cent. I would have been rich from that show alone. But me and business—oogly-boogly—that's my big trouble."

Cukor remembered that she never talked a great deal about her trips abroad. " 'I went to Europe because it was the place to go,' she told me many times," he remembered.

"The first time I went to Europe," Fanny wrote, "without Nick, I went to France. There was some man on the boat who told me he could speak French. Now, I had gotten the address of my cousins in France. I was going to look them up. This man on the boat tells me he's stopping at the same hotel I'm stopping at in Paris. So when we got to the hotel, I asked him if he would call these cousins of mine, since he talked French. So he gets on the phone, and I hear him talking to somebody. I had told this guy my cousins were very rich, which is what my Mom had told me.

"When he finishes talking, he says to me: 'That's funny, your cousin's husband is a valet. He is sick and he wants you to come and see him.' Well, I pictured a little room some place, and I thought: 'This is going to be a touch, and my Mom had it all wrong about them. They must have lost their money or something.' So I thought: 'Okay, I'll stand for a small touch,' and I dress very simply, put no jewelry on, just a black, plain dress. When I get to the address, it's the wholesale district and my cousin's husband has a big wholesale business there.

"And I tried to explain to him that I was the cousin of his wife. Now he looks at me, and he thinks *he's* going to stand for a touch, because I look so poor. Well, finally we found somebody in the place who could speak English and French, and we made some sense.

"My cousin's husband explained that his valet had told my friend on the telephone that the mistress was sick and resting down at their home at Fontainebleau. She would like very much to see me. So the next day up comes a big Rolls-Royce and they drive me down, the biggest house I ever saw. Well, I dressed this time, put on my best as long as I knew they weren't going to touch me.

"We were staying at the George V Hotel in Paris, and Bea Lillie was with us. And in the meantime Jenny Dolly, of the Dolly Sisters, called me up and wanted me to come out to their house and see her children, the two kids she had adopted. So Sunday I went out to see her. I'm ushered into the drawing-room and some old guy is there who is taking Jenny out then. And he was sitting in the chair.

" 'Why don't you ply with me, Granpa-pa?' the kids ask.

"When I got back to the hotel, I told Bea the whole story.

"In about three weeks we go to Cannes, and we are in the gambling-rooms playing *chemin de fer* and Bea has the deal. There's an old man around eighty-six years old playing with her. He's all dressed up, white tie and tails, and white hair, and real classy. She deals him a card. And he is looking at his card, peeking under it, thinking, peeking again, thinking some more.

" 'Why don't you ply with me, Granpa-pa?' Bea asks him, and I fall right off the chair.

"While we were moving around, the children would stay with the governess in her home town in the south of France. From Cannes we went to Venice and Cole Porter has this big *palazzo*, I don't know how many rooms. I'll bet five thousand people could dance in the ballroom. We are at the Lido, at the beach, and Cole is getting a little bored, and he says: 'Come on back to the house, Fanny, I'm going to write some songs for you.'

"We went to the ballroom in this *palazzo* and there was a piano at each end of it. And all those paintings of the families who had lived in this *palazzo*. Cole and I are at one end of this big ballroom, sitting at the piano. And he gets an idea for a song to be done with a Jewish accent. All of a sudden I look up and see this little guy at the piano and me with him, in this big ballroom where God knows who had lived, and he's trying to write me a little Jewish song. I just couldn't get over it. I guess I broke the mood, and I never did get that song."

In George Cukor's house, the sun had found every corner of every room. The director talked on about Fanny, his face lighting and his eyes smiling as though, by so remembering her, he brought her back to this house where she had spent so many days.

"We were right here in this room," Cukor said, "talking about her, just Fanny and me alone one night. I asked her if she was sorry about anything in her life."

"I'm not sorry," Fanny replied. "I don't think I ever made a move in my life that one minute after I did it I didn't ask myself: 'Why did you do that?' I always analyzed myself until I was sure I knew why I had done a certain thing. Even with Nick. I don't miss Nick," she told Cukor, "I miss loving Nick. Because when you are in love, the man you are in love with is the last thing you think of before you go to sleep and he is the first thing you think of when you wake.

"And when you're not in love," Fanny continued, "you stay up as long as you can because you're afraid to go to sleep, and you don't give a good goddam if you ever wake up."

She spoke then with the bitter wisdom bought by the toll of many years' loneliness; but those months when Nick was in Leavenworth, when, as she told Will Rogers, "I'm happy because I know where he's spending his nights," she was as much in love as she had ever been. She signed to star in "The Music Box Revue" for the 1924–5 season, and for a time she was at ease in her heart. With Nick's nights accountable, she spent more and more time with her children. When Frances wrote a poem:

> *The corn is shaking,*
> *Because the chickens are waking,*

Fanny displayed it as proudly as though it were a new libretto in which she was to star. Young Frances later told a sob sister: "My name is Frances, but I want to be called Fanny, because it is my mother's name and my mother is a great actress. I don't want to be a actress. I want to be a opera singer."

"That's great, kid," Fanny said. "We'll do a double at the Met."

One day she found her son, Bill, drawing figures with chalk on the sidewalk. He had covered the block from West End Avenue to Riverside Drive, and Fanny sensed his determination to continue his sidewalk silhouettes across the length of Manhattan Island. She was preparing to remove the menace to the city's beauty when a panel of neighbors appeared to defend the promising Picasso. Somewhat pleased, despite her determination that her daughter and son be at all times the young lady and gentleman, she agreed to let Bill continue his artistry.

"Maybe the only time she really had Nick was the years he was in jail," Cukor reflected that Sunday in his home. "God knows she saw little enough of him when he was a free man. Actually, you know, she was terrible about her love affairs; any five-and-dime clerk could manage her beaux better. She was suspicious, argumentative, and terribly, terribly possessive. Although in Nick's case I don't imagine anything would have helped.

"You know," he continued, "she was a very contradictory human being, was Fanny. She had this superb taste, she knew instinctively what was right and what was wrong, and yet very little of the world touched her.

"She had been abroad so many times, and she regarded Europe as about as much fun as Long Island. Once, talking about France, I said: 'Fanny, you speak French, don't you?'

"Mind you, she had spent as much time in France during the twenties as any expatriate."

" 'No, I don't, George,' she answered. 'I believe in talking one language good.' "

JOHN CROMWELL: "*I Can't Understand a Goddam Word.*"

A sk Jack Dempsey, who lost to him twice, if Tunney was a better fighter, and the old ex-champion will tell you Gene never knew the day when he belonged in the same ring with the Manassa Mauler.

Ask Tom Dewey if Harry Truman is a better President than Tom might have been, and the squire of Albany and Pawling, New York, will look at you as if you'd just taken leave of your senses.

Ask Ralph Branca, off whom Bobby Thomson of the New York Giants hit that heartbreaking home run in 1951, if the latter is a troublesome batter, and the Dodger pitcher will guarantee to strike him out in any ball park you name.

For if you are really good at your trade, then a loss is only a lapse of luck; a defeat is something you bounce back from; a bad review will be in yesterday's newspaper tomorrow.

If the ghost of Hamlet haunts the hearts of all clowns, if the desire for drama must be filled by all those who make the customers laugh, Fanny Brice was no exception, for in

May 1925 the following appeared in the theatrical section
of the *New York Times:*

> *David Belasco, it was announced yesterday, has taken
> Fannie Brice under his management and will star her
> in a play without music. Miss Brice, who appeared for
> many years in the "Follies" is at present in "The Music
> Box Revue." Her contract with Mr. Belasco will become
> effective at the end of the Music Box engagement, prob-
> ably a year hence.*
>
> *No definite plans have yet been made, but it is under-
> stood that Miss Brice will be seen in a semi-serious play
> containing emotional possibilities.*

Along the Rialto, the announcement was greeted with in-
credulity. "They thought she was crazy," Trixie Wilson remembers. "Here she's the biggest thing on Broadway, and
all of a sudden she has to emote."

"So . . ." Cantor said, when he talked of the Belasco undertaking, "so . . . she wanted to do a straight play. Is it
such a crime?" he asked with no more sorrow evident in his
voice than if one of his daughters had embarked on a bull-
fighting career.

"Maybe she wouldn't have done it," Cantor continued, "if
anybody but Belasco had asked her. Belasco," he said, rolling the big eyes, and shaking his head in awe and wonder-
ment.

For in the turbulent twenties, when Ziegfeld was Broadway's Barnum, David Belasco was the Main Stem's Michel-
angelo. He of the cockeyed collar and the uncombed silver
locks, with the face of a sorrowing choir boy, was a kind of
magic maestro of the American theater. He spelled it Art
with a capital A. If you come to New York now you'll find
the Belasco Theatre housing a television studio, but when

Fanny appeared there she walked the boards in the foot-prints of all the great leading ladies of the American theater.

Belasco began his campaign to woo Fanny from her comedy in a carefully thorough fashion. One night when Fanny arrived at her dressing-room in the Music Box Theatre she found her maid arranging a dozen magnificent American Beauty roses in a vase. The card that had come with the flowers held only a big bold "B."

Fanny dismissed it as the secretive signature of another shy swain who carefully guarded his unrequited romance with the star he worshipped from afar, and thought no more of the flowers. But the next night a matching dozen appeared. This time the card read "Belasco."

While Fanny had gone a long way from the day when she ran screaming out of Ziegfeld's theater, cavorting across Broadway with her first Follies contract clutched in one hand, she could not help but be excited by the great man's overtures. She thought only that Belasco had seen the show and was thus characteristically expressing his appreciation for a good evening of theater.

Until a third dozen arrived on the following night. While Fanny was not a girl to be kept in the dark long, she was determined to wait. She didn't have to wait long. After that night's performance, a Belasco emissary arrived at her dressing-room to ask that she meet his boss at his office atop the theater he had, with no false modesty, named the Belasco.

"Sure, I signed with him" Fanny wrote of that initial meeting with Belasco. "What the hell, he bent over and kissed my hand."

" 'You're a rare jewel of an actress,' Belasco told me.

"What am I going to say to that?

" 'I want to get you a wonderful, beautiful play,' he told me.

"What am I going to say to that?

" 'The world is waiting for you, Miss Fanny,' he told me.

"Jesus, what am I going to say to *that!* I signed right then in his office."

And left New York within a few weeks for an extended vaudeville tour. She was as highly paid a variety performer then as there was in the world. Cantor saw her once in Los Angeles, having come with Ida and having warned her not to let Fanny know they were in the audience.

"I wanted to see for myself," Cantor said. "I wanted to be sure she wasn't putting on anything because she knew I was out front. I will tell you without any reservations that Fanny was as big a hit, as big a headliner, as I have ever seen. Fanny came out dressed like a society dame and did a song. They applauded for that, and no performer would have to be ashamed of receiving such applause. Then she would walk out half a chorus later and do her stuff: the eyes rolling, the goofy walks, the comedy face. They rocked the theater. They just tore the building apart, but when she was through, she was through."

Late in December, when Fanny was playing a theater in Milwaukee, she sent for her children. When they arrived, she dispatched her maid to Chicago, ninety miles away, where she had engaged a large suite in a Loop hotel. The maid bought a big Christmas tree, set it up in a corner of the parlor, and decorated it. She bought wreaths and hung them in all the windows and on all the doors. She hung mistletoe, she bought candies, and fruits, and nuts, and cakes, and champagne. Telephoning daily from Milwaukee, Fanny supervised the preparations, sending the maid on tour after tour of Chicago's toy departments and men's shops, ordering gift after gift. To her children, to her friends appearing at the theater, to her manager she said not a word until December 21, 1925, when newspapers across the country printed a story from Leavenworth:

Prison gates will swing open here tomorrow [said a Chicago newspaper] *for Jules (Nicky) Arnstein, one of the central figures in a $5,000,000 New York bond theft and husband of Fanny Brice actress.*

Nicky was received at the Federal Prison on May 16, 1924, under a sentence for two years for conspiracy. Seventy-two days have been subtracted for good behavior.

In Milwaukee, Fanny told newspapermen: "Now I believe in Santa Claus."

And, finishing her engagement, took the first train to Chicago.

But would not go to the train to meet Nick.

Would not let the newspapermen spoil this meeting for her. She had wired Nick the name of the hotel and she waited there with Frances and with Bill, the tree decorated, the wreaths hung, the gifts on the floor, the champagne cooling, as she listened for the sound of the buzzer.

And took each child's hand as she went to the door.

Stood at the door and said: "You're home, Nick," and felt his arms about her at last, felt his mustache tickling her as always.

They let the champagne cool while the children took over. They let it cool while Mam'selle fed Frances and Bill and led them off to bed. Fanny was too emotional to think of dinner. When at last the champagne was drunk, the suite quiet, the rooms dark except for the soft lights of their bedroom, Fanny said: "We'll never be apart, Nick. We're a family again, and we'll stay that way. We're going back to New York after I finish here, and we'll be together forever."

"Fanny," Nick said, "I have a very good proposition here in Chi . . ."

"No, Nick," she said. Until that moment she had forgotten

his absent nights, his empty chair, her lonely bed. She had not thought of the savage scenes when he reappeared after being away one night or two nights, with talk of a "big game" or of an "important deal."

"No," she repeated. "You can find something in New York. You can go into business. You could be my agent, Nick," she said, struck with this new scheme to keep him. "You'd get ten per cent of me, and I'll bet a lot of people would want you to be their agent. Why, you could clean . . ."

"I don't like charity, Fanny," Nick said coldly, but he agreed to return to New York with his wife and children.

Where he immediately objected to Fanny's appearance in a straight play. Writing of it many years later, Nick said he told Fanny: " 'You're a big star now. Perhaps the highest salaried woman on the stage. Did you ever hear of a "heavy" earning four thousand dollars a week? What can you gain by it? The more I think of this proposition, the more I think it would be fatal. Don't be carried away by Belasco's name.'

" 'I'm going ahead with it, no matter what you think,' Fanny snapped at me. At last she believed her ambitions were to be realized.

" 'Nick,' she said to me when she got her part and brought it home, 'I want you to let me read it to you.'

"I wanted to be fair so I ensconced myself in the heaviest cushioned chair in the house while she cleared her throat and started. For several tedious hours she read on. When she turned over the last page, she paused and her eyes were raised to mine.

" 'Well, what do you think?' she inquired.

" 'Rotten,' I retorted. 'It's just as I thought. As for the plot, words fail me. For one thing, it's twenty-five years old, and I've seen much better in the old blood and thunder days. No, it won't do, Fanny.'

"But Fanny was still unconvinced and, in her anger at my

sarcasm, she became personal. I, in turn, amplified my criticism of the play. She became more and more furious, for her heart was set on this play."

While Nick's modest admissions of furthering Fanny's career have as much truth, for the most part, as the Russians' claims of inventing the telephone, he may, in this one instance, have been sticking pretty close to facts—except that Fanny would not have argued with him about the merits of the play, since she knew from the beginning of the venture that it was a fiasco.

"Belasco got Willard Mack," she said of her venture into drama, "with a play he [Mack] must have found at the bottom of his trunk.

"Belasco said the play should be about a Jewish girl. So Mack put an 'oy' in front of every line, and we're in business. He must have looked a long time for the title. He called it *Fanny.* At the first reading I fell asleep. Belasco could see I wasn't enthusiastic. He said: 'Don't be discouraged,' and told me all he was going to do to the play. Enough had been done to it when it was written. I couldn't back out. I had signed this contract with him."

Belasco had also signed Warren William as the good guy and John Cromwell, who was to become a top-drawer Hollywood director, as the bad guy in this hot and heavy horse-opera of gold on the ranch and dirty work in the bunkhouse.

Sitting in his walled garden in an old, old section of Los Angeles, a thin, slim-hipped, middle-aged man, Cromwell remembered the rehearsal of *Fanny* twenty-five years ago with the same clarity and attention to detail that he might have were we talking about yesterday's rushes of the picture he was currently directing.

"Belasco," Cromwell said, "was accustomed to directing experienced dramatic actors. He knew nothing of Fanny's technique, and could not believe that she actually never knew what she was going to do until she was there before the footlights.

"He made Fanny and Warren William do the second-act curtain scene over and over and over again, interrupting after every reading from his seat in the theater, lecturing Fanny, telling her what he wanted, insisting that it be done his way. When he gave them a break finally, Fanny joined me in the wings.

" 'I probably could have done what he wanted,' she said, 'but I can't understand a goddam word he's saying.' "

Fanny was more than a little puzzled by the proceedings. "Belasco gave me the play a couple of weeks before we went into rehearsal," she wrote. "The first thing I noticed was that the curtain scene of the second act was a very dramatic scene, and that was the first scene I learned.

"He rehearsed differently than anybody I ever worked with. The scenery was all made and every prop was in at rehearsal. You would rehearse a week or ten days in the set of the first act. After you knew that, he would set up the second act.

"I couldn't wait until we got to the curtain of the second act. I had rehearsed and rehearsed it by myself. When we got to it, I got up and did it, and he jumped up and said: 'That's the worst thing I ever heard. I could get somebody for fifty dollars a week to do it better than that.'

" 'Then you should have hired one of them,' I told him.

" 'Do it again,' Mr. Belasco said.

" 'Just stop yelling at me,' I told him.

" 'You stop declaiming, young lady,' Belasco said.

" 'All right,' I said.

"Everybody is watching Warren William and me now.

Nobody is even breathing loud, because all the stagehands and other people who worked for Belasco, they could have lifetime jobs as long as they remembered he was God.

"So we do the scene again, and right in the middle of it, he jumps up again, and throws his hands in the air.

" 'That's just awful,' he said.

"I didn't say anything this time. He went into a long speech and told us to do it again.

"We did it again. And again. And twenty times, and each time he stopped us in the middle of it, and bawled the hell out of me. Finally I couldn't take it any more, and I just walked off the stage. John Cromwell was very nice to me.

" 'Don't take it so hard,' John said. 'I've heard this about Belasco: he likes to break you up to see if he can get a better performance out of you.'

" 'That's not why I'm nervous,' I said. 'I don't know what declaiming means,' so John explained to me what declaiming was. From John's explanation, telling me what I was doing that was wrong, for the first time I knew what straight acting meant. I didn't even learn how to close a door from Belasco. If it wasn't for John Cromwell I wouldn't have known what he wanted from me. All I was doing was making a sad sound. I wasn't feeling it. I was listening to myself, which is the most deadly thing to do. Well, after John explained it to me, I went to Belasco.

" 'I'd like to do that scene for you again,' I told him.

" 'Please do, young lady,' he said.

"Now I knew where the hell I was going. When I finished everybody in the cast applauded. Belasco applauded. He came up on stage. 'My dear Miss Fanny,' he said, 'why didn't you do it that way the first time?'

" 'Because I didn't know what declaiming meant,' I told him.

"There was no trouble from then on. It was so funny to

me to think that one person could explain one thing that I should have learned all through the years, and through that one explanation that John Cromwell gave me I saw it all, and it was such an awakening for me as an actress. All I knew about acting was doing something with the hands or with the feet. I thought that was it. I never found any trouble in singing a ballad with feeling. I found myself really throwing myself into it. You had the music to carry you and make you feel it. I knew about singing. I knew how to throw myself in the mood of a song, but I didn't know about words without music.

"I learned a lot from rehearsals, but it was all wasted on that play. What I didn't realize was that Belasco was just about finished then, and the things he asked me to do were a little exaggerated. When a comic starts to act, he must always underplay. If he overplays anything dramatic, it becomes silly. You can't go from comedy to tragedy, but from comedy to pathos is all right.

"Oh, it was just a terrible play."

The critics agreed wholeheartedly. *Fanny* opened in the fall of 1926, and in his review in the *New York Times* the next morning Brooks Atkinson, the newspaper's drama critic, said:

> *When word spread around that Miss Brice was to abandon base comedy for the pure gold of emotional histrionics, the prospects for raucous entertainment in the theatre seemed to be growing alarmingly dimmer. For as a sort of animated newspaper comic strip . . . she has no peer nor rival. "Fanny" contrives now and then to manage an emotional scene or two to humor . . . [her] whim. As the groveling general factotum of a kind-hearted old woman, Miss Brice expresses undying devotion, gratitude beyond words and affection unmatched*

*in its purity. During a little religious interlude she sings
a Jewish lullaby with her hand tenderly stroking the old
lady's head. Once she delivers an impassioned jeremiad
about honor between friends with tears in her eyes and
a choking throttle in her throat.*

*But it cannot rival for a moment the Fannie Brice of
the slightly crossed eyes, the broad grin and the comic
awkwardness. With a huge sombrero on her head she
sits down to a game of poker with the cowboys, does
tricks with the cards, deals off the bottom of the pack,
and thus for a few restful moments she puts the play out
of her mind completely. With a rose in her hair and another in her rolled stockings, she tries her absurd blan-
dishments upon the villain who has unearthed the bur-
ied treasure. Delightfully vulgarized by her accent and
stupendously shrill voice and by her broad grimaces and
stiff-jointed bucking and plunging, these episodes reveal
Miss Brice playing confidently on her home grounds.
Most of us are content to see her at her best. At her best
she is unparalleled.*

In the walled garden in Los Angeles twenty-five years
later John Cromwell sat quietly for a time, watching a spar-
row at the birdbath. He raised his arm slowly, cautioning
silently against speech or movement while his tiny guest
quenched its thirst, throwing its head back in instinctive
grace as it savored the cool, cool water in this pleasant twilight.

For a few moments the city was far away; here, with the
night's breeze stirring the trees, with the soft ripple of the
water in the cement bowl, with the small bird completing
the almost contrived beauty of this peaceful garden. Cromwell could very nearly feel Fanny's presence. She seemed,
for a short, still time, to be among the living once more.

Cromwell sat motionless, not daring to move, feeling himself the interloper until, with a sudden, thin, almost inaudible whirring motion, the bird left the garden, the semaphore at the intersection changed from red to green, the waiting automobiles charged forward in a roaring cacophony, and to the right a door opened, freeing a narrow carpet of light to run across the grass. Cromwell was told that dinner was waiting.

He answered reluctantly, running his hands through his hair while he stood beside the birdbath. He seemed unwilling to leave the garden; for here in this secluded space the past had returned pleasantly—all regrets, sadness, heartbreak, even tragedies considerately removed—so that for a brief interlude one was young again, one was strong again, one knew that a lifetime lay ahead containing all joy and happiness.

❄ 14 ❄

FANNY: *"I Went After Something I Didn't Want, and Got It."*

I DON'T think Nick would have ever paid any attention to me," Fanny wrote once, "but I never really found out. I never gave him the chance. I really went after *him* from the first time I saw him, I guess. I think that if I hadn't chased him, he would have met me, and I think I would have passed out of his life. I don't ever remember any guy really making a play for me. I wasn't the cutie type.

"All my years with Nick I had a dream that I could change him. I thought if I worked at it long enough, and waited long enough, and tried hard enough, I could change Nick into what I wanted. He had every quality that was fine, you know, except he wouldn't use them. That was something for me to work on, to make him use the good qualities. And it is a funny thing, because everything in my life that I ever wanted, if I tried for it, I can say that I got it. But with men, the harder I tried, the harder I flopped."

In the spring, after the opening of the Belasco fiasco, Fanny, Nick, and the children moved to the house in Huntington, Long Island. Since his release from prison Nick had been an abnormally, for him, attentive husband, but with their arrival at the country house his old habits returned. Fanny would be driven to the theater nightly, never knowing whether she would find Nick home when she returned after the performance. Remembering their quarrels of a few years ago, she said nothing of his absences, hoping in this silently suffering fashion to outstay his wandering feet and roving eye.

Until a warm Sunday when Fanny had invited a houseful of guests. While Fanny looked after lunch, she suggested hiring a boat to take their friends fishing.

"What do you think, Nick?" she asked. "Wouldn't a boat be fun?"

"An excellent idea," Nick replied, sitting comfortably in a chair overlooking the water.

"I'll send the chauffeur," Fanny said. "He can rent one for us right down the block."

"Why, I'll do that, my dear," Nick said. "I'll want to check the captain's fishing gear anyway."

"Well, all right," Fanny said. "But the people are due any minute, Nick. Maybe we'll send the chauffeur and you can be here when they come."

"Good Lord, Fanny," Nick said sharply. "The dock is no more than a hundred yards from here. I'll be back in five minutes."

"I learned one thing about men," Fanny wrote long afterward. "When they argue over nothing, it's usually over something they're hiding."

But that day she wanted no quarrels; no scenes and no harsh words before the people coming down from New York.

"Sure, honey," she said. "You go get the boat."

Nick had not been gone five minutes when the guests arrived. Fanny herded them into the dining-room for the buffet lunch, explaining that Nick had gone to hire a boat and that as soon as they were finished with the food everybody was going out on the briny.

Except that Nick didn't return. Not after lunch, not after the sun had disappeared, not after Fanny had exhausted herself entertaining the guests, not after the children had appeared for their good-night kiss, not after she had eaten a solitary dinner, not after she had gone to bed, lying wide awake and angry and hurt, with an unread book beside her.

Only when she was sick with fear that he might be ill, injured, dead in an automobile accident, only long after midnight, did he appear, remove his jacket, hang it carefully, and turn to stare in apparent surprise at his wide-awake wife.

"I thought you were asleep, darling," he said, sitting down to untie his shoelaces.

"Where were you, Nick?" Fanny asked quietly.

"The car broke down, my dear."

"You didn't take the car. I sent the people to the station in the car."

"I took the small car, Fanny," Nick explained patiently.

Fanny glanced at the clock on the night-table beside her. "Fourteen hours and the car broke down?" she asked. "Can't you do better than that?"

Nick didn't answer.

"Am I not even worth a good lie?" she asked.

Nick went into the bathroom. Fanny lay in bed, listening to him brush his teeth, waiting while he washed his face and hands, saying nothing until he returned, wearing silk pajamas.

"Good night, my dear," he said, getting into his bed.

"Is that it, Nick?" she asked.

"Is that *what*, Fanny?" he said irritably.

"Good night," she repeated, "and I'm supposed to forget

it, is that it? Just another day between Nick and Fanny?"

"I don't know what you're talking about," Nick said, turning his back to her as he pulled the blanket high around him and stretched his legs for sleep.

Watching him, she knew he would never stop foraging in greener fields. Watching him, she knew the hurt inside her would never leave her, but that it would remain constant, like a low, steady fever. Watching him, she saw not Nick alone but Nick's nameless companion; saw them living through the day together; saw them with all the fertile imaginative resources of the actress, until the hurt became unbearable, and she said aloud what she had never said aloud to him before.

She said: "I hate your guts, Nick. I hate you!"

He turned in the bed, staring at her with the now-familiar indignation.

"You don't mean that," he answered.

—Then tell me I'm wrong, she begged silently. —Come over here, she didn't say, and prove it's a lie. —I'm a cinch for you, Nick, she didn't say, but don't fall asleep on me, that's all.

"Don't I?" she asked.

"You and your town house and your country house," Nick said. "I can get a house on Long Island any time I want one, and don't you ever forget it, my dear."

That was it. She had the word now. He had never come closer to admitting infidelity. To anyone else, it would have sounded more like male braggadocio. To Fanny, who knew Nick better than she was ever to know herself, he had turned up his hole card.

—Why did you tell me? she said to herself. —Why did you say it? she asked herself. —Why did you have to say it? she demanded silently. —Why didn't you swear at me, or just not talk at all?

For there is an unwritten law for all philanderers, whether they cross the matrimonial line once or a hundred times: *Don't admit anything.* Don't talk, and don't hang your head. Don't confess and expect forgiveness. Don't counterpunch and don't go on the defensive, for your wife wants to believe you, *wants* to *believe* you.

Nick had broken the law, and so Fanny said the second thing aloud she had never said before.

She said: "I want a divorce."

And Nick said: "Go to sleep."

And she heard her words again, although she did not speak again. She heard them again and again, while he turned away from her once more and slept, and the house became still, and she lay holding the book she had not read at all, hearing the clock strike the hours away, as she walked with delicious fear through the imagined ruins of a life divorced from Nick.

"I knew he had somebody on Long Island," Fanny wrote in her memoirs. "I knew she was rich. The next day I went into New York early and I hired a couple of private detectives to trail him. For a couple of weeks they found out nothing, and I was glad. I was glad to pay them to trail Nick forever, just so they would prove me wrong, but in my heart I knew.

"Will Rogers was the only man I ever met who I would have sworn was true to his wife. Nick wasn't Will Rogers.

"After about a month, the detectives come to me with a report: Nick is meeting a woman on the Manhattan side of the Queensboro Bridge on 59th Street. She picks him up in her car, they go someplace on Long Island for lunch, stay two or three hours, then go for a ride in the country, and she brings him back to the bridge.

"It was like a disease, that divorce. Once I let the word

come out, I couldn't shake it off. It got hold of me and I would think all the time: Get rid of him, get rid of him, get rid of him.

"I would think: Why do you need all this misery? Where is it taking you? You haven't got a husband. All the things that everybody else knew, I now began to admit to myself: He doesn't earn a living, he isn't strong and protective, he doesn't give a damn for the children."

But what she never wrote about were the delaying tactics she successfully employed against herself. She never remembered the delight in his prompt appearance for dinner, nor her happiness when she saw him waiting with her car at the stage door, nor the security and comfort his presence in the Huntington house gave her.

Until, some six weeks after his abortive attempt to hire a boat for their guests, he didn't come home at all one night. He didn't come home the next night either, but telephoned from New York just as Fanny reached the door, calling from their house in town to tell her he was spending the night there.

"He timed it," Fanny wrote. "If he'd wanted me with him, he could have called the theater, instead of waiting until I had come all the way out to Huntington. I knew he was alone, and I didn't know he was alone. I knew he wouldn't bring a woman into our house, but I couldn't stay out there when he was in town."

Fanny didn't even take off her coat. She didn't look into the nursery that night. She summoned the weary chauffeur and ordered him to drive her into New York. When she arrived at their West 76th Street home, Nick was in his dressing-gown, sitting in the library.

"Why, Fanny," he said, rising to greet her. "What brings you here at this time of night, my dear?"

"Cut out that stuff," Fanny replied. "Where were you last night, Nick?"

"Are we going into that again?"

"All right." She nodded for emphasis. "All right, Nick, if that's your answer. But I know all about your meetings with this woman."

"What woman?"

"You know what woman. Don't give me that, Nick. You know who I'm talking about."

But her name was never mentioned. Not then by either of them, not later in either's memoirs, not ever in all the newspaper accounts of their affairs. The detective agency is mum about its clients. All anyone knows now or knew then is that Fanny had learned there *was* a woman.

Nick, however, admitted nothing. He returned to his chair, refusing to talk to his wife, and Fanny said it again. "I know it's all over between us and I want a divorce."

But Nick didn't. And Fanny didn't. There was no dramatic reconciliation. There were no soft words and new promises and fervent affirmations of lasting love. They slept in separate rooms that night, but they slept in the same house. Fanny called off her detectives, and Nick announced he was going to open a gambling-house in Chicago with a Leavenworth pal. Since the detectives' reports had mentioned only one woman, Fanny took it as proof of his fidelity that he was putting half a continent between himself and his trysting-mate.

At the close of the theatrical season Fanny journeyed to Chicago. They had been separated too long for her to remember night-long absences, private detectives, lies and deceit and anger. She wanted Nick.

And Nick apparently wanted Fanny. He met her at the train, he took her back to his hotel, he ordered dinner in their suite, he waited on her, and he told her of his success

with the new casino. He made her comfortable, insisting
that she rest after her journey, and he promised to return
from his gambling-house as early as possible.

He was adjusting his Panama hat when the phone rang.
While Nick admired himself in the mirror, Fanny picked up
the receiver.

"Hold on for New York," the operator said. As the cold
fingers of fear gripped her heart, Fanny smiled at Nick's reflection in the mirror, and he winked at her. Then: "Jules?"
asked a woman.

"I didn't say a word," Fanny wrote. "I handed him the
phone and I said: 'Your girl friend.' He got as white as a
ghost and tried to hang up quick, but I started to pack while
he spluttered all over the place, trying to duck out of the
call.

"He just watched me pack. He didn't try to stop me, and
that's what hurt me the most. I said: 'I'm going to Paris,
Nick, and now I will get my divorce in Paris.'

"He didn't say anything. He just watched me packing like
I had watched him packing. I walked out on him, and went
to Paris with Norma Talmadge. The kids went on the same
boat, with the governess, and they stayed in the governess's
home town. Norma and I took a big apartment in Paris. I
would go from there to Lido or someplace and Norma would
go someplace else. It meant we could just pack a bag and go,
keeping the apartment for a base."

Once, long afterward, Fanny was asked about the high society with whom she customarily stayed and spent her time,
both on the Continent and in New York.

"I suppose," she answered, "that I met almost every person in the society world there was to meet. I never thought
anything about them, or cared much, unless they actually
touched my life. I'd see show people who took the society
people very seriously, and thought they were one of them,

which they never were. Those society people are clannish. I
never cared who anybody was. I had society people in my
house, and I had anyone else I liked in my house. If I liked
them, that's all that counted to me.

"I was always amused by the high-society people as much
as they were amused by me. They were just a big study to
me. I never kidded myself. I never said: 'Oh, kid, you're in
society now.' I knew I didn't belong there. I was looking at
them, and they were looking at me. They were like an audience to me. And, you know, I was always surprised the way
that society people were aware of society. Since they were
really in it, I would have thought that they wouldn't be
aware of it. But you have no idea of how aware of it they
are. And how impressed a big name is with another big
name. Like the Americans in society; as soon as they meet
somebody with a title, I could see their reaction. It was
somebody they looked up to. Most of those titles, though,
they were just good-looking con men like Nick.

"When society gave parties, they always liked to have on
the list Lady this and Lord that, people I wouldn't give a
bone to, they were so phony. So I always knew there was
always somebody looking up to somebody and somebody
always looking down at somebody.

"I always knew where I belonged and I knew who I
wanted to be with. I am sorry for those performers who get
to meet a couple of society people and think they are really
in. And, you know, when society sees anyone act like that,
they blow him right off. I knew they liked me because they
knew I didn't give a damn for them, except if they were interesting. If a person is not interesting, I don't care if he
built the highest building in the world, I don't want to be
near him. I don't want to see him. But the society people,
if I liked them, I would talk to them just the way I'm talking to you. And I would even get lower and lower with the

things I said, to get under their skins, see how they really ticked. It was always people that interested me, not the spot they were in."

"When I came back from Europe," Fanny wrote, "I couldn't think of work. I didn't want to go into a show, or do anything. People came to me with shows, and I tried to tell them I was in no shape to work. I told Flo no that year. It's funny, when you don't want something, then everybody tries to give it to you. I didn't want to work, but that year [1927] I turned down more offers and better offers than I ever had.

"It got so I couldn't stand the house. I couldn't stand the servants. I couldn't stand being around people. I would go to a party and some of the funniest people in the world would be there, and I'd sit like a deadhead all night. I wasn't interested in the children. If the cook asked me what I wanted for dinner, I'd chase her out of my room. I forgot antiques. I forgot clothes. Some days I didn't even get dressed. I just had him on my mind and it was making me nuts.

"So I knew that I had to do something, snap out of it some way. Because the way things were going I was a cinch for the booby-hatch. I wouldn't call him in Chicago because I thought it was up to Nick to call me. Well, so there were no calls from anybody. One day I packed up, and told my chauffeur to drive me to Grand Central. All the way out to Chicago I made up my mind to have this divorce. And I decided to make him give me the evidence for it.

"If he gave it to me, I wanted it. If he didn't give it to me, I didn't want it.

"In other words, I went after something I really didn't want, and got it. I had proved my love for Nick every day for fifteen years. Now I wanted him to prove his love for me."

But he didn't. Fanny checked into the Congress Hotel in Chicago and telephoned a lawyer, engaging him to represent her. While her arrival in the city did not escape some notice, most newspapers and her friends in the Windy City assumed she was in Chicago to see her husband.

She saw him, all right. In what followed, Nick's own account has the corroboration of several friends of both his and Fanny's.

"She had her lawyer call me," Nick said to me in his Beverly Hills apartment. "She wouldn't call me herself, and I didn't like that a little bit."

Watching him that afternoon, you would have thought Nick Arnstein was talking of a divorce that had been granted the day before. It was the only time he really came alive. He sat up in the Queen Anne chair, pointing his forefinger into the air, his face red, and his voice harsh and filled with anger.

"That lawyer of hers thought he was a real wise guy," Nick said. "He told me to get over to the Congress on the double. He said Fanny had come to Chicago for a divorce and I damned well had better give her one. I hung up on him. Nobody talks to Nick Arnstein that way.

"I was in no hurry," Nick continued. "I took my own time. A few days later I met Fanny at the hotel. Her lawyer was there. I had a lawyer, but I didn't bring him.

"Fanny had worked herself up to a fine state. She was a nervous wreck. She was sitting on the sofa, and when I came in, the lawyer started to talk rough with me. I said: 'You're out of this.'

" 'I'm representing Miss Brice,' he said.

" 'Right now there is no Miss Brice,' I replied calmly. 'Her name is Mrs. Arnstein, Counselor, and I'd advise you to button up and button up quick.'

" 'Miss Brice wants a divorce,' he said.

" 'I want to hear it from her,' I said, looking straight into her eyes. I was never afraid of her. I wouldn't give in to her if it meant my life.

"I waited. The lawyer buttoned up. There was a deathly silence. Fanny faced the most dramatic moment of her life. The lawyer coughed. Fanny seemed to choke back a sob. I knew people had inflamed her against me, but I was prepared, as always, to face the world with fear for no man.

" 'I haven't got all day,' I said.

"Fanny spoke. 'I want a divorce,' she said. That was the first thing she said. 'That's the least you can do for me,' she added.

" 'You've got it,' I told her. I wouldn't bend to her.

" 'You'll never see the kids, Nick.'

" 'If you feel that way, Fanny,' I replied, 'I'll never go near you or the kids again.'

"And I never did. I didn't even go back to the New York house for my clothes. She auctioned them off with her furniture later. I was through.

" 'You'll have to give me evidence, Nick,' she said.

" 'Let your lawyer arrange it,' I said. They arranged everything. I went to a hotel with a woman for the adultery evidence. I never saw that woman before, and I never saw her again."

"I watched him leave that room," Fanny wrote long years later, "and I didn't believe what was happening. I didn't believe we were through, and I didn't believe I'd never see Nick again as my husband. The lawyer went away to arrange the hotel-room thing, and I knew I was just as much in love with Nick that day as the day I first saw him.

"I waited for Nick to stop the divorce. Even when the lawyer came to take me to court, I thought Nick would be downstairs to call it off. I thought he would be outside the

court to stop it. I thought he would be in the court to tell
the judge: 'Forget it, Judge. My wife and I made a mistake.
We're in love. Why, we don't want a divorce.'

"But he never showed up. All I remember is that it was a
beautiful day. I was like in another world. I was like watching me standing there in that courtroom. I didn't hear my
lawyer. I didn't hear what the judge said. All I know is they
gave me a bunch of papers to sign, and I signed, and they
gave me a copy.

"I had to get out of that town. I got a compartment on the
first train for New York. I knew I would go crazy if I sat in
that compartment, so on the way to the train I stopped at
Marshall Field's and bought a yard and a quarter of gabar-
dine, a needle, thread, and scissors. I made a skirt. I made
the same skirt a dozen times. I didn't sleep. I told the porter
not to make up my berth. He brought me some tea. Every
fifteen minutes he poked his head in to see how I was. If it
hadn't been for that porter, I would have gone out of my
mind, I think. When I got back to New York, I didn't think
I could make it out of the train, but I saw those newspapermen and I made up my mind to show them."

But she couldn't quite make it this time. Reporting her return from Chicago, the *New York Times* said:

> *She was dressed in black crepe, with a close fitting
> black toque.*
> "I'm all in," *she kept saying.* "I want to get home and
> see the children."
> *Then she made a comic grimace, although her eyes
> were filling with tears.*
> "Haven't I had enough?" *she pleaded.*

She hadn't. The newspapermen would not let her go. They
bombarded her with questions. The *New York Telegram*
said:

*As she talked of Arnstein, she impressed the inter-
viewers with her sincerity, even as she had once impressed audiences, while her husband was in Leavenworth, with her song, "My Man."*

*Nicky Arnstein is still her man. For Miss Brice be-
lieves, in this day of many matings, that there is just one
man for every woman.*

*"They asked me Monday in Chicago if I loved him,"
she said. "This is Friday. My answer is still yes."*

"Will you ever love anyone else, do you think?"

She shook her head.

*"If a man wants to go, you can't hold him," she said.
"In trying to help him, I didn't. I've always been weak
where he was concerned. I think he believed I wouldn't
go through with it, but for once I showed him my
strength."*

That day, as she returned from Chicago, the newspapermen followed Fanny crosstown and uptown to her home near
the Hudson River. The photographers were waiting, and two
policemen were there to keep the curious back from the entrance to her home. Upstairs, the governess stood before an
open window with her children, while Fanny had to pose
again for pictures, listen again to questions that ripped the
lid from the secret chambers of her life. She needed the help
of the police to get into her house, and she needed the aid
of her maid to get her clothes off.

Later—much later—when the children were asleep, when
Fanny had sent back the broth her cook had brought her,
when the house was still and she was all alone in the bedroom she had shared with the man who was no longer her
husband, she lay on the chaise longue.

In the dim light she could see Nick's suits hanging in the
open closet. She could see Nick's slippers below his bed. She

could see his cigarette holder on his night-table. She could see his toothbrushes beside her toothbrushes and, like a child who stares in masochistic awe at the needle it pushes through the skin of its hand, she looked again at the stiff-papered document she held:

". . . *that subsequent to their intermarriage the De-fendant has been guilty of* committing adultery with a certain lewd woman, whose name is unknown to the complainant, at the Berkshire Hotel, 15 E. Ohio St., Chicago, on to-wit the 10th day of September A.D. 1927, and also has committed adultery with divers other lewd women at divers times and places to the complainant unknown.

and:

It is further ordered, adjudged and decreed that the complainant be and she is hereby given the sole care, custody and education of the minor children of the parties hereto, Frances, aged eight years and William Jules, aged six years, with the right of visitation to the defendant at all reasonable times.

It is further ordered, adjudged and decreed that the question of the support and maintenance of said minor children be reserved for the future consideration of this court, and that the defendant be and he is hereby barred of and from any and all claims for dower, homestead or other property rights in the estate of the complainant.

ENTER:

JUDGE

15

BILLY ROSE: *"She Was Thunder in the Mountains."*

TELL me what's easier than hitting a guy when he's
down? What's simpler than taking a stick to someone
who's got no stick? Who's the noble soul to turn away from
the mob? Why does everybody want to get into the act when
a fellow's on his uppers? What's the pleasure they get from
watching a man take the long count?

They're on Billy Rose now: the Broadway bums, the bis-
tro boulevardiers, the L.A.-New York weisenheimers, the
columnists with their typewriter Tommy-guns. Everybody's
belting Billy, it's the biggest thing since canasta.

Billy's come a cropper! Billy's getting his! Billy's gonna
get taken! Watch that wife of his! Billy blew a wrong note!
Rose is not so sweet! Billy drew the joker! Let's all give Rose
some heat!

He was a stationary target during those months, having
been locked out of home; having his secret strife exposed;
having his marital mess washed in a Broadway bath and
hung out to dry in the public eye. Billy was in bad trouble
and they were all taking punches.

At the little man who wasn't there. If he was a loser that day last winter, he was the fightingest loser you ever saw. He was cocky, he was agile, he was ready, he was strong. He'd had enough shots taken at him to have dropped the Empire State Building, but his head was on his shoulders, his eyes were clear, his fingernails were manicured, his hands were steady, his lounging pajamas were handsome, his telephones were ringing, and he was plotting.

In his apartment-office atop the Ziegfeld Theatre, which he owns, Billy Rose looked as beaten as an untamed tiger. He looked as soft as steel, as deceptively sleepy as a king cobra. And you can believe this: he looked also as if he was having fun.

Because things were happening. Because the Ferris wheel was turning, the merry-go-round was whirling, the colored lights were shining, and the barkers were barking. And if he picked up the empty shell, if it turned out he had to pay for the candy—well, he'd had a good ride, he'd had action for his money, he'd lost this one, but tomorrow there'd be another.

He was right where he wanted to be, high above the Main Stem, in the only seat that fit him. The butler brought coffee, Billy scratched his chest, lit a cigarette, and said, "Who's kidding who? What's this all-washed-up talk? I'm just starting. Who's going to short-count me? Where I grew up, I was ahead the day I reached my twenty-first birthday. Just staying alive was victory. I've been around this town too long to quit now. Why, I was making money when piano rolls were a big item.

"How did I feel about Fanny? Well, in 1927 I was a song writer and she was Fanny Brice. She wasn't an entertainer. She was an institution like Prudential Life Insurance. Fanny didn't do just one thing well. She did everything better than anybody else did anything. She was great in each department. Fanny was thunder in the mountains, lad, thunder in the mountains.

"I met her, really shook hands with her, in 1924 when I was twenty-four years old. I wrote a song called 'In The Middle of the Night' which all the speakeasy tenors used to sing. Then I opened the Backstage Club over a garage, hoisted Helen Morgan onto a piano, and sat behind the till doing my own counting. Fanny came in one night with a party. Did you ever see her walk into a joint? She made the waters part, sonny, and don't you ever forget it.

"She said she wanted to meet the guy who wrote 'Night,' and I went over to her table and introduced myself. I could see her face fall. I said: 'I know, you thought that anybody who wrote a song like that would have eyes like the searchlights on the Albany night boat.'

"I didn't see Fanny again," Billy continued, "except from a fifth-row seat, until 1927, after she divorced Nick. I always went to her opening nights. She was a . . ."

One of the three telephones atop the semicircular, antique, wine table he uses for a desk rang harshly, and Billy wheeled and hurried to it. Maybe *you* don't listen to telephone conversations when you're sitting five feet from the instrument, but maybe you're deaf or carry a set of ear plugs around with you.

This was a California call. Billy was questioning the legality of Eleanor Holm Jarrett Rose's divorce from Art Jarrett, and he asked the California lawyer he was talking to more questions than a covey of newspapermen hot on a story. He asked questions, he gave orders, he outlined strategy, and he hung up the phone to return to the precise point where he had interrupted himself.

"Fanny was a gal who was afraid of nobody in show business. Most stars who sign for a show want no competition around them. I know, I've had more trouble with casting

than Tevya had marrying his daughters. Sign a star and his
or her idea of a cast is a bunch of storewindow dummies.
Not Fanny. Get her in a show, and she wanted every headliner in America with her. The more stars, the better the
show. She worried about none of them, and she didn't have
to. Chevalier was the only performer who could touch her.

"She had what the great ones have: the magic to take you
away from yourself and make you her obedient servant. I
watched Al Jolson walk out on the stage and send sparks out
into the theater. It was there, it came from somewhere inside of him. If you were sick, it made you well for an hour.
If you were old, it made you young. If you were sad, it made
you happy.

"I watched Harry Lauder, a little old man wearing a skirt,
stand before a New York audience, the most sophisticated
audience in the world, and tell them to sing. He told them
to sing with him, and they sang with him.

"I watched Fanny. She had it: the magic. It came from
her eyes, from her hands, from her just *being* on the stage.
She was one of the goose-flesh specialists, and you can't ex-
plain that quality, you have to see it. Watch Garland [Judy
Garland] on a stage if you ever get the chance. She and
Chevalier and Durante are the only three left.

"Writing for Fanny was a romp. All you had to know was
how to fit her. That's how I met her the second time, you
know. Ballard MacDonald, the writer, brought me up to the
house on 76th Street."

Of that first meeting with Billy in her home, Fanny says:
"A few days after I got back from Chicago with the divorce,
I kept thinking: 'Nick loves me. This whole thing will be
straightened out and we will be married again, but it's a
good lesson for him. Now Nick will prove his love for me

and then we will live a better life than the first time we were married.'

"But a week went by and no Nick. Two weeks went by and I heard he was in California. Three weeks, a month passes since the divorce, and I get no calls from Nick, no letter, nothing. Now, I know that if I sit in that house looking at his clothes I will go crazy. Everything reminds me of Nick from morning to night. I decided to get rid of everything, every stick of furniture, every spoon, every suit of his, *everything.*"

So Fanny arranged her auction. Announced that she was selling, announced that she was moving, announced that she was preparing new material for vaudeville.

"I had to get to work," Fanny wrote. "This sitting around, that was bad. I had to get out and do something, be with people, get into action. I sent for Ballard MacDonald and I gave him a deposit to write my act for vaudeville."

Meanwhile Billy Rose, looking then as now for new worlds to conquer, had signed to write the lyrics for a new Broadway musical comedy. He went to MacDonald, an experienced librettist, and asked him to work on the show with him.

"Billy," said MacDonald, "I'd like to but I can't. I've just agreed to write a new act for Fanny Brice."

"What's to stop you from writing the show *and* Fanny's act?" Billy asked.

MacDonald, who was as well known for his tippling as for his writing, seemed reluctant to burden himself, but Billy is a most persuasive fellow when he wants something.

"I'll help you with Fanny's act," Billy offered, "and then you can do the show with me."

At the Brice home Billy was impressed: with Fanny, with her well-mannered children, with her well-ordered staff of

servants, with her superbly furnished home, with everything
he saw. When the butler announced dinner Fanny led them
to the dining-room, placed Billy on her right, MacDonald
on her left, and sat in Nick's chair at the head of the table.

As she pressed the buzzer with her foot to summon the
soup, Billy clapped both hands to his nose.

For he was bleeding like a stuck pig. Fanny tilted his head
back over the chair. She put ice to his nose. She made him
swallow three times. Nothing helped. The blood poured.
Holding the napkin, which was now as red as a matador's
cape, Billy at last made his way to the bathroom, more embarrassed than he has been before or since, until, mercifully
and abruptly, the crimson torrent subsided.

And the three had sandwiches and coffee in the library.

Billy remembers the evening as he remembers everything
else: with photographic clarity. He's a very famous man
now, as familiar to Americans as, say, Spencer Tracy. It is
part of his biographical ballyhoo that he was once a shorthand speed-champion, but what not many people know is
that he takes notes in his head as well. He doesn't forget
anything, our Billy: not victories or defeats; not flattery or
favors; not friend or foe.

"It wasn't one of my best nights," he said that day in the
Ziegfeld Theatre, "let's put it that way. By the time my nose
stopped bleeding I was as weak as though I'd just come out
of an all-night session in a Turkish bath. I'm not a guy who
takes kindly to his size, but that night I felt about as big as
a bug. The funny thing is, the thing I can't figure out to this
day, I never before had a nosebleed, and I haven't had one
since that night."

Fanny was not at all impressed with Billy. When, finally,
they began to talk business, Billy told her he had an idea for
a song to be called "Riverside Rose."

"It was no good," Fanny wrote. "I told him it was no good.

I told him that I never did a Jewish song that would offend the race, because it depended on the race for the laughs. In anything Jewish I ever did, I wasn't standing apart, making fun of the race. I *was* the race, and what happened to me on the stage is what could happen to them. They identified with me, and then it was all right to get a laugh, because they were laughing at me as much as at themselves. It is the same with any race, and it is something I always knew from instinct. There is good taste in humor like there is good taste in clothes or furniture. It is okay for one Irishman to call another Irishman anything, any kind of name. But if you are not an Irishman, keep the mouth shut. The same with all people.

"Now I tell Billy that, and he gets mad. He's had the nosebleed and he wants to be a big man, but now he argues with me. It ends up we're not talking at all. I thought: 'This is a smart-alecky little guy. This little guy I can be happy without.'

"About a week later Billy calls me up. 'Have you seen Ballard MacDonald?' he asks.

" 'I've been looking for him for three days,' I say. 'Where is he?' I say.

" 'I don't know,' Billy says, 'but he promised to write this show with me.'

" 'He promised to write me an act,' I say.

" 'Well, I will try to find him,' Billy promises.

"The next day Billy calls again. He looked high and low for Ballard MacDonald but no Ballard.

" 'I've written a couple of songs I'd like you to hear,' Billy says.

"At that time I would have listened to a song if a guy in a loony-house had written it. 'Come on up,' I told him.

"Well, he came up. Well, they were just so great, so wonderful. We talked for quite a while. I told him about a couple of ideas I had, and do you know he took down everything I said in shorthand. Before Ballard ever shows up again my act is finished by Billy Rose, and I think it was the best act I ever had. You know, here is a girl sitting there with a broken heart, and I'm thinking: "This is a clever kid. I think I'll keep this kid around, he's smart. He might make life very easy for me.'

"I felt I didn't have to push myself with Billy around. I didn't have to find material. He was a good whip for me, because he made me think, made me work harder to keep up with him. I had a great admiration for his talent. Later on, Billy told me he felt the same thing."

Billy accompanied Fanny when she took to the road, to break in her act out of town. Such procedure is *de rigueur* for all new theatrical ventures. By playing before a live audience, the performer learns from the act's reception what is good, what is not so good, and what is downright bad. During the out-of-town run an act—or a play—can be edited, tightened, strengthened, until, when the New York opening-night audience arrives, they are seeing something that has had its baptism in the "sticks," to quote *Variety*.

The day after she opened at the Palace, on November 21, 1927, the *New York Telegram* printed this review:

> *Fanny Brice wouldn't sing "My Man" at the Palace last night, although the audience stopped the show for 20 minutes and shouted at her to let them hear it.*
>
> *They remembered it was the song she had sung up and down the country while her husband, Nicky Arnstein, was in prison.*
>
> *She came back to the stage yesterday for the first time since her divorce.*

But the newspapers didn't say that she stood smack in the middle of the stage, looking straight at the audience, for fif-

teen minutes, while they did more than shout at her to sing
it. They were out of their seats and stamping their feet.
They were whistling and clapping their hands. They were
pleading with her to sing it, and they dared her to sing it.
The manager stood in the wings and begged her to come off
the stage, but she had never run from an audience, and she
was not running that day. There was only one boss in a
theater when Fanny Brice came out on the stage, and she
didn't propose to have command taken from her now.

Fifteen minutes! Do you know how long fifteen minutes
is, just sitting in your easy chair and watching television, or
reading, or staring at the fire? It's almost half of a ten-round
fight. It's a fifth of most motion pictures. It's longer than the
time it takes you to undress, get into the shower, get out of
the shower, dry yourself, get into pajamas, and pull the covers over you.

But she wasn't being told what to sing. She waited until
they were back in their seats, until the clapping had ended,
the feet were still, the voices exhausted. Then she went on
with her act.

The following year, however, she sang "My Man" once
more. In Hollywood the "talkies" had created a revolution in
picture-making. Al Jolson had made *The Jazz Singer*, the first
full-length talking picture. Warner Brothers, who had pio-
neered sound, were looking for another winner after Jolson.
They signed Fanny for her first movie.

Writing of her career in motion pictures Fanny said: "I
will say that I never learned the camera. You have to be able
to forget the camera. And I found it very hard to lose myself
with all those guys around with those machines. Before
they shoot a scene, they prepare like for a war. If there had
been thousands of people around watching me, then I could
forget the camera. But wherever I looked, there is that eye
staring at me. Like a peeper. Making pictures is like mak-

ing love in public, you can't be at ease when somebody is watching.

"Because if there are five thousand people in an audience, it's like they were one person watching me. But if there is one person watching me who didn't pay to get in, then it's like five thousand. Because in a theater the people belong there, that is my job, to amuse them, but on a movie set they don't belong there, and I could not accept it that they were there. Maybe that is why I could never perform in a living-room. There are performers who are great in a living-room. Now Eddie Cantor, in a living-room he is great. He knocks me out. I die when Cantor is on in a living-room.

"And I will say that in the theater it was different for me. I made a deal with the audience every time I came out: I look at them, and I smile at them, and I tell them—by looking at me they know—that this is a private party between them and me. In the theater I was always at ease, but in pictures there was that camera following me around like a cop.

"It's whatever you get used to. Of course, the great advantage I had—the main thing, I think, in life—is a ladder. The first step, the second step, till you get to the top. All those steps. Then when you get up there, you can balance yourself, because you know how. But if you go from the first step to the eighth step—Honey, you're in trouble, because you'll say: 'Jesus, I wish I knew how I got here!' And in my day there was a great training-school: burlesque and vaudeville were such a school. There's no school now. And who took the school away? Moving pictures. And yet it's so strange about moving pictures. I have seen people start that didn't know anything about acting, and you know in two or three years they really could act. And why? Because they knew the camera. It's a new medium. It's whatever you get used to."

If Fanny was inclined to disparage her endeavors before

the magic eye, her audiences and critics were not. Warner Brothers capitalized on Fanny's private life and provided her with a story that might have been written from the front pages of the nation's newspapers. It was called *My Man,* and in it she sang the song for the first time since her divorce from Nick.

When it opened on Broadway, the *New York Telegram* critic said:

> *Not yet having seen Mr. Jolson in the talking-pictures, Miss Brice registers better than any other Vitaphoner these eyes have seen. In "My Man" she is, as always, first-rate and effective. Even her burlesque stepping to Mr. Mendelssohn's "Spring Song" comes refreshing from the tin. Audiences adore it. "My Man" is the best talking-picture I've ever seen. Thanks, of course, to Fannie Brice, that fine comedienne.*

Fanny had another explanation of her success in that first movie. "In the picture," she wrote, "I have a younger sister. And of course she is a no-good little bitch, and I am the big-hearted jerk who takes care of her, and gives her everything she wants. Now I fall in love with a guy, and of course my bitch sister falls in love with him, but I don't know that. And one day, when I am not expected home from work, I walk into the house and find them together. She is in his arms. I grab her by the wrist and slap her and chase her out of the house. Then there is a scene of me looking out of the window while she leaves, where I sing 'My Man.' I am supposed to stand at the window, sing the song and cry. In my mind I think of Nick leaving and the tears just come."

This, remember, was several months after her divorce. Billy Rose was a constant guest in her home, and she was his constant companion along the Rialto. Their names weren't being "linked"—they themselves *were* together. Fanny was seeing him all the time—but if she wanted to weep tears for the cameras she had only to think of Nick.

Until, summoning courage from an apparently inexhaustible reservoir, she put the furnishings of the New York house under the auctioneer's hammer and stood by while the streets of New York emptied themselves into her boudoir.

> *At the rate of two a minute* [began a *New York Telegram* account of the proceedings], *actresses, housewives, flappers, and ordinary females romped into the . . . domicile at 306 West 76th St. until 10 o'clock last night to discover why Nicky Arnstein left the happy home he occupied for years with Fanny Brice.*
>
> *These women might have told their husbands that they went to size up the bargain to be had at the auction beginning today of Miss Brice's bric-a-brac, but they couldn't fool a "Telegram" reporter. True, they did nose among the belongings, but 10 to 1 every woman was looking for some trace of Arnstein.*
>
> *As the evidence now discloses, Nicky couldn't have moved a foot inside the door on stormy nights without stumbling against a Sèvres vase, hand-painted and placed precariously on a green marble pedestal."*

Another reporter itemized the furnishings:

> *Here they are* [he wrote], *as explained by the guide:*
> *A Chickering piano, mahogany, suggestive of a lady's boudoir. There should be magic in that piano. On it the comedienne must have rehearsed her "Mon Homme" song, unequalled in appeal in the present generation of Broadway.*
>
> *A torrid Chinese embroidery, scarlet background heavily encrusted with blue and gold.*
>
> *A Chinese Chippendale desk and bookcase, majestic in size, airy in design.*

Fanny and Beatrice Lillie attending the opening of Billy Rose's Music Hall in 1934.

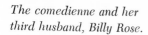

*The comedienne and her
third husband, Billy Rose.*

Polly Moran and George Cukor watching Baby Snooks.

Joe E. Brown at the same party.

A painting in oil, "Pursued by Wolves," by the Russian Storloff.

A Tabriz (Persian) rug of large dimension, brilliant with reds and golds.

A Chinese teakwood screen, showing embroideries of pine trees and flaming grasses.

A bedroom suite—here we come to another solemn moment in the personally conducted tour of our guide— Circassian walnut, ormolu trimmed, Louis XVI—twin beds, chiffonier, dresser, Princesse dresser for Madame, two chairs. Rose brocade coverings scrolled with Princesse lace. A little matter of $7,500.

For the forgotten arts—a set of Bohemian crystal cocktail glasses delicately stemmed bearing on their bowls bright chanticleers in all the gorgeous colors of the Coq d'Or.

A Court Lady looking out from her canvas with wide dark eyes, wondering eyes that somehow assure us the feudal days were barren in comparison to the things she has seen in this astonishing century.

Such objets d'art *were noted with approval by Miss Brice's oldest friends. Flo Ziegfeld, one of her entrepreneurs, passed through, dropping a salty tear. Fred and Adele Astaire moseyed around behind him.*

The house was as choked as the Bronx [subway] Express when the bidding started at 10 a.m., but the bidding for the first item—a discarded silk hat and evening suit of Nicky's—was desultory. After much plugging, the auctioneer raised the price two-bits to $2.75.

Fanny had already rented an apartment across town in the fashionable East Sixties. With the auction behind her at last, she set about furnishing her new home and refurnishing Billy Rose.

There in his suite in the Ziegfeld Theatre Billy examined himself carefully in the bathroom mirror as he brushed his hair with a gold-backed brush. You could see the "BR" etched in the gold of the brush. You could see the initials in the gold of the matching toilet-set that the butler had carefully laid out beside the washbasin.

"A few weeks after she moved," Billy said, "we're sitting around one night. She points her finger at me and says: 'Tomorrow you're going to get some new clothes.'

" 'I got clothes,' I told her.

" 'You got blank, not clothes.'

" 'They fit.'

" 'Well, tomorrow there's going to be a change. I'm going to get you some decent stuff,' Fanny said.

" 'You're not going to get me anything,' I told her.

" 'I'm not going to buy you anything,' Fanny said. 'You're buying it. I'm just going to tell you *what* to buy.'

"She did just that," Billy remembered. "She was with me half the day. We started with shoes and we ended with hats. When we finally got to Lindy's for dinner, she was happy, and I was out about eighteen hundred bucks."

Fanny may have been happy for another reason, for, as she says, "I was never bored with Billy. The life with him was very stimulating. It was a different kind of a thing, and of course we had that much in common—our work. I could never stop and talk with Nick about my work. I didn't want to anyway. Billy and I used to sit in Lindy's a lot. I liked being around writers. The difference was that my life with Nick was away from show business. There was no conversation with Nick regarding show business. It would have been a bore to him. And I found that Billy Rose was a companion in my own work. And a very ambitious person, who I knew would get places. I would tell everybody: 'He's going to be a big man.'

"You see what I found thrilling with Billy was that I was with a man who was creating all the time—doing something. After *Nick!* Who was just *talking* and never doing *anything!*

"And Billy wanted to learn *everything*. When he was doing his first show, he said to me: 'I'm doing a show and they are talking costumes to me. And when they say satin, taffeta, and talk about qualities, et cetera, I don't know what they mean. I don't like to talk about anything if I don't know what I'm talking about.' He asked me to go around to the stores and get him samples of every material and quality. I went around for three days until I got a big box of samples of every kind of material in every quality. I sat down with Billy for three or four hours and explained to him how you know satin, how you know taffeta, what makes this quality, and what makes that quality, et cetera. The next day he stayed in bed from morning to night with that box of material, studying it. Then he came over and said: 'Sit down here.'

"I sat down. He put the box in my lap.

"'Take the price tags off,' he told me.

"I took them off.

"Then he said: 'This is taffeta. This is the cheaper one. This is the good one.'

"He knew every piece of material, what it should cost and everything.

"Billy had a seven-track mind. He could talk to seven people on different subjects and remember everything—never forget anything. And that was very stimulating, to be around somebody that bright."

Bright—and not too romantic. To a Boston newspaper-woman who interviewed her during the out-of-town run of *Fioretta*, a musical comedy produced by Earl Carroll, Fanny confided:

"I'm done with men. Talk about being reconciled with Nicky is just bunk. No, I'm not going to marry Billy Rose or any other man. I'll tell you what—if I ever saw a romance coming in my direction that looked dangerous, I'd run the other way. No more husbands."

A few days later she called Billy Rose in New York. "This is a show with a lot of words," she told Billy, "and none of them are funny."

Remembering *Fioretta,* Billy agrees with Fanny. "She was right," he says. "I took the next train to Boston, and looked at the show. This was another one of those bean feeds where everybody was in costume and wrote letters with a feather.

"Earl Carroll buys Fanny at her price and then plays her straight. It's like buying Lindy's and throwing out the bagels and lox. I wrote Fanny a couple of songs, and hung around Boston trying to help her. One night I'm in her dressing-room waiting for her. We're going to get some supper. She sent her maid back to the hotel and there is nobody around. She was sitting in front of the dressing-table, and I'm standing behind her.

" 'Let's get married, Fanny,' I said.

" 'A-a-a-a-a-h-h-h-h-h,' she said. She finished taking off the stage make-up.

" 'What do you say, Fanny?'

" 'What do I say about what?'

" 'About getting married?'

" 'Who?' she said. She put on her street face.

" 'You,' I said. 'You and me.'

" 'You and me what?'

" 'You and me getting married.'

" 'You and me?'

" 'Yes. You and me,' I said.

" 'A-a-a-a-h-h-h-h-h.'

" 'Ah, what?' I said.

"She got up and went for her coat. 'Quit your kidding,' she said.

" 'I'm not kidding, Fanny.'

" 'We'll talk about it some other time,' she said, and turned her back on me.

Nobody had to tell me I was no Clark Gable. I knew that every morning of my life when I shaved. But when a man offers a woman his name, he expects at least a polite refusal, not this 'We'll talk about it some other time' routine. I was so burned up, I wanted to boot her right in the behind.

"Fanny turned around. 'Okay, sucker,' she said, 'if it means that much to you, we'll get married.' "

Which they did on February 9, 1929, one year, four months, and 139 days after her divorce from Nick. "She told me once," Billy remembers, "that she married Frank White, the barber, because he smelled so good; she married Nick Arnstein because he looked so good; and she married me because I thought so good."

Reporting the marriage, the *New York Telegram* said:

> *When Fannie Brice stepped out of her blue Minerva landaulet in front of City Hall today, she had her head cocked to one side.*
>
> *But it wasn't coyness at being married, for today's (to Billy Rose, the song writer) was her third. It was just a stiff neck.*
>
> *"My," lamented Fannie, "that I should have such a stiff neck on my wedding day!"*
>
> *That was about all she had to say for publication. The "I do" was pronounced in the privacy of Mayor James J. Walker's office.*

The *New York World,* however, sent a rhyming reporter to the wedding, for his story began:

> *What's all the crowd, what's all the crowd,*
> *The Civic Virtue wondered,*

It's Fanny Brice. She's married thrice,
A park bench warmer thundered.

While Fanny herself wrote of the wedding:

"Going down to City Hall, Billy said he forgot to buy a ring. 'Don't worry about it,' I told him.

" 'What do you mean, don't worry?' he said. 'We've got to have a ring.'

" 'I've got a ring. I figured you'd forget,' I said, and took a ring out of my purse, and dropped it into his pocket.

"It was a gold, carved ring, and that's the ring Billy Rose put on my finger.

"And inside of the ring it was engraved: 'To My Darling Fanny—with Love, Nicky.' "

That's not the way Billy spells it. "Fanny has been telling that story for years," he said recently. 'I'm not the kind of fellow who would forget a ring for his own wedding. But you ought to use her story. It's too good to kill."

16

MR. BRICE: "*You Know, Fanny's Husband.*"

WHILE the newspapers regarded Fanny's marriage to Billy Rose as a most felicitous event, to her children it was a catastrophe.

"The last thing I ever got from my father was a picture of himself," Frances Brice Stark said recently. "One to me and one to my brother, Bill. On each picture he had written: 'Be Seeing You Sometime.' That was in 1927. I was eight years old and Bill was six. Then Billy Rose began writing songs for Mother. He came around to the house more often. I remember him then perfectly well.

"To some extent our French governess poisoned our minds against Billy Rose. She said he wasn't the gentleman my father was, according to her. She respected my father because he was well-mannered.

"The day Mother and Billy Rose were getting married, I was upset. When they and a few friends came home to celebrate, she called for me. I wouldn't come out. Mam'selle was gloating. Mother called again. I ran into my room and locked the door. Mother called again. You see, when Mother was angry, she was really angry. She would explode. Mam'selle went out to tell her that I was in my room. For Mam'selle it was a personal triumph.

"Mother came charging into my room. I had never heard her so angry before. 'Frances,' she said, 'open that door!'

"I was crying.

"She pounded on the door again. 'Open that door!' she shouted.

"I said: 'I'm not coming out.'

" 'If you don't open that door, I'll break it down.'

"I didn't answer.

" 'One more chance, Frances,' Mother said. 'Are you going to open that door?'

" 'You'll spank me.'

" 'Not if you open it this minute.'

" 'Promise?'

" 'I promise,' Mother said, so I opened the door. She just turned to Mam'selle and told her to get me washed and into another dress and then bring me out.

"Which Mam'selle did. I came out and I was polite, but for the first three years that Billy Rose was living in our house, my brother and I never called him anything but 'Mr. Rose.' "

To Fanny's friends, her third marriage was even more puzzling than her years of loyalty to Nick. They could understand her love for Nick, who may very well have been the most handsome man on the North American continent in those years, but they could not—ever—fathom her attraction to Billy Rose.

Fanny says of her third marriage: "There was revenge in

my mind. I thought, 'What will this do to Nick? How will he feel about my getting married?' "

Perhaps she never knew what it did to Nick. Perhaps for the rest of her life she believed, as the world believed, that Nick had taken what he could from her and been glad to leave her when she asked for it.

But there is evidence to disprove this prevailing theory, and the evidence comes from Nick himself. That day last year in his Beverly Hills apartment he was shown this story from the *New York Times* of January 7, 1930:

> *Quebec, Jan. 6. . . . Jules W. Arnold, widely known under the name of Nicky Arnstein, was married to Mrs. Isabelle McCullough, divorced wife of Charles McCullough, millionaire resident of Chicago, on October 18, 1929, records here show.*
>
> *The wedding ceremony was performed by the Rev. W. H. Stevens. Mrs. McCullough was accompanied by her mother. Arnold and his bride remained for some time in Quebec, following their marriage, and also visited Murray Bay before returning to New York.*

And below it, in the same article:

> *Chicago, Jan. 6. . . . Nicky Arnstein's bride is the daughter of Mrs. J. C. Matlack of Great Neck, L.I. Arnstein is said to have met her at a garden party given in Chicago in 1927 in honor of Fannie Brice, then Mrs. Arnstein.*
>
> *The present Mrs. Arnstein is reported to have been beneficiary of half of the $5,000,000 estate of her father, the late John C. Matlack, who was in the rubber tire business here. The other half was distributed to charities.*

Nick flung the newspaper clipping from him as though it had dirtied his hands. He was as angry with Fanny at that moment as he might have been had she just slammed a door in his face and walked out of the room. His voice shook with anger, his eyes flashed with anger, and his face was free of color and ghost-white.

"I married to burn Fanny up," he said, and these are his exact words, remember, for there was a stenographer in the room. "I didn't want to get married," Nick continued. "What the hell did I want to get married for? Women were a dime a dozen. I was young then, well, I wasn't so young, but I looked young. Straight as an arrow."

For Fanny, who never knew that she had got the revenge she wanted, those first years with Billy Rose were pleasant years.

"I enjoyed his company," she wrote. "Billy was a very bright man, amusing and ambitious, and it was quite a change from Nick. I can't say I wasn't happy. I had a whole lot in common with Billy—but nothing physical."

To which Billy said a few months ago: "All I know is that we slept in a double bed."

For the rest of her life Fanny believed that she and Billy Rose were just two good friends who had obtained legal sanction to share one roof. "I realized there are only two things you can be," she wrote. "You can be gloriously miserable or miserably happy, and I was gloriously miserable with Nick and miserably happy with Billy Rose. So much is involved when you are in love. So often I thought: 'I wish my life could have been with Nick as sensible as it was with Billy, with none of those silly emotional things that happened—to have a man come in at two or three in the morning, and not care.'"

"She's right as far as she goes," Billy said when he was told of this portion of her memoirs. "There was never a scene, she never threw a wing-ding, but she'd give it to me just the same.

"One night, when I was rehearsing a show, I came home quite late and Fanny was awake. I told her a funny story that one of the chorus girls had told me.

"When I finished, Fanny just looked at me. 'Did you fall out of bed laughing?' she asked."

She displayed a rare talent for infuriating Billy. "When he was working," she wrote, "he'd come in and say: 'Will you listen to this, Fanny? I want you to tell me what you think.' And he'd sing the song for me.

"And I'd say: 'I like it. I like everything but this one line.'

"And without exception he'd say: 'That's funny. That's the best line in the song.'

" 'Well, I'm very sorry, but I don't like that line.'

" 'Why don't you like it?' he'd ask.

" 'I don't know why,' I would tell him. 'I can't say why. All I know is that it goes against me in here,' and I would point to my heart.

" 'You and your goes against you,' he'd snap at me. 'I must be nuts to ask your advice about anything. You don't like it, but you can't give me a reason. To hell with it. I'll do it my way.'

"So there would be a big argument. He'd leave my room and go back and work some more. I would hear nothing from him for a while. Then he would return. He would always come back. It would take an hour or two hours and he would be there with the song. 'Listen to it now,' he would say. So I would listen. And it was always without the line, or phrase, or word that I didn't like.

"And I would never say: 'See? I'm glad you took my advice. That should have come out, the way I said.' I wouldn't say that. I would say: 'Gee, I think it's a swell song, Billy.'

Wouldn't mention anything about the line I didn't like. And he wouldn't mention it either.

"And what I liked about Billy, he never asked the same question twice. Not of me, and not of anybody else. He was a fast learner, that Billy."

He learned quickest that he had become above all else Fanny Brice's husband. "We had been married about a year," Fanny wrote, "when Elsa Maxwell invited me to a party. I brought Billy. This was one of those specials of Elsa's. Everybody in the country is there. So what happens? Elsa meets us, and she gives me the big hello, and she just looks at Billy like he brought a delivery or something.

" 'Elsa,' I say, 'this is my husband, Billy Rose.'

" 'How *nice!*' Elsa says.

"So she goes away and now we get rid of our coats. And we're moving around the party. And I know a lot of people there, but Billy knows nobody.

"So we come to one guy, a society guy, and we stop beside him.

" 'Mr. ——,' I say. I can't remember the guy's name any more. 'Mr. ——, I want you to meet my husband, Mr. ——,' and I can't remember Billy's name. I stand there with them and Billy's name doesn't come to me.

" 'Rose,' Billy says. 'Billy Rose is the name.'

"So of course they shake hands. We talk for a while, and then we walk away.

" 'That's not funny, Fanny,' Billy says to me. 'I'd rather it didn't happen again.'

"So ten minutes later, I go to introduce him again, and again I say: 'My husband, Mr. ——,' and I'm standing there, snapping my fingers, trying to remember his name. Figure out that psychology, will you?

"Well, Billy turned around and walked out on that party; just left me there."

Billy was not a fellow to give up his name without a struggle. As he himself wrote in his book, *Wine, Women, and Words:*

> *A few months later, I ripped the insides out of Arthur Hammerstein's pretty theatre on 53rd and Broadway and opened another cabaret called The Billy Rose Music Hall. Its feature number was a potpourri of old-time vaudevillians—fire-eaters, acrobats, and Swiss bell-ringers—who did an abbreviated version of their turns. This was my first meeting with the pretty lady called "Nostalgia" and we've been big buddies ever since.*
>
> *The electric sign on this music hall was a seven-day wonder on Broadway. It was eighteen stories high and the mazdas spelled out just two words—*BILLY ROSE. *The first night it was burning, I went outside to admire it.*

While Billy stood smack in the center of the sidewalk, a half block from the sign, his head up and a big, big smile on his face, he heard two men talking behind him.

"I was a proud little pumpkin that night," Billy remembered, walking around his office-apartment last winter with the unceasing, desperate regularity of a tiger in a cage, moving rapidly from one end of the antique-filled room to the other, gesturing, pointing, waving his hands as he spoke. "I'm a little guy and I've got the little guy's need for big things. Well, that sign, don't forget, was bigger than most buildings in most towns in the U.S.A. I'd spent a lot of money on those blinking bulbs, and I spent it for myself. If you think that sign brought in any customers, you're smoky in the head. There I stand with the two yokels behind me, and I tilt my head back even more so that I don't miss a word.

" 'Billy Rose,' says one. 'Who's Billy Rose?'

" 'You know Fanny Brice?'

" 'Sure I know Fanny Brice,' says the first farmer.

" 'That's Fanny's husband,' says the other.

"I got it like that for a long, long time."

In the Ziegfeld Theatre that winter's day, Billy lit a fresh cigarette from a dying cigarette. "I took money from Fanny once, for a couple of days, and I took plenty. I'll never forget her for it, and it shows you what kind of a dame she really was."

A few nights after the stock-market crash, Black Thursday, in October 1929, Billy found his wife sitting in the kitchen alone, holding a cold cup of tea in one hand. He lit the gas under the kettle and sat down at the white-enamel table.

"Some day," he said.

"I don't want to talk about it," she said.

"How big a loser are you?" Billy asked.

"Big enough."

"How much?" he asked again.

"I don't want to think about it," Fanny said.

"Good enough," he said, rising to prepare a cup of tea. He carried it to the table and they sat for a time in silence, staring at the bare tabletop as though there, on its brilliantly white surface, lay the reason for their losses. Billy sipped his tea, Fanny held her cold cup, and after a time she said: "How much did you go for?"

"Fifty thousand bucks," Billy said.

"Chicken feed," Fanny said.

"Not to me," Billy replied. "It's every dime I had."

"You got the song royalties."

"It isn't so much the money. I just don't like to take a beating."

"That makes you *different*?"

"Fanny, I got an idea."

"For stocks?"

Billy nodded.

"I don't want to hear it."

"We can get even, Fanny."

"Don't tell me."

"I figured it out."

"I'm going to bed," Fanny said.

"Listen, Fanny, have you got any money?"

She looked at him. She had been married to Billy Rose long enough to know that he never spoke idly. "Certainly I got money."

"Lend me fifty thousand dollars," he said.

"What for?"

"This afternoon I studied the stock-market charts for years back. After a big break, the market usually snaps back about one third. If I had fifty thousand dollars, I'd load up when the market opens tomorrow. With any kind of luck, I figure to have all my money back by one o'clock in the afternoon."

"And if not?"

"I'll sign over my song royalties, Fanny. You'll take no licking from me."

She was silent for a moment. Then: "We'll go to the bank the first thing." Fanny rose and left the kitchen, with Billy trailing.

"How about you?" he asked. "You can do it too."

"I know when I'm beat," she said. "I've bought my last stock."

The next morning Billy accompanied Fanny to her bank, where she withdrew fifty thousand dollars from her savings account and gave him a cashier's check for that amount. Billy scurried to his broker and bought five hundred thousand dollars' worth of stock on a ten-point margin. His guess was right on the nose. By two that afternoon some of his stocks were up almost twenty points. He sold when he was even. The next day he gave Fanny her fifty thousand dollars.

"What makes Fanny stand out in my book," said Billy, "wasn't so much that she let me take the fifty grand. What I'll always remember is that she gave me the money the day after she lost half a million herself."

To a reporter for the *New York World-Telegram* who interviewed her after the crash Fanny said:

"I was on the inside, but I forgot to get out. When did my stocks flop? When they all flopped.

"No, I never heard of Morgan. Does he sit on a piano? I was on the inside of the inside. My cousin's husband was a customer's man.

"Do you know, for four years nobody spoke to me above a whisper. 'Buy this, buy that.' The lower they whispered, the more authority it had. How much did I lose?"

At this point Mr. Rose entered the conference.

"Don't stress your losses, darling," he said.

"What I lost, it doesn't need any stressing," said Miss Brice. "I was on the inside. I started with Kayser Silk. That was something close to me, I could understand it. Everybody has got to have silk underwear. It's a necessity. So gradually I worked outward. I like to talk a long time on the telephone, so I bought American T. and T.

"Then I got on the inside. I met a big man. 'Listen,' he said to me, 'I lost five fortunes already, so I ought to know something about this game.' After that I didn't even know the names of the stocks. I had 30 or 40 different kinds.

"Anaconda I can't forget," she said. "It's a beautiful name. I remember I went into my broker's office with Jay Brennan, and a big fellow, one of the real insiders,

with a low mumble, said to me, 'Miss Brice, you must
have some Anaconda.'

"So I said: 'Uh-uh, I prefer American Consolidated
Foreign Investment Corporation,' or something like that.
I don't remember exactly. But he said, 'Give Miss Brice
500 shares of Anaconda.' Just like that.

" 'What a nice man he is,' Jay said to me. 'He gives
you that stock.' It cost me 158. The next day it went
down to 154. So I said to this insider, 'What does that
mean?' He said, 'It means you should buy 500 shares
more.' Finally I sold the 1,000 shares for 12."

The living-room atop the Ziegfeld Theatre was filled with
as much smoke as Madison Square Garden on fight night.
New York was quite dark now and Billy Rose had a date for
dinner.

"Maybe I'll get married again," he said, "and maybe I
won't. From where I sit, I'd say I won't. I've been married,
as the boys say."

He walked into his dressing-room, getting out of his pa-
jama top as he stood before his hanging suits. "I've got a
date for dinner," he said. "I'm looking to do some important
eating at Luchow's tonight, but we can talk while I'm
dressing.

"A couple of years after I married Fanny," he continued,
"I was actively and violently unhappy about being her husband. At home, let's face it, I wasn't winning any popularity
contests with the kids. Remember, I was the fellow who came
in after such a good-looking Daddy had left. On Broadway,
I was Fanny's husband, and I was getting damned sick and
tired of being Fanny's husband.

"I'd be around town with Fanny and I saw that the fellows who got the biggest respect were Dillingham, Ziegfeld,

Sam Harris, George M. Cohan, all the producers. I decided
to be a producer. Fanny was all for it. I signed her, I signed
Jessel, I hired a sketch-writer, and I picked a title for my
show: *Corned Beef and Roses.*

"Fanny was my star at three thousand dollars a week
against ten per cent of the gross.

"And when the show opened in Philly, all it proved was
that I was still a good song writer. I changed the name to
Sweet and Low, wrote some more songs, and brought it into
New York."

Billy paused to knot a burgundy tie over his white shirt.
He stood before the mirror, observed his efforts with satisfaction, lit another cigarette, and continued.

"Jessel got out," Billy said, "and Ted Healy came in. He
was living with a chimpanzee, and I had to buy food for the
chimp. That was part of the deal. Healy was on a gold kick.
He said, and he was damned right, that the country was
headed for a depression and he wanted to be ready. I had
to pay him in gold. That was also part of the deal.

"We came in with *Sweet and Low,* and the critics kicked
the bejabbers out of us. Ziegfeld came to see it and told
Fanny he was ashamed of her for being in such a turkey.

"I asked Sam Harris to see the show and give me his
advice.

" 'Close it,' was his advice.

"I asked George M. Cohan to see the show and give me
his advice.

" 'Close it,' was his advice.

"So I kept it open all that spring. If I closed it, I went back
to being Fanny's husband again, and I was a mite tired of
that."

While *Sweet and Low* lumbered along, its cash drawer as
empty as Mother Hubbard's cupboard, Billy worked fever-
ishly to inject life into it. One day at brunch Fanny said:

"Will you do me a favor? Go down to Philly and see Waxey Gordon."

Waxey Gordon, born Irving Wechsler, who died recently while serving a life sentence as a habitual criminal, was then one of the kings of America's hoodlum empire. He owned breweries, he owned cafés, he owned hotels, he owned ships, and he owned a floundering musical comedy called *Forward, March!* which was going nowhere. Waxey, who had recently become an entertainment entrepreneur, was upset because he could not force customers to buy tickets the way he persuaded others to buy booze.

"What do you want with Waxey?" Billy asked.

"Go down and see him as a special favor to me," Fanny replied.

Billy got the next train. Arriving at the Philadelphia theater, he was immediately led down the aisle to Mr. W., as the gangster was known by those in the know.

Mr. W. explained his trouble. He was hiring the comedy team of Smith and Dale to bolster up *Forward, March!* and he had no material for the pair. Could Billy help?

"I've got two sketches," Billy confessed, "but I need them for a show I'm preparing."

"I need them worse," Waxey said. "How much?"

"I can't guarantee they're funny," Billy said.

"How much?" Waxey asked again.

"Five thousand," Billy said.

"Pay him," Waxey ordered, dismissing Billy, as a gent in a blue serge hurried forward with a black satchel. Out of it came five thousand dollars in hundred-dollar bills, and out of the theater went Billy. He was driven back to New York in a black car, escorted to his office, and relieved of the two sketches.

Some months later, Billy got a phone call. "Mr. W. wants to see you," he was told.

At the hoodlum office, Billy was told to wait in the ante-room where several dark-jawed Dillingers sat in chairs pushed back against the four walls, like unescorted girls at a country-club dance.

After ten minutes Billy said: "What's up, fellows?"

Getting a load of silence for answer.

After thirty minutes he said: "Does Mr. W. want to see me?"

Receiving a load of scowls for answer.

After sixty minutes, the door opened and the man who had handled the black satchel in Philadelphia nodded at Billy and jerked his thumb inward. "You," he said. "Inside."

Billy went inside, the door was closed behind him, and he was alone with Waxey, who sat behind a desk.

It is one thing to reminisce about the old days of the booze barons, talking of them affectionately, describing their charmingly murderous peccadilloes nostalgically, as though adding a pound of soft-nosed lead to an associate's weight was no more offensive than hanging a pot atop the campus flagpole. It is quite another thing to be standing before one of those amoral thugs in his own back yard when he is surrounded by a dozen killers carrying their killing equipment.

There is a current tendency to remember these hoodlums as playboys of a pleasant, almost-forgotten era when money flowed freely and when you could rub shoulders with a racketeer who was really a nice guy, kind to his mother, and gentle with children.

It is a rotten tendency and a sickening one, for these were not nice people. They were cruel, they were vicious, they were contemptuous of the law; they killed, they crippled, they burned, they bombed. They were liars, they were cheats, they were bound by no rules of decency or honor, and nobody knew it better than Billy Rose when he stood before Waxey Gordon. But he knew something else: gangsters killed other gangsters. They didn't customarily shoot song writers.

"The sketches flopped," Waxey announced.

"I know," Billy said.

"You owe me five big ones," said Waxey.

"I told you . . ." Billy began.

"Five big ones," Waxey decided. "Get 'em up."

The only thing Billy had not hocked at that point was his family jewels, and his family jewels were worth eighty cents. Eighty cents, that is, if he found a demented pawnbroker. He didn't know where he would beg or borrow five thousand dollars.

For several suspenseful seconds, Waxey glared at Billy. Then Billy said: "If you say I have to get it up, I will. But," he added, "I'm going to tell Fanny you're a welsher."

The anger mounted in Gordon's face: a red spot high on each cheek, like beacons flanking an airport. Gordon leaned forward, his hands on the desk, his fingers twitching convulsively on the surface. "Get out of here, punk," he ordered.

Walking toward the elevator in the Ziegfeld Theatre Billy said: "That's the kind of standing she had with the hoodlums in this town. In this town and all over the country. They had a big respect for Fanny.

"That summer," Billy continued, stepping into the elevator, "I rewrote my show, changed the title to *Crazy Quilt*, and sent it on the road."

Before the show embarked, however, Billy asked the stars to take a temporary cut of two thirds in salary, so that the show might stay alive. When Fanny willingly accepted one thousand instead of three thousand dollars each week, the others followed suit. The cut was restored after nine weeks.

"We played whistle stops," Billy said, "that hadn't seen flesh-and-blood entertainment for years. When we got back to New York, forty weeks later, I was $240,000 to the good. What was even more important, I was no longer Fanny Brice's husband. I had my name back."

�֍ 17 ✦

PHIL RAPP: *"She Had Raw Guts."*

HILLCREST in Los Angeles has, in common with other private golf courses in America, splendid fairways, strategic traps, formidable bunkers, immaculate greens, and a superb clubhouse. Continuing: the floors are carpeted, the showers are soft, the bartender is discreet, and the chef is a remarkable artist.

Where it differs, where Hillcrest stands apart from similar establishments in the republic, is in its membership. Danny Kaye belongs. George Burns belongs. Jack Benny belongs. George Jessel belongs. Groucho and Harpo Marx belong. The membership rolls are a kind of blue book of America's entertainment business, and the portals of Hillcrest on Pico Boulevard are no less impassable to any but the top rank of tragedian, comedian, writer, director, producer than are the gates of Bailey's Beach in Newport to all save the highest echelon of social lights.

To sit *near* Jessel's table at lunch is no mean accomplishment, and to play a round as the guest of a member may become the most important single day's activity in the life of an ambitious—and talented—young man.

At eight o'clock on this summer's morning, Phil Rapp, one of the country's most successful radio-comedy writers, had finished eighteen holes, had showered, had drunk his orange juice, had ordered breakfast, and was talking about Fanny Brice, for whom he had written several seasons of scripts.

"She was strong," Rapp said. "She was the strongest woman who ever lived. She had raw guts, and she was afraid of nobody in the world."

In 1933, after the death of Ziegfeld, the Shubert brothers revived the Follies, starring Fanny and Willie Howard. Rapp and the late Dave Freedman, a by now almost immortal gag-man, wrote all the sketches for the show, including one bit they titled "Sailor, Behave," a parody of the current hit play, *Sailor, Beware*.

"In this skit," Rapp said, "Fanny was Upright Annie, of virtue intact, and Willie Howard was Dynamite Moe. This skit was written around a bed. Willie wants to get Fanny into the bed, and Fanny wants to get him out of the room.

"In this skit we had one big worry: that the laughs would not be evenly distributed. When you are writing for two heavyweights like Fanny and Willie, you have to please them both. If one makes a damn fool out of the other one, you are in big trouble.

"We were in big trouble opening night on the road. Dave and I are standing in the back of the theater in Boston. When Fanny and Willie do the skit, she is getting all the laughs. The audience loves Fanny and pays no attention to Willie.

" 'Dave, we have to rewrite that skit,' I said. 'We have to go to Willie after the show is over and pacify him. He'll be ready to tear the theater down.'

" 'Maybe you're right,' Dave said, 'but let him come to us. We've got two long weeks up here with enough work as it is. If he complains, we'll rewrite.'

"After the show," Rapp continued, "There's not a word out of Willie. We wait half the night in the hotel, but there's peace all around us. The second night Fanny gets the laughs again. Again we wait. Again silence. The two weeks go by and Willie is peaches and cream, and we come to opening night in the Winter Garden in New York. I'm in the wings and it comes to the 'Sailor' sketch.

"They start around the bed and Willie times it just right so that he delivers his first line when he is at the foot of the bed, facing the audience, and Fanny is at the head of the bed, facing the wall.

"The audience dies. Now he chases her again, and Fanny can't stop, because if she stops he catches her and that's not the skit. She has to throw her lines over her shoulder, into the wings, up against the wall, and Willie don't deliver a line unless he is standing on top of the footlights rolling his eyes at the audience.

"Fanny didn't get a laugh. *Not one laugh.*

"The skit is over, the curtain starts down, and it isn't half-way to the floor when Fanny grabs a night-table that is part of the set and starts for Willie. She's got the night-table up over her head and she screams: ' You sonofabitch!'

"But Willie is moving.

"'Come here, you sonofabitch!' she screams, as Willie goes past me.

"'I'll kill you, you no-good thieving sonofabitch!' she screams, after him with the night-table, and she meant every word. She chased him through the wings, down the stairs, into the dressing-rooms, out into the alley, and up Seventh Avenue, swinging that night-table, but Willie got away."

Rapp dropped his toast there in the Hillcrest dining-room, bowing his head and holding the table for support as he laughed uproariously, remembering that night at the Winter Garden.

At last he wiped his eyes and leaned back in the chair. "Willie wouldn't come back to the theater that night," Rapp said. "But Fanny came back. I'll tell you what kind of a showman that girl was. She came back, still carrying the night-table, gave it to the grip, went to her dressing-room to change costumes, and came out on the stage alone to sing a song, her big number of the show.

"And her voice cracked. Now that can happen to kids, to beginners singing in saloons, but to Fanny Brice—nobody ever believed it.

"She stopped cold. Motioned to the orchestra conductor to start again.

"And cracked again.

"And motioned to the conductor again, looking up at the audience. 'Just stay in your seats, you've got no place to go,' she told them. 'We'll get it this time.'

"She got it, all right. And when she finished, she got the biggest ovation I ever heard a performer receive anywhere, or any time.

"Then she walked off, went down to the stage door, and sat there waiting for Willie."

Of that Shubert Follies Brooks Atkinson wrote in the *New York Times*:

> *Something constructive has been accomplished toward the welfare of nations. Fannie Brice and Willie Howard have been lured into a production of the Follies, which was staged at the Winter Garden last night. It would be pleasant enough to have only one of them among the graces and tunes of a Broadway musical arcade. The combination is extraordinarily cheering. For Miss Brice and Mr. Howard are well met in the theatre—both racial in style, both given to the rolling, roguish eye and both mighty good company.*

*Fannie is in top form. Early in the show you will dis-
cover her introducing the huckster's note into evangeli-
cal racketeering with a song entitled, "Soul-Saving
Sadie." Toward the end of the first act she is Countess
Dubinsky, who right down to her skinsky is working for
Minsky, whereupon she performs a hilarious travesty
upon the sinful fan dance. Or behold her as Baby
Snooks in short, starched dresses, listening dubiously to
the story of George Washington and then shamelessly
lying to her father.*

Robert Garland, reviewing the show for the *New York
World-Telegram*, began:

*To start out on a strong, sweet note of cheer, let me
assure you that Fannie Brice is in fine form in the diver-
tissement at the Winter Garden. Given half a chance she
is as funny as she has ever been. Given a pair of feather
fans, she is funnier.*

*Year in, year out, Miss Brice has been walking away
with shows. Year in, year out, Miss Brice has been dis-
proving the Broadway saying that no artiste can be better than her material.*

*Following an old Briceian custom, she is better than
her material at the Winter Garden, walking away with
the rough-and-not-quite-ready entertainment to which
Mrs. Florenz Ziegfeld has lent her late lamented husband's name. From the square known as Times to the
Circle known as Columbus, there are few things more
hilarious than Miss Brice's manipulation of the feather
fans.*

*As the Countess Dubinsky who is working for Minsky,
she is a fan dancer to end all fan dancers. Here is burlesque with the bite of satire in it. Here is good mean
fun.*

Understand something about New York's drama critics, please. Their reviews make or break a show, period. No discussion, that's just the way it is. They are as incorruptible as nuns, as inflexible as the Supreme Court of the United States, and, compared to the critics, the nine men in black robes are about as tough as your mother. This was twenty-four years after Fanny's first Follies, and these are gentlemen about as easy to please as an adder. But twenty-four years after her first Follies she was better than the night at the New Amsterdam when she stopped the show cold.

She was nostalgic too. In an interview given Jimmy Cannon, now a sports columnist, a few days after the opening of the Winter Garden Follies, she said:

"This Follies is like the old days. We never felt it was the Follies though until we came into New York. In Boston it was just like any other show. But as soon as I stepped out on that platform opening night in New York, I knew it was the Follies.

"I used to think the Follies formula was all washed up. You know what I mean—extravagant sets, swell-looking dames, all that. But after this show I don't think the Follies will ever be washed up.

"Mae West had a lot to do with it, I guess," said Miss Brice, who is thin. "But liquor and big showgirls belong together. Little ones are okay, but it takes a big dame to wear clothes with class—and charm.

"The big naked things in the Follies wore bathing suits you see on the beach every day now and never give a tumble to," she laughed. "They were much longer, even, than the ones we wear now. But it was certainly something in those days. I used to think only the people change. But I guess times have, too."

Rapp complimented the waiter on the eggs, and waved a hello at Phil Harris as he entered the dining-room. Rapp spread marmalade on his toast, and talked for a time of Fanny during the run of the show.

It was shortly after the opening that Fanny met with Nick, seeing him for the first time since Chicago. Of that meeting Fanny writes:

"A friend called me one day and said Nick wanted to see me. He said Nick was moving to California with his wife and that he wants to say good-bye to me. I said: 'I'll see him. Why not?' So we arranged the meeting at this friend's apartment, and I went to see him."

But Nick said of that episode:

"My wife and I were living comfortably and quietly on Sutton Place. We were surrounded by family and friends. Our one and only desire was to live in seclusion and avoid publicity. No matter how hard we tried to live quietly, the press every now and then blasted me on the front page. Lacking spectacular news, they made me the goat. However, in the main we succeeded in keeping our lives private. It was then that Fanny sent an emissary to me, asking that I see her. I bore her no ill will, and so I agreed."

They met in late afternoon at the friend's apartment, Nick having arrived first, the intermediary having left, and Fanny entering to see Nick in profile as he stood at the windows looking down on mid-Manhattan. He turned as the door closed and came forward, breaking into a wide smile, his arms out.

"Fanny, my dear," he said. "This *is* pleasant. How are you, Fanny? How have you been?"

"I'm okay, Nick."

"I'm delighted to hear that, Fanny. Come, let's sit down, old girl. You and I have a lot to talk about." He led her to the sofa, made her comfortable, offered her a cigarette and lit it for her. He sat half-turned toward her, his legs crossed.

"I'm reading great things about you, Fanny," he said.

"The same stuff."

"The same Fanny," he said, laughing. "You haven't changed a bit."

"Neither have you."

"I keep myself fit, old girl. I'm thinking of entering the air-conditioning field, you know, and the preliminary surveys have kept me on my toes."

"You haven't asked for the children," Fanny said.

"How are the dear ones, Fanny?"

"You don't give a damn."

"Why, Fanny, of course . . ."

"You haven't changed, have you?"

"What do you mean, Fanny?"

"You know goddam well what I mean." She rose from the sofa and strode to the windows. "Your own kids, and you don't even ask for them. You're no good, you're a lying . . ."

"I'm leaving, Fanny."

"Leave," she said. "Go ahead, leave. Get out of here," she shouted. He found his hat and coat and calmly and deliberately dressed himself for the street.

Then he was gone, leaving her alone in the almost-dark apartment, holding a dead cigarette in her hand.

The morning after her meeting with Nick, Fanny began legal proceedings to change her children's last name to Brice. Within a few weeks she had removed the last remaining reminder of her life with Nick.

Except in the newspapers, which coupled her constantly with her ex-husband.

"The big animation I get out of Bill," she wrote of her son, "is that he looks so much like Nick.

"I always hoped I'd have two children, and I had them. I always hoped I'd have a boy and a girl, and I had them. I always hoped the boy would have the talent, and not the girl, and it worked out that way. Because, as I realize it, I didn't want my daughter to have a career. Because if a woman has a career, she misses an awful lot. And I knew it then, that if you have a career, then the career is your life. The hell with anything else. It is the biggest part of you and you can be married, have children, have a husband, but it isn't enough for you, because the career is always there in your mind, taking the best out of you which you should give to your husband and kids. You want your husband to have success, but it has to come after your own success. Who are all these actresses kidding that they take pictures in the kitchen? When you work a full day—or night—and you come home afterward, do you think that you want to sit down and listen while your husband tells you he had a big day, sold eighteen washing machines? In a pig's ear. You want quiet, you want rest, and you want him to rub your feet and bring you a cup of tea. And if he won't do it, you're paying the maid, let her bring the tea. Let her pull the shades. Let her tell the cook to wait an hour for dinner. What's this with the washing machines he sold?

"So I was happy when Frances didn't have the talent. Then I watched Bill. And I waited for the talent. Oh, boy . . . I see him drawing. He's doing automobiles and airplanes and everything he sees. And I asked him if he liked it. He said he did. And I asked him if he would like a teacher. And he wanted a teacher. So I got Henry Botkin, George Gershwin's cousin. So Botkin came two or three times a week and worked with Bill. And the one thing Botkin taught him was to learn to work—that it's a full-time job. You just don't start and then stop when you feel like it. The thing I was worried about in regard to Bill, I was afraid he would be like me. I wouldn't study for anything. I would make it come by itself, and I knew that was no good for painting. Because I got everything from the heart, and I knew that if he painted it had to come from the head as well as the heart. And he didn't disappoint me."

Frances doesn't know what drove her to devote her leisure time to riding. Frances joined a Long Island riding club and soon was spending more time in the stables than at home. She was a better-than-average pupil to start, and within a few months was showing marked abilities atop a horse.

Frances began competing in shows and winning the events she entered. When, a few years after donning jodhpurs, she won her place in the Good Hands Cup competition at Madison Square Garden, she asked Fanny to attend. Fanny, whose interest in horses had waned considerably after she had signed checks for the mahogany stables at Huntington, reluctantly agreed to watch the show from a ringside box.

Fanny dressed for the occasion in customary *haute couture*. Her entrance was as provoking as her appearance before an audience, and to Frances, watching from the runway leading to the ring, it was the night of nights.

She rode with all the skill she could command, wanting to win for her mother.

And did win. Was summoned to the center of the ring for her cup and, when the sterling was handed her, rode out to the applause of the audience.

She could not return fast enough. She wanted to gallop the horse to its stall in the basement. She wanted to leap from its back and run all the way back to the ringside box and stand before Fanny to give her mother the trophy.

Which Fanny accepted, remembering the cost of outfitting Frances, boarding the horse, paying for the riding-lessons, writing checks for saddles. She looked carefully at the trophy and she said: "All that money for a cup?"

Fanny shows Eddie Cantor a Tamayo in her Holmby Hills home.

Grandma Brice and her three grandchildren.

A late picture of Fanny with Elsa Maxwell and Beatrice Lillie.

Many years later, Frances—as well groomed as Fanny ever was, and sitting in her home in California with her son and daughter sleeping upstairs, and having been married for twelve years to Ray Stark, a successful young agent in Hollywood—was asked what she felt that night at her mother's reaction to the cup she had won.

"Mother hated any show of emotion in public," Frances answered evenly. "That was all fine when alone, but in public it embarrassed her. Even with us she was that way. I have the same quirk, so I know."

In Hillcrest's dining-room, that lovely summer's morning, the early risers had long since disappeared, and Phil Rapp's table was the only one occupied. The ashtray had twice been emptied by the attentive waiter, and now it was full for a third time. Rapp sat with his elbows on the table, carefully destroying a book of matches as he went back more than twenty years to his first meeting with Fanny.

"I wrote her first radio show in 1931," he said. "Radio was like television is now: trying to scoop up everybody, trying to fill the broadcast schedule with headliners. Well, she was a headliner, but she never gave a damn for radio. She always said: 'It's stealing money.' She wouldn't rehearse except under the strongest pressure, and then only on the day of the broadcast. She thought radio was a lark, and I guess to her it was."

Lark or not, the critics welcomed her appearance as happily as they welcomed her presence in the theater.

Of one of her early radio shows the *New York World-Telegram* said:

> *Fannie Brice, the nimble-voiced comedienne with the eternally skidding feet, was on the Dixie network for WABC Saturday night and her quavering voice, her*

slyly savage imitation of a creaky voiced singer of red hot songs, her bewildered Jewish Juliet, rocked this reviewer with laughs—and he has heard it time and again.

On another occasion, appearing in a radio show with George Olsen's orchestra, Fanny stepped to the microphone to sing one of her sad ballads. The music began and Fanny began, but as quickly stopped. "That's no good, George," Fanny said, talking to him as well as several million listeners. "Start all over, I made a mistake." Olsen's muddled musicians began again, Fanny started from the beginning, and the broadcast continued to her satisfaction.

But not to the sponsor's. And not, it was soon apparent, to the network's. Both wanted Fanny, but both wanted something other from her than her stage material. The days were gone when a headliner could play, say, a Denver vaudeville house for the umpteenth year and not only use the same material but be afraid to change a line or an inflection for fear of incurring the patrons' disfavor. Radio wanted new material and new sketches, and it was willing to pay. That's all Fanny needed to know.

"I first did Baby Snooks," Fanny wrote, "in 1912, when I went in vaudeville. At that time there was a child called Baby Peggy and she was very popular. The hair was all curled and bleached and she was always in pink or blue. She always looked like an ice-cream soda or something. Then I had talked to people about doing a baby—I thought I could be very funny with it. Because when I did a character I *was* that character. When I made like Madame Pompadour or Camille, I was both of them. So when I started to do Baby Snooks, I really was a baby. And when I think about Baby Snooks, it's really the way I was when I was a kid.

"I didn't do it again after that, on the stage; but the idea

stayed with me, that some time I would need Baby Snooks
again. One time in Detroit I was asked to somebody's house
for a party. And, as everybody knows, I never could do anything in a room that I did on the stage. And they asked me
to sing. There was a song when Pearl White was doing *Perils
of Pauline,* and the song was "Poor Pauline." And these people asked me to sing that. Now I couldn't get up in the living-room floor and sing it like I do on the stage, so I sang it
as a child would sing it, like Baby Snooks. And they just
screamed and died. When I went back to the theater the
next day I thought: 'What the hell, I'll sing that baby song.
They laughed so hard at the party last night, I'll try it on
the audience.'

"Well, I did it as a baby, and it was a big success, so I
kept it for an encore. And after that engagement I knew this
was a good character, this baby, and decided I wouldn't use
it again until I needed it.

"Then I never touched it again for years and years, until
the radio came along. Now I began to feel there was something wrong with the kind of characters I was doing. I told
my writers I wanted to do a baby. And they didn't know
what I was talking about, what kind of a baby I wanted to
do, and looked at me as though to say, 'The old girl wants
to be cute.' And they always brushed it aside.

"There was another reason why I thought the baby was
good. You know the way they have to go over your script
for censorship? I found out when I was doing Mrs. Cohen
at the Beach. We'd be ready to rehearse, and they'd say:
'You can't do this, you can't do that. This will offend, and
that will not sound nice.' And I knew this couldn't happen
with a baby. Because what can you write about a child that
has to be censored? Well, the writers didn't get excited about
it until one day one of them read a story in a book about a
child with a father. The father catches the child in a lie. And

the writer thought it was funny, and brought it to me to read.

"I said: 'That's the kind of kid I want to do with my Baby Snooks.' So they agreed, but we needed a father."

Hanley Stafford, who was not Snooks's original father, but the longest in point of tenure, remembers that for a long time Fanny changed Daddies with the regularity that some of her friends employed in changing husbands.

Stafford, a radio free-lance, was rehearsing a drama with Ethel Barrymore one afternoon in New York when his agent asked if he wanted to audition for a job with Fanny Brice. Stafford had a mind's-eye view of himself playing a life-guard to Fanny's Mrs. Cohen at the Beach; or a Nijinsky to her Pavlova; or an Armand to her Camille.

"I think not," he told the agent.

"They'll pay fifty dollars a week," the agent said.

"How much?"

"Fifty," said the agent, and this in the bottomless depths of the depression.

"A week?" asked Stafford.

"*A week.*"

"Every week?" asked Stafford

"Each and every week."

Stafford looked quickly at Miss Ethel, who seemed inclined to continue the recess for some time. "Where is the audition?" he asked.

"Two floors down."

"Lead on," said Stafford.

He was taken to another rehearsal studio where he saw Fanny Brice for the first time in his life without paying for the privilege. He was given a script, told to read the lines marked: "Daddy," and to read them straight.

"I hope you've got something," Rapp said quietly. "We've listened to everybody except the janitors in the building."

Stafford, who was unaware that Fanny had already read Baby Snooks with eighteen Daddies that day, was not at all concerned about his part. He could not shake from his head the dollar sign followed by a five that was followed by a zero.

"Are you ready, Fanny?" Rapp asked.

"Come on," she said.

Stafford took his place beside her. Since she had not even looked at him, he decided not to look at her. He was, he assured himself, gainfully employed at the moment with Miss Ethel upstairs, and he could not imagine one female star being any more difficult than another.

He read straight, as he was told; and when the audition was finished, he waited at one end of the room with his agent while Fanny, Rapp, the account executive, and the other brains of the show huddled together at the other end.

As they conferred, Stafford had a vision of Miss Ethel upstairs, deciding that she had rested enough. He had a vision of Miss Ethel rising from her chair, looking about her for her leading man, and turning slowly to regard the director. He heard her asking: "Wh-e-ah . . . is that dolt whom you've given me fo-a-ah a leading ma-a-n?"

Touching his agent's arm, Stafford whispered: "Let's get out of here."

"Wait," whispered the other.

"Miss Ethel," whispered Stafford.

"Fifty bucks," whispered the other.

Thus torn between steak and potatoes, or just potatoes, Stafford moved nearer the door, prepared for a quick get-away in the event the word he got was the wrong word.

Watching the group at the other end of the room, Stafford was surprised to see Fanny start toward him.

"Just a minute," she said, when she was halfway across the room. "You got any kids?"

"Me?" asked Stafford.

"Yes, you. You got any kids?"

"I have."

"Young kids?"

"Yes," said Stafford.

Fanny stopped and turned to Rapp. "That's the guy, Phil," she said.

Hillcrest's dining-room was filling up with the luncheon crowd. George Jessel appeared, coming from Twentieth-Century-Fox across Pico Boulevard, walking in the midst of a surrounding group to his customary table, and Rapp greeted him.

Phil Harris appeared from the locker room, having finished his round of golf, and Rapp greeted him again.

Danny Kaye appeared, lean and tanned, and Rapp said: "He's the one who reminds me of her: the same sure talent; the same ability to handle an audience all by himself.

"But Fanny . . . Fanny," he said, signing the check, ". . . Fanny was something all by herself. She wanted Stafford for Daddy, and she got him," he snapped his fingers, "like that. He never left the show, and at the end he was getting $1,350 a week. Fifty bucks to start and go to that kind of money."

☼ **18** ☼

BEN HECHT: *"Like an Indian Takes to Hot Coals."*

ILLY ROSE is a ready-made villain," said Ben Hecht on a sunny spring day last year. "There are people whose personalities lend themselves to public prosecution. Billy leads the roster. Recently a New York newspaper scheduled Billy for its dissecting table. It was to be a series of articles telling the truthful truth about him. A reporter called on me.

" 'Did Billy Rose ever cheat you?' was his first question.

" 'No, and he was never arrested for sodomy,' I replied, sending the young man on his way.

"The world doesn't understand Billy," Hecht continued. "He is a sensitive man. A poet, really, writing in letters ten feet high. He is a dreamer in a box office, weaving multicolored fantasies full of dollar bills. Billy wants to do good. At the present time he is succeeding. He is almost virginal in his relationship to women. He puts them on pedestals and they show their gratitude by kicking him in the teeth. He has great talent and great violence in that small chest and he has always had a kind of salmonlike instinct for the main chance. When he gambles, he gambles everything and he gambles it himself. And he seldom loses. You have to respect such a man."

Hecht paused to light a fresh cigar. He was in New York's "21," a restaurant where he is both king and court jester.

"I'm growing old perceptibly," said Hecht, co-author of *Front Page*. He looked about him at the patrons of the eating-place. "I have the constant feeling that the dust is settling on me. Everybody is dead or dying. Not only my friends are gone, my enemies are gone. I find no one worthy of insulting. Meanwhile I continue to amuse myself. I am writing a musical comedy, my first, and an autobiography, also my first. There are a few things left to say, even though the world has made laughter illegal."

Hecht led the way to the second floor of "21" and entered the large dining-hall that is his throne room. At the table he looked at the menu with no more interest than this year's best-dressed woman finds in last year's gown. He ordered luncheon quickly and, when it was served, ate it quickly, as though the intake of food was an unpleasant chore to be dismissed with as little ceremony as possible, holding the lighted cigar in his right hand and wielding the flatware with his left.

"I was a frequent guest at Fanny's parties while she was married to Billy," Hecht said. "But I cannot remember him then. He was inconspicuous by his presence."

Hecht said hello to Dana Andrews and turned in his chair to cross his legs. "She had one other great complaint about Billy," Hecht said, talking with the delicious delight of a window-peeper. "She maintained that, since Billy was shorter than she, *she* should hold his arm on the street. Billy, on the other hand, felt that such a switch in the marital manual would be a reflection on his manhood. Fanny lost.

"She was," Hecht continued, "forever analyzing herself on the most personal level."

Hecht chuckled. "So many things she said stopped you cold. You had no answer for her. She had great prescience. She was about people the way those carnival fellows are about your weight. She loved the occult. Once she found an Indian from India, one of those swamis who have powers. Fanny immediately brought him to her apartment and invited everyone she knew. I was there. Billy was there. Her children attended. First she gave us all dinner. Fattening us up for the kill. Then, with the dessert, she demanded silence and gave up the floor to the swami."

That night in Fanny's apartment the dark-skinned, slender Indian rose and stood without speaking for a long moment, looking at each of the guests and at all of them, but regarding Fanny longest: fixing her with a sad, poignant smile. When there was silence, when only the rapid breathing of his audience could be heard, the swami said: "My ladies and my gentlemen, please. In my native land of India we have known for centuries that there is born, now and again, a son of the gods, possessing powers beyond the pale of human limitations.

"Such a son, my ladies and my gentlemen, am I."

And paused.

And looked mournful.

While the others stared at the swami breathlessly, Fanny grinned at her magic-master with the delight of a child who has been promised colored candy.

"Now," continued the swami, "we are to adjourn into the parlor," and led his pilgrims out of the dining-room. Stopping before a huge, heavy table several feet from the entrance hall of the apartment, the swami ordered the vases and other objects atop it removed.

Fanny rang for her servants. "Clean it up!" she shouted.

"Get everything off of it! Everything!" she said, meanwhile smiling confidently at the swami.

That worthy was no less confident. With the table bare, he grouped his patrons around three sides of it, placing himself in the center, facing the unguarded, free side.

"We shall now," he said, and his voice seemed to fill every corner of the room, "place our hands gently on the table. We shall think on this table. We shall think this table will soon move. We shall be assured it will move.

"Move slowly out from under and away from us!" he announced, as the guests gasped and Fanny grinned and her maid tiptoed into the room to whisper in Fanny's ear: "There's a phone call for you, Miss Fanny."

"Not now!" Fanny hissed.

"Move slowly," repeated the swami, lapsing into a strange, singing language.

"Miss Fanny, it's important, that call," the maid insisted.

While the Indian chanted and the table stood firm and Fanny contemplated homicide.

"Miss Fanny, please come to the telephone," the maid pleaded.

"Who's on the damn telephone?" Fanny shrieked.

The swami stopped abruptly. The table stood firm. Her guests stared. The swami smiled sadly. The maid trembled with fear.

She stepped back, loyal to her mistress but aware of Fanny's spleen. "Who the hell is it?" Fanny demanded.

"It's . . . it's . . . it's," stuttered the maid. "It's . . ." looking about her, "it's Charley Young, Miss Fanny."

"I don't know any Charley Young," Fanny answered, turning to smile assuredly at the swami.

"You know this Charley Young, Miss Fanny. Oh, yes, you surely do, ma'am, and he's waiting now."

Fanny surrendered. She placed a friendly hand on the

swami's black serge. "You wait here," she said. "I'll be back right away."

Following the maid, Fanny hurried to her bedroom and picked up the receiver. "Hello! Hello!" she said. "I don't know any Charley Young. Who is this?"

"How are you, old girl?" asked Nick.

She had not heard his voice in several years. She had not seen him, nor would she let her friends talk about him. She had continued a campaign to remove Nick from her life; but at any other time, in any other place, she would have seized the telephone with both hands and continued the conversation until one of them dropped from exhaustion.

But this was magic night.

"What do you want, Nick?" she asked impatiently. "I'm busy!"

Nick, believing himself witness to a theatrically brave front camouflaging an aching heart, said softly: "Just wanted to know how my little girl is getting along, Fanny."

"I'm getting along fine, kid. Good night."

She hung up on Nick and turned to her maid. "What the hell were you talking about with this Charley Young business? What's the matter . . ."

"I just invented that name, Miss Fanny. I thought you wouldn't want all the people knowing it's Mr. Nick."

"Say," said Fanny, breaking stride. "That's pretty good, kid. Yeah. Next time he calls just say it's Charley Young."

Whereupon she hurried back to her impatient Indian. "Some producer," she explained.

The swami once again wordlessly commanded his waiting audience to silence. Once again he quietly told the guests to place their hands on the table. Once again he began to tell them the table would move. Once again he began to use the strange, singsong language.

There followed several moments of this gibberish, while

the room seemed to grow darker and a lassitude enveloped the assemblage, with the exception of Fanny, who studied the swami steadily.

As he chanted, the swami closed his eyes. The others followed suit. Not Fanny. If anything, she opened her eyes wider and saw the maid and the cook standing across the room, clutching each other for safety.

"It's moving!" someone cried.

"Sssssshhhhhhhh!" Fanny warned.

"It's going!" a woman screamed.

"Shut up!" Fanny whispered.

The swami paid not the slightest attention to his terrified audience, but continued to chant away at the same singsong.

"I feel it!" a man exclaimed.

"*I* feel it!" shouted another.

"There it goes!" said a third, and indeed, the table began to float slowly out of the parlor and into the hall.

Hecht saw it float.

Billy Rose saw it float.

Frances Stark remembers that it floated.

While Fanny, not at all surprised, slapped the swami on the back. "You did it, kid," she said. "I knew you could do it." And, turning to her guests: "How do you like that, huh? Is that guy great, or is he great?"

In "21" Hecht chuckled as he remembered that evening. He puffed on his cigar for a time and then, inexplicably, began to talk about Hollywood, about Broadway, about the sad state of American *belles lettres*. For a few minutes he became, however, feebly, once again the *enfant terrible* of the American literary scene, laying about him with satirical and parodying bitterness, and then abruptly stopped, grinning self-consciously like an old grad at his class reunion who has been caught scrawling on a blackboard.

"Fanny loved her magic," Hecht announced, no mean devotee himself. "At any gathering she wanted to show her powers. One of her favorites was to leave the room after telling someone, say me, to pick an object in the room, animate or inanimate, and concentrate on it.

"In a few minutes she would return and study me. I would feel as though I were being offered up for sacrifice. Then, walking toward me with her eyes always on my face, she would, as she later explained, *will* me to send out thought waves telling her which object I had chosen.

"Behind me now, she would place her hands on my shoulders, ordering me to walk slowly about the room. I would begin my tour. Slowly she would follow, hands on me. Then, when I was certain I had fooled her, she would dig her fingernails into my back and announce the object of my choice.

"When I would ask how she did it, she would answer: 'It's no secret, kid. It's my power.'

"But nothing hit her like hypnotism," Hecht continued. "She took to it like an Indian takes to hot coals."

It was in Cleveland, where Fanny had many friends, that she was first exposed to hypnotism. At a party one night she watched a man hypnotize several people. When the entertainment was over, Fanny bombarded him with questions. The hypnotist graciously explained the details of this ancient art, and suggested that Fanny use an envelope adorned with a tiny ink dot, if she washed to join the fraternity. She must ask her subject to held the envelope and concentrate on the dot while she softly and continually suggested that the other was going to sleep . . . going to sleep . . . going to sleep . . . going to sleep.

Delighted with her discovery, Fanny journeyed to Chicago, where the Follies played its next engagement. All day she waited in her hotel suite, like Svengali. At last, late in the afternoon, a male friend came to call.

"Fanny," he said as the maid opened the door, "you look wonderful. Haven't changed a bit."

"Come on." Fanny said, taking his arm.

"Where are we going?"

"Come on, come on," Fanny said, tugging at the man's arm, pulling him into the suite and depositing him on the sofa. "Lie down," she ordered, thrusting the envelope in his hands. Her mentor had told Fanny that a subject was more pliable if he was relaxed.

"Lie down, kid," Fanny said, seizing the man's shoes and hoisting them onto the sofa. "Now I want you to concentrate on that dot. Just look at the dot and concentrate, you understand?"

"Fanny, what's the matter with you? Don't you feel well?"

"Concentrate!" Fanny insisted, and called for her maid. She wanted a witness to this, her first venture.

With the maid standing fretfully beside the sofa, Fanny began her powers. At first the gentleman caller resisted, torn between his affection for Fanny and his growing suspicion that she had taken leave of her senses.

But a determined Fanny was not easily thwarted. Steadily she overcame his resistance, until at last the man was completely under.

Turning triumphantly to the maid, Fanny said: "There! You saw it, kid. Now watch!"

"Miss Fanny, he's dead!" the maid exclaimed.

"He's hypnotized."

"Oh, Miss Fanny. Oh, Miss Fanny. Oh, heaven above. Oh, Lord!" the maid wailed.

"Keep still and watch," Fanny ordered. Whereupon she told the man to rise from the sofa, go to a vase on the piano, take a chrysanthemum from it and return to his resting-place.

As the man rose slowly in his trance, the maid moaned and fell over in a dead faint.

Fanny made certain that her domestic was breathing and returned to the more important work at hand: bringing her first subject out of the trance.

She accomplished that chore with alacrity, explained her new-found power to her friend, and then the two of them lifted the maid to the sofa and revived her.

"Gee, kid, you passed out," Fanny said.

"He's alive!" the maid wailed, pointing at Fanny's friend.

"Sure, he's alive," Fanny said. "I hypnotized him. That's why I brought you in here, to see me do it."

"I didn't see nothing, Miss Fanny. I didn't see a *thing*."

"You just said you saw him dead," Fanny declared. "Well, he isn't dead, is he?"

"No, Miss Fanny."

"Then he was hypnotized."

The maid looked wildly about her. "Yes, Miss Fanny," she said. "You're right, Miss Fanny," rising from the sofa, and edging away from her mistress. "You're right, you're right," she repeated, backing out of the room.

That was the beginning of her hypnosis jag. Returning from the road that year, Fanny took a house on Fire Island, a long, narrow spit of land which lies a few miles off Long Island some forty miles from New York. That summer she began to hypnotize wholesale. One weekend, Hecht, who had become an insomniac, begged her to hypnotize him into sleep.

"Sure, kid," Fanny said, producing the well-worn envelope with its faded dot. Ordering Hecht to concentrate, Fanny began to suggest sleep to him. After ten minutes of monologue, Fanny saw that he was still as wide awake as a young terrier.

"You're not concentrating, Ben," Fanny complained.

"Of course I'm concentrating."

Fanny shook her head. "No, kid. You've got something else in your head. You've got to get everything out but sleep."

Whereupon she lapsed once more into her spiel. But Hecht was not to be put under. As he continued to repulse her, Fanny's resentment mounted. Suddenly she grabbed his arm. "Too goddam much light in here," she announced, taking him to a closet in her bedroom. Pushing a chair into it, she bade Hecht sit down. She drew the shades, closed the bedroom door, and pulled the closet door very nearly shut. Standing before him, she told him to close his eyes and began her powers again.

She had never worked so hard. Hecht's eyes began to water as the dot started to waver on the envelope, but he showed no more signs of going to sleep than did Fanny.

"I don't feel anything, Fanny," he said at last.

"That's because you're too goddam dumb!" Fanny shouted, slamming the door in his face, and leaving him in the closet.

Hecht was her only recorded failure, and the only blemish on a riotously happy summer. Fanny seemed to have forgotten all troubles completely. Her children remember that every weekend brought a fresh horde of guests: the Hechts, George and Ira Gershwin and the latter's wife Lee, Lillian Hellman, Jimmy Durante, Lou Holtz, George Jessel, Harry Pilcer, and Bea Lillie.

Fanny, in her efforts to understand her son Bill's talents, took up painting. She would spend afternoons on the beach, standing or sitting before an easel. Since she hated to do anything alone, and since she could not commandeer her guests to join her, she bought an extra set of paints, an easel, and a brush for Herman, her German cook, and ordered him to accompany her. The two became a familiar sight on Fire Island, Fanny walking determinedly ahead, searching out fresh scenes, and Herman following with the paints, brushes, easels, and chairs.

Billy Rose would also appear on weekends, but Hecht remembers that he would wander quietly about the house and the Island, forgotten in the crush of some of the world's most talented and high-priced personalities.

Hecht remembers also that Fanny was particularly annoyed with Billy because he had never bought so much as a candy bar for the children.

But Frances recalls the Christmas that followed as a happy one, and names Billy Rose as the one who helped make it possible.

Fanny was in Kansas City with the Follies. It was her custom to have one of the servants bring the children to her for the holiday season. That year Billy told Mademoiselle that she could make her own plans for Christmas. For several days he returned to the apartment each evening laden with packages wrapped in gaily colored paper. Then one day he told Frances he wanted her to accompany him on a shopping trip.

"Oh, just a few gimcracks and gewgaws I need," Billy said. "I'd appreciate your help, Frances."

The two rode a cab to Fifth Avenue, where Billy ordered the driver to stop before one of the most famous jewelers in the world. "We're off to the races, Frances," he said, leading the young lady into the shop.

Billy roamed through the establishment for a time, with Frances following. He paused finally before a showcase filled with strings of pearls. A salesman appeared and Billy pointed at a superb string.

"That one," he said. "Let's have a look-see."

The salesman brought forth the pearls. Frances gasped. Billy grinned. "How do you like them?" he asked.

"They're beautiful! They're just absolutely beautiful."

"Do you think your mother will like them?"

"Like them?" Frances exclaimed. "She'll just love them! She'll just . . ."

"Check," Billy said. "Wrap them up," he ordered.

With the box of pearls stuffed into Billy's coat pocket, the two walked up Fifth Avenue toward 57th Street. It was a cold crisp day, the sun shone in a blue sky, the women—the lovely, long-legged, lavishly dressed, beautiful, beautiful women—strolled the Avenue, the shopwindows sparkled with the wares of a hundred countries and the craftsmanship of a thousand artisans, and the two of them—Billy Rose and Frances Brice—caught the fever, the happy, heart-swelling, exciting fever.

"One more stop," Billy said.

Frances, unwilling to spoil the next surprise, asked no questions. At 57th Street Billy turned to his right and they walked to Gunther Jaeckel, the New York furriers.

As a salesman approached, Billy said: "Now it's your turn. Now you pick something for your mother."

Frances picked, all right. She chose a magnificent fur for Fanny and, turning to Billy, she said: "Do you like it?"

Billy shook his head. "It's your party. Do *you* like it?"

The young lady looked at the salesman and she looked at Billy. "I think it's just the most beautiful thing I ever saw. I think it's just . . . just . . . just . . ."

Billy nodded. "You like it. Wrap it up," he ordered.

A day or two later Billy packed Frances, Bill, himself, Fanny's presents, and all the mysterious packages into the compartment of a train bound for Kansas City. As they began the slow journey underneath New York's Park Avenue, Billy seated the pair opposite him.

"Now," he said. "We've got to have rules on this train. Here's how we'll do it. There are going to be periods for everything: sleeping periods, eating periods, reading peri-

ods, playing periods, looking-at-the-scenery periods, and,"
he tapped a box beside him, "Monopoly periods. Okay?"

The children nodded.

"We had a wonderful trip," Frances recalls. "We had these
periods for everything and when we wanted to do something
else, we voted. Billy told us jokes and played with us. He
was a different person, gay, funny, and he never ran out of
ideas about what to do next."

Until the train halted beneath the Kansas City terminal
where Fanny waited for her two children, who were being
brought to her for the holiday season by their governess. She
saw her children first, and had eyes only for them, throwing
an arm around each and drawing them to her.

"Hey, you grew some more!" she said to her son. "What
are you studying to be, a giant?" And to Frances: "Too much
lipstick, kid." Fanny shook her head. "Oogly-boogly, that lipstick. Well, let's get up to the hotel. Come on, we'll eat and
then . . ."

Then she saw Billy Rose.

She stared at her husband.

Just stared at him.

"Well, for Christ's sake!" she said at last. "Where did you
come from?" She looked from her husband to her children.
"He brought you?" she asked them. They nodded and she
shook her head mournfully. "All the way from New York on
a train with them?"

She lapsed into silence as they waited for the porter to
remove the voluminous contents of the compartment. But
she was pleased. She fooled neither her husband nor her
children; not then and certainly not Christmas morning,
when the three watched her unwrap the furs Frances had
chosen.

She kissed Billy then, while her children busied themselves with the Christmas presents that Billy had mysteri-

ously deposited in the New York apartment in the weeks before their departure. She kissed him again when, at the very
last, when the center of the drawing-room was a vast mound
of Christmas wrappings, Billy drew the long, flat box from
his inside pocket and offered it to Fanny. She wore the
pearls around her neck and the furs about the pearls and
over her robe until it was time to dress for the theater, and
if she thought of another Christmas in another hotel in Chicago, nobody knew it.

Fanny wanted her family out front that Christmas night
in Kansas City. The three watched her from the fifth row
that evening, and if the paying patrons found a funnier, happier, more spirited, more satiric comedienne in that performance, they could well have thanked the boy and girl
and man down front in the center aisle.

It was a glum, silent, suddenly saddened Fanny who saw
the trio off for New York ten days later. Ordinarily Fanny
would joke and gibe with her children, never once betray-
ing the desperate need she had for their presence, but that
day on the station platform she was solemn and seemed anxious to be gone.

And when they were gone, when the train had left the station, hurried to a department store to buy gifts for her son
and daughter.

"Mother had charge accounts in every good store and shop
in the country," Frances said recently. "She loved to shop,
for us as much as for herself, and we were always getting
gifts: from Kansas City and Cleveland and Pittsburgh and
Chicago and Seattle and everywhere."

It was as though, by sending these gifts, Fanny remained
close and near to her children. She was a frequent correspondent as well, but an impatient one. She would receive
a ten-page letter from her son and reply as follows:

"I love you. It is rain . . ." The "ing" would be barely

legible as her pen stroke bled off the page, to be followed by
this:

> "xxxxxxxxxxxxxxxxxxxxxxxxxxxxxxxxxxxxxxxx
> xxxxxxxxxxxxxxxxxxxxxxxxxxxxxxxxxxxxxxxx
> xxxxxxxxxxxxxxxxxxxxxxxxxxxxxxxxxxxxxxxx
> xxxxxxxxxxxxxxxxxxxxxxxxxxxxxxxxxxxxxxxx
> xxxxxxxxxxxxxxxxxxxxxxxxxxxxxxxxxxxxxxxxxx"

However perfunctory her correspondence, when Fanny
was playing a theater in New York, her children were always with her. In the 1936 Follies, which the Shubert brothers produced, they were at the theater on weekends until
ten p.m., when Fanny's chauffeur drove them home. Fanny
did not have to urge her children to accompany her to the
theater, for Frances was stagestruck and Bill was stage-girl
struck. The object of his adolescent affection was a girl who
was appearing in the Follies.

At this time Fanny arranged for her daughter's first and
last appearance on the stage. One night when a chorus girl
became ill and the stage manager decided to close ranks,
Fanny suggested Frances as a substitute.

"She's just a kid," the stage manager protested.

"She's no kid, she's sixteen!"

"But Fanny, she doesn't know the routines!"

"She knows every line and laugh and dance step in the
show. I'll make her up," Fanny said, ending the discussion.

In Fanny's dressing-room Frances was sitting before the
mirror when her mother entered. "Fran," Fanny said, looking at Frances's reflection, "you want to be in the show tonight?"

Frances gasped and turned to her mother, staring at
Fanny. "Mother! I would love to!" she said.

Don't you know how she felt, this girl of sixteen who had
watched her famous mother for as long as she could remember? She was full of delight and full of fear. She was full of

anticipation and full of hesitation. She would not have gone on for all the money in the world and she would not have stayed off for all the money in the world.

Fanny dispatched the maid to fetch the chorus girl's costumes for the show. Waiting for her maid to return, Fanny began to make up her daughter.

After she had removed Frances's dress and stockings and shoes, Fanny began to accentuate her eyebrows. She darkened them and she applied lipstick. She rearranged Frances's hair and then, at last and finally, she reached for the grease paint.

When the maid returned, her arms laden with the spangled and sequined costumes, Frances's head jerked upwards to see the finery.

"Sit still," Fanny cautioned.

Frances tried to sit still, but her right foot twitched convulsively until Fanny was finished, when she leaped forward, reaching for all the costumes at once.

"Okay, kid, get into your costume," Fanny said, seating herself before the mirror. When the maid had dressed them both, when the curtain call had echoed and re-echoed through the corridors, Fanny rose from the dressing-table and walked to the door that the maid had opened.

Turning to Frances, she smiled. "You're nervous, aren't you?" Fanny asked. "It's your first time and you're nervous."

Frances nodded.

Fanny extended her hand. "It's my millionth time and I'm nervous too," she said, and holding hands, mother and daughter left the room to appear on the stage together.

It was mid-afternoon now in the New York restaurant and Ben Hecht was silent for a time. The cigar had grown cold and he made no attempt to relight it. He seemed solemn for a moment, this irrepressible, aging imp, who knew only the laughing road through life. He watched the waiters changing table linen and he turned a half-full glass of water around and around and around.

"The last time she was at Oceanside [a coastal town approximately one hundred miles south of Los Angeles, where Hecht has a home], I gave her that part of my autobiography which I had finished. She read it and told me she liked it. I was very pleased. I would rather have had a favorable reaction from her than a score of sophomoric judgments from the literarians. She was a tough critic."

Hecht chuckled suddenly and reached for a match. The solemnity vanished and, after he had lit his cigar, he said: "One time at Oceanside there was a flock of people down for the day. The house was full. A Broadway producer, a young fellow who had been highly successful and was then just beginning to run his meteoric course, was thinking of trying to revive the Follies. Knowing Fanny was my guest, he asked to be invited."

Hecht shook his head, laughing as he remembered. One of the owners of "21" passed, signaling him an invitation for a hand of gin rummy, and Hecht nodded his acceptance.

"Well, this young man—I won't name him for I have no wish to start another feud—this young man sidled over to Fanny in the hope of convincing her to return to Broadway.

" 'You know, Fanny,' he whispered in her ear, 'you and me, we'd be a hell of a combination. Just the two of us, on the stage and off.'

"Fanny rose from her chair and regarded this punk. Then, in a voice that competed adequately with the surf, she said: 'How dare you talk to me that way?'

"There was dead silence in the room. We all turned to watch them. The budding Belasco began to turn not red, but purple. Fanny raised one arm majestically.

" 'Get out of this house!' she ordered.

"And out he went. Fanny was not at all concerned that it wasn't her house. She just didn't take that kind of talk from tyros."

Hecht rose from the chair and offered a limp hand in farewell. He was about to join his cardmate when he appeared to think of something more.

"You know," he said, pointing the cigar, "if she had ordered me out of my house that day, I would have gone too."

✹ 19 ✹

FANNY: *"Until You Fall in Love."*

FANNY wrote:

"Once I said to Billy Rose: 'You will be with me until you fall in love.' I said: 'I'll know when you fall in love: when you go out and buy two or three new suits.' Because that is what love does to you. When you are buying something, you think of how it is going to look to them. Without love it is like having a good song without an audience."

She wrote:

"And had Billy never fallen in love, we would have still been together. Because we were good together because of the lack of emotion. After the emotion is ended in your life, I found I got great joy from just being myself and relaxing. When love is out of your life, you're through in a way. Because while it is there it's like a motor that's going, you have such vitality to do things, big things, because love is goosing you all the time. I found, after the love, that I needed help to keep going. Billy Rose gave it to me. Before, when I was with Nick, I didn't need any help. I had all that push. But now Billy Rose gave me the push. I know I helped Billy just as much as he helped me. We both realized that."

There is a prevailing legend, which has circulated for
many years along the Beverly Hills–Broadway axis, that
Billy's marriage to Fanny was the only reason for his later
success, since he was awful tired of being called "Mr. Brice"
and this unhappy circumstance spurred him to great heights.

It is a little presumptuous to short-change the mighty
mite in this fashion. The five-foot-three Billy would
probably be sitting exactly where he sits today, full of
money, property, and antiques, no matter whom he had
married.

You need no more proof than to sit with him for an hour.
Sit with him, watch him, listen to him, and you can almost
hear the wheels turning in his head, and the spotlights clicking on and off.

But if you can't sit with him, then hear what he has to
say. To a *Time* reporter interviewing him for one of the
magazine's cover stories a few years ago Billy said: "I spent
the first 40 years of my life in the buck hunt. There was
nothing in the world but Billy Rose and he was going to get
his. It's a tough street, I told myself, and you'd better learn
how to count."

To another interviewer he said: "I always figured myself
smart as the next guy, but I had an added starter; I was
willing to work. I learned a long time ago that the hardest
job is to *find* the dollar. Getting it is a lead-pipe cinch."

Billy might still be called Fanny's husband, but they were
beginning to know what he looked like.

They knew what he looked like in Fort Worth, Texas,
where the city's millionaire fathers were looking for someone to stage a spectacle to out-colossal the Dallas whoop-
de-do thirty-two miles away. They sent for Billy and Billy
came running—at one thousand dollars a day.

He stayed one hundred days, and for three of them Fanny
visited him, pausing on her way to California. Billy was in

bachelor quarters at the Fort Worth Athletic Club. Fanny was in a near-by hotel. Remembering that interlude, Billy recently recalled an evening when they had dined together. After dinner he escorted his wife to her hotel.

"You know, this is no good, Fanny," he told her.

"What's no good?"

"This phony life of ours."

"What do you mean, phony?" Fanny asked.

"The only people we're making happy with our marriage are the stockholders of American Telephone and Telegraph," Billy replied. "I'm in Fort Worth, you're in New York. When I get back to New York, you'll be in Hollywood. When I get to Hollywood, you'll be in San Francisco starting a vaude-ville tour."

"So?"

"So it's no good," Billy repeated. "What am I doing living alone in a bachelor's club? What are you doing running around the country?"

"I'm going to make a picture for Metro-Goldwyn-Mayer," she replied innocently.

"That's just what I mean," Billy said. "One of us ought to stop running around."

Fanny continued to California where she rented the es-tate of the Countess di Frasso. She had signed a five-year contract with Metro-Goldwyn-Mayer, and while she made her first picture for that studio Billy was busy in Cleveland with his first Aquacade.

And with Eleanor Holm, then married to Art Jarrett, the orchestra leader. "I told Fanny it would happen," Billy says of his meeting with Eleanor Holm. "When Fanny went to California, she left me with a thousand beautiful women. How long can you leave a hungry kid alone in a candy store?"

When word of Billy's attachment to the star of his show

reached Fanny, she said unconcernedly: "I can do anything she can do better, except swim."

For several weeks, while reports of Billy's romance drifted back from Cleveland, Fanny was silent, in public and in private. Then late one night she reached for the telephone.

"I want to talk person to person to Billy Rose in Cleveland," she told the operator, giving her the name of Billy's hotel.

"I'll hold on," Fanny said, listening while the operator rang for Cleveland information and asked for the number of the hotel. It was a hotel where Fanny had often stayed during her Follies and vaudeville tours.

Fanny heard the woman at the hotel switchboard say: "I'll ring Mr. Rose."

She heard the woman say: "Mr. Rose doesn't answer."

And she very nearly fell out of bed when the woman said: "Is this Miss Brice?"

"Yes," Fanny said.

"Just a moment, pl . . ." said the California operator.

"You don't know me, Miss Brice," said the switchboard woman, "but in 1926 you . . ."

"I'm sorry," said the California operator, "but you are not allowed to . . ."

"Ah . . . shut up!" Fanny said.

". . . in 1926," continued the switchboard woman, "you gave me tickets for your show when you stayed here."

"Yes," said Fanny. "Sure, I remember," she said, she who did not remember at all.

"I am sorry," said the operator, "but I will have to disconnect . . ."

"I'll pay for the call," Fanny said.

"I think I know how you can find Mr. Rose," said the woman in Cleveland, "but please don't say I told you."

"Don't worry," Fanny said.

"I . . ." said the operator.

"SHUT UP!" said Fanny.

"Call Miss Holm at the . . ." said the switchboard woman.

"You got that, operator?" Fanny asked.

"Yes, ma'am."

"Thanks, kid," Fanny said to the switchboard woman. "All right, operator, ring that hotel, station to station."

The operator did as she was told, and at the second hotel Fanny asked sweetly for Eleanor Holm.

"Ringing Miss Holm," replied the second switchboard woman.

And after a time, a woman's voice said: "Hello."

"Is Billy Rose there?" asked Fanny.

"Who?" asked the sleepy voice. "Who do you want?"

"Billy Rose."

"Who's calling?"

"Mrs. Rose," said Fanny and hung up.

On Eleanor, on Billy, and, for many months, on the press as well. She had had her fill of newspapers and of reporters and of her picture in the papers—and always, always, of the receiving end of trouble.

"When the Billy Rose divorce came up," Frances said recently, "Mother didn't say a word. There was never a statement made about it by Mother. It is an amazing thing. All through her lifetime she could have been associated with the greatest scandals of the country. She knew gamblers and racketeers. Many of the people she knew and saw could have involved her in terrible things. But she had such integrity, such honesty, and always conducted herself with such complete knowledge of what was right in life and what was wrong, that these people and what they did never touched her. Mother never played ambitious in order to have anybody like her, but the funny part of it was that everybody liked her anyway even though you couldn't tell her anything. She really strove to present herself in relation to her own image; to be herself with complete honesty. I don't think that she tried to affect characteristics that were not to her mind a part of herself. Now, naturally, if you go on the basis of who you *think* you are, the quality of your honesty is questionable. Rationalizing for your activities is a part of a scheme of fooling yourself. Still, I would say Mother had an extraordinary desire to be direct and frank, brutally so."

To a *New York World-Telegram* reporter who interviewed her over the long-distance telephone at that time Fanny Brice said: "I know nothing about the reports of Eleanor Holm and Billy. The wife is the last one who hears anything like that."

The newspaper story continued:

"Miss Brice laughingly denied that Rose had asked her for his release from their marriage while the couple were at the Fort Worth Fair.

" 'If there was any truth to the reports linking Billy and Eleanor, I'm sure Billy would say so.' "

For several weeks all parties concerned denied everything and then, in the tenth year after her divorce from Nick, Billy was interviewed in Denver by a United Press correspondent.

That story began:

"Billy Rose and Eleanor Holm Jarrett will be married as soon as Fannie Brice divorces Rose and Mrs. Jarrett divorces bandleader Arthur Jarrett, Rose announced today.

"Rose and Miss Brice," the story continued, "have been estranged for several months. So have the Jarretts.

"The trouble with both couples, Rose said, was that Miss Brice and Jarrett spent too much time in the spotlight while he and Mrs. Jarrett believed that a wife's place was in the home. 'Mrs. Jarrett has promised to be a wife and nothing more,' he said.

" 'I want Miss Brice to get a divorce as soon as possible, and I think she will, although I haven't talked to her about it,' Rose said. 'Miss Holm will file a divorce from Jarrett very soon. After the divorces are granted, we'll be married just as soon as the law allows.' Miss Brice, in Hollywood, declined comment.

" 'I imagine Miss Brice will say something today,' Rose said. 'After all, I guess she's pretty tired being around a guy that smells like elephants all the time.' He referred to his production of 'Jumbo,' which has been playing in the New York Hippodrome.

"Rose said he had not seen Miss Brice for about six or eight weeks, 'and then only for two days,' when he was visiting on the West Coast. He said he had not mentioned a divorce to her then.

" 'But the writing's been on the wall for some time,' he said. 'It's no fun being married to an electric light. Miss Brice is one of the brightest and cleverest stars the stage or screen has ever had, but our careers clash. I have to travel a lot and I want my wife by my side.

" 'No one has been fouled in this case. It's just an instance of four bull-headed careers clashing.' "

To Fanny a matrimonial crisis, however slight its emotional impact, could be weathered in one way only: selling her furniture and moving. After appearing in *Everybody Sings* and *The Great Ziegfeld*, Fanny's contract with Metro-Goldwyn-Mayer was terminated to the mutual satisfaction of both. As Baby Snooks Fanny had appeared on several radio programs in which that studio's stars were featured, and the brat had quickly gained great popularity. Maxwell House Coffee offered Fanny a large fee to appear in a weekly show as Baby Snooks; the offensive child was soon a national favorite.

As the program originated in Hollywood, Fanny decided to stop renting and to buy a house. She had a good reason, but no matter how good the reason, it is something more than coincidence that whenever a man of hers strayed, she looked for new quarters. In the midst of her troubles with Billy Rose she bought the magnificent house in the Holmby Hills section where she was to live the rest of her life, and set about furnishing it with her usual zest.

After making Billy wait nearly a year, she at last filed suit for divorce. On October 2, 1938, the *New York Herald Tribune* reported:

> "Hollywood, Calif., Oct. 1—*Fanny Brice sought a divorce from Billy Rose today in a complaint that avoided mention of the producer's romance with Eleanor Holm, the Olympic swimmer.*
>
> "*Her closest reference to the Rose-Holm affair was the charge that she was deserted approximately a year ago. It was about this time that Rose was publicizing Miss Holm across the country as his latest stage attraction.*
>
> "'*All I have to say is in the complaint,*' *Miss Brice said.*"

Three weeks later Fanny had her divorce, but under California law Billy had to wait a year before the divorce would become final.

During which he heard not a word from Fanny, Billy recalls. "She played it like a champ from start to finish," he said. "There was a lot of talk about Fanny suing me for a hundred-thousand-dollar settlement. The newspapers were full of it. It was just talk. I'm telling you now, none of it ever started with Fanny.

"Eleanor and I were married twenty-four hours after the divorce came through. A week after the wedding bells rang, I got a bill from Fanny for eighteen thousand dollars.

"I'd forgotten it, but she hadn't. It was for that nine-week salary cut everybody took when 'Crazy Quilt' was 'Sweet and Low,' and I was losing almost ten thousand dollars a week.

"What did I do? I paid. What else could I do? I sent her a check and I saw her every time I came to California, but she never mentioned that money and I never mentioned that money."

☼ 20 ☼

FRANK PERLS: *"In This Desert of Culture, She Was a Beacon."*

FRANK PERLS, fat and friendly, sits like a benevolent Buddha near the open door of his shop on Camden Drive in Beverly Hills. The sun shines upon his shapeless shoes and his hands lie motionless in his lap. He nods, or smiles, or shouts his hello to most of the people passing the shop, and you would think from the number of persons he knew that he sold ice cream, or candy, or fruit, or that he repaired shoes, or pressed pants, or cut hair.

Frank Perls sells paintings. His shop is an art gallery. His patron was Fanny Brice.

"She came to my gallery the first day I opened it, in October 1939," he said. "I was hanging my pictures and this strange woman enters to tell me I am hanging them wrong. I was a German alien, fresh from Germany, fresh to California, fresh to Los Angeles. I do not know this woman from Gypsy Rose Lee.

" 'I will show you how to hang pictures, so they'll sell,' she said.

" 'I think I know a little something about hanging pictures myself,' I said.

" 'You know a little nothing,' she said.

"She continues moving my pictures around my gallery, and I am now very hostile to this woman who is taking over. I did not send for her, and I did not want her there, but she did not care what I wanted. When she was satisfied with the pictures, she left the shop. They remained the way she hung them. I do not know yet why I left them hanging her way. I think on it. I cannot tell you. It simply did not occur to me to override her decision.

"I was a young man trained in art, devoted to art. I had spent my life with art. This woman to whom art came late in life, and was an important part of her life, knew somehow instinctively where each picture should go.

"Of formal art training she had nothing, and knew nothing. But of rightness and taste, she had a natural sense."

Perls paused to answer the question of a young man who had been browsing in the gallery. The young man thanked him, and Perls said: "She returned to the gallery that same evening with John Decker, the artist, and with Thomas Mitchell, the actor. She was from the first the barker for my gallery. She brought in these two like she was showing off her own gallery which she had built from the ground, stone by stone, window by window.

"On the wall was a Modigliani—'Portrait of Lolotte'—and Fanny said: 'How much is that?'

" 'Five thousand dollars,' I told her.

"She turned on Mitchell like she had found him a nice tie. 'There's your picture, Tommy,' she said."

Mitchell did not, Perls remembers, share her enthusiasm for the Modigliani. "My picture?" he asked.

"It's yours, Tommy," she said.

"It's Mr. Perls's," Mitchell replied.

"You're going to buy it," Fanny said.

"I'm not buying anything," Mitchell countered. "I didn't

come here to buy. You asked me to visit a gallery with you and . . ."

"He'll take it," Fanny told Perls.

"I assuredly will not take it," Mitchell said.

"The hell you won't," Fanny decided. "I've been thinking of you and that picture all day, goddam it, and now you start arguing with me."

Mitchell looked helplessly about the gallery. Decker, thankful that Fanny hadn't taken a fix on him, was no help. Perls, new to the country, the state, the city, was assuredly no help.

"It is a very fine specimen, sir," he told Mitchell.

"*There,*" Fanny said, as though Perls had just offered Mitchell the Mona Lisa for forty-nine cents. "It's a very fine specimen."

"But I don't want a picture," Mitchell said.

"Of course you want a picture," Fanny said. "Wrap it up," she told Perls.

"I haven't got a check," Mitchell said desperately.

"I have a blank check, sir," Perls said.

"*There,*" Fanny said, beaming at Perls, as though his offer of a blank check was no less an achievement than a cure-all for cancer. "See? He's got a blank check."

In his shop Perls chuckled as he remembered the muddled Mitchell writing a check for five thousand dollars, his price for a casual evening with Fanny.

"He was not the end," Perls said of Mitchell. "She sold at least fifty pictures for me. She would come into the gallery with someone, anyone who could afford to pay, and take off her shoes, and begin to sell. She could connect, instantaneously, a painting with a purchaser, and she could not rest until she had the person in the gallery and giving her sales speech. Nobody got away from her.

"She was a tout for me, but I believe she was a tout for

all the galleries in Los Angeles. Fanny was in this desert of culture not only a light, but a beacon, and without her this town would not have been as art-conscious as it now is."

Howard Warshaw, the young American painter who is a colleague and friend of Fanny's son, Bill, agrees with Perls.

"Another thing," Warshaw says. "She was a full-fledged contemporary. She thought as we did. When Bill brought me up to the house, I was polite, because I figured she was a generation removed, like everybody's mother. But after talking with her for five minutes, we were friends with all barriers of age and specious social taboos removed.

"In any discussion of painting she was a willing and active participant," Warshaw said. "A painting had to strike all her senses favorably, or she didn't like it."

A few days later, as Fanny was being driven down Sunset Boulevard, her chauffeur stopped at a red light beside an automobile in which sat Howard Warshaw. The young painter invited her to his studio.

Warshaw, a careful, slow workman, had labored for months on an extraordinarily large picture, a canvas several yards long. Now he stood beside it as Fanny regarded his painting carefully. She cocked her head first to one side and then to another. She pursed her lips. She frowned. She squinted. She smiled.

"I'll tell you, kid," she said finally. "Cut about three feet off that left side and you've got a picture."

For many months after Perls opened his gallery, Fanny was an almost daily visitor, he remembers. When she could not come to the gallery, she summoned Perls to her home.

"After the war began," he said, "There was a curfew in California for all aliens. Since I was a German, I, of course, had had to be home by an early hour. How many times did Fanny herself make dinner for me and feed me in her home, practically shoving the food at me so I would eat and get to my home before the curfew?

"Of course I knew that her son was studying painting, but she did not talk to me of Bill. I did not know what she thought of the life the boy had chosen. She would go to Glendale, and there rummage for hours in second-hand stores buying pictures for seventy-five cents, for a dollar, for two dollars. These pictures she would bring to me for my opinion.

"She comes one day with two armfuls of these pictures she has bought in Glendale which she arranges in the gallery for my critique."

" 'Get away from here, Frank,' she said, 'I'll call you when I'm ready.' "

She was on her knees, propping the pictures against the wall at regular intervals until she had a long line of the dirty, dusty paintings. She was still on her knees when she called Perls.

She was on her knees when he stood against the opposite wall, staring for a moment at each picture, examining the entire group silently while she waited.

"That one," he said, pointing his pencil. "That one there is interesting."

"What do you mean, interesting, Frank?" Fanny asked, sitting on the floor now, her right arm out for support.

"It has something. There is a freshness about it. There . . . did all these pictures come from Glendale, Fanny?"

"I just bought them. What about *this* one, Frank?"

"I see talent there, Fanny," Perls said. "Young talent, but good talent; solid talent."

"Are you sure, Frank?"

"Of course I am sure. Certainly I am sure," he said, as Fanny pushed herself up from the floor and went to Perls. She seized Perls's wrists and held them tightly, laughing

in his face. "That's Bill's picture," she said. "The one you
picked is Bill's, he painted it."

"Fanny, I am very happy."

"*You're* happy. Jesus, how do you think I feel?" Fanny
asked, going back to the pictures and kneeling once more
to gather them, leaving her son's for the top.

Call it creative talent, or artistic ability, or what you will—
it was what Fanny admired above all things in this world.
What she loathed above all things was to witness the dis-
sipation of such gifts, and Bill's complete devotion to painting, his passionate desire to exploit his talent, his dedication
to his work, gave her great happiness.

But she could not be a silent spectator. "When I was going to Art School," Bill remembers, "she would periodically
examine my work and, far from expressing herself as a dot-
ing Mother, she would submit me and the work to clear-
headed, shrewd criticism. Sometimes, if she looked at a
picture which I had considered almost completed, she
would have a suggestion of some extremely small change or
addition. If I agreed with her criticism and made the altera-
tion, she would always, upon seeing the picture again, triumphantly exclaim: 'Now it's a picture.' She was nearly always right. She had a feeling for what was needed to make
anything complete. Also she had to be a part of it, she had
to be helping create even if she herself wasn't creating."

In his sunlit gallery, Frank Perls sat contentedly near the
entrance, waiting for his first sale of the day, or week, or
month, and he seemed loath to stop talking of Fanny. "She
was not one woman," he decided, "but a hundred women.
I knew a generous, kind, mothering Fanny. I knew a young,
vital, alive, curious Fanny. I did not know a tired, lonely,
frightened Fanny.

"She was with everyone a different woman," he continued.

"She was a study. You could study Fanny for years like a painting, and this is the truth I am telling you for I myself have studied her.

"She was not one," he said, "whom you could dismiss with a word, a sentence, an adjective. She was"—he shook his head—"she was . . . she was"—nodding at last, the smile triumphing over the frown—"immense."

❋ 21 ❋

EVERETT FREEMAN: *"Fanny Must Be President of the Chase National Bank."*

EVERETT FREEMAN has been a boy wonder for more than twenty years. He was a prolific—and fantastically successful—short-story writer for the nation's top magazines at the age of eighteen. He was a toiler in Dave Freedman's New York radio comedy vineyard before he was nineteen. He was Baby Snooks's boss man—writer and director—before he was twenty-five. He was a scenarist in Hollywood before he was thirty, and a producer at Warner Bros. before he was forty.

He is in his very early forties now, and looks like a featherweight ten years after hanging up the gloves. He has quit being a producer to return to writing. He seems impatient of small talk and he *is* impatient of small talk. He seems direct—direct to deal with and direct to converse with—and he *is* direct.

On that Sunday in June 1952 he had finished a difficult week with a script that he was preparing for Twentieth Century-Fox Film Corp. Over the telephone he said he had a date for golf. He said he would be glad to talk about Fanny Brice, but he could not talk about her today. He mentioned the round of golf.

But an hour later, having canceled his date, he sat in the patio of Frances Stark's home on Stone Canyon Road, talking about Fanny.

"She taught me something," Freeman declared. "She taught me many things, but this in particular: we don't grieve, you and I, for the death of a friend. We grieve for ourselves, having lost that friend. We grieve selfishly, knowing we cannot replace that friend. We are not at all concerned with that friend's passing. We're concerned only with our own little lives and what the death has done to our lives.

"When Fanny told me that, I listened and nodded and went home. So many things she said hit you with such a shock that no answer was possible. Then I began to think on it: *really* think, with my mind and not with my emotions. She was right, you know. Think of it for a while yourself and you'll know she's right. She could speak only in truths. Truth is often shocking, but Fanny knew no other way. She devastated some of the most sensitive men of this generation with the things she said in their presence.

"To Fanny," Freeman said, and his voice softened perceptibly, "I was a combination of friend, son, and pal. I was with her six years, writing and directing Baby Snooks, and I never spent a worthless or profitless minute with her. She never deviated. She was a pure character, the strongest human being I've ever known. Had Fanny been a man she must be president of the Chase National Bank.

"When television stormed the country a few years ago, many top-notch performers in radio took pay cuts. Not Fanny. Told that her salary would be slashed to three thousand dollars a week, she went off the air, although, after taxes, it would have made little difference to her. She had made up her mind that she would not take the cut. Her personal representative Abe Lastfogel, Sam Berke her business manager, myself, everybody she knew, pleaded with her, trying to show Fanny her error. She would sit in that living-room of hers listening, nodding, seemingly agreeing. When the case had been presented, she could offer a two-word decision:

" 'Not me.'

"She stayed off the air a year. She had made up her mind not to go on, and wrong or right, that was it. And when she returned," Freeman continued, "she was immediately in the first ten most popular programs.

"If she was for you," he said. "If she was really your friend, there was nothing, absolutely nothing, she would not do." Freeman unbuttoned his shirt and removed it, wanting some sun on his body, as he remembered his oil adventure.

"I was the wolf of Wall Street," he said. "I was going to be a millionaire. I was going to surprise Fanny."

For no reason that he could explain, the thought of surprising Fanny was uppermost in his mind when Freeman invested many thousand dollars in a "proven" oil field. He was in Oklahoma with the company of *Jim Thorpe, All-American*, which he had written and was producing for Warner Bros. Somebody introduced him to a prospector who knew a spot where oil was just waiting to be taken out of the ground. All that was needed was money. Freeman graciously obliged.

He returned to Hollywood with several thousand feet of film depicting the life of Jim Thorpe, and several thousand shares of stock in an oil company for which he had purchased most of the equipment.

Freeman told his wife, swore her to secrecy, and waited

for the oil. Waited and telephoned to Oklahoma, until one day, while he worked on a script, his colleagues in Oklahoma called. Their land was lousy with oil. They were all rich. He had done it. He was the wolf of Wall Street.

Freeman immediately called Fanny, exultantly telling her of his good fortune. Fanny's scream could be heard around the block.

"Oh, my God! Oh, Christ! Oh, you fathead! Don't you know you're not the kind of guy who strikes oil?"

"What's the matter with you, Fanny?" Freeman demanded. "They just called me. The place is lousy with oil."

"If there's oil in that well," said Fanny flatly, "I'll go down to Oklahoma and drink it."

"I'm sending you the first barrel," Freeman replied coldly, somewhat nettled by her skepticism.

"Keep the goddam barrel," Fanny replied. "You'll need it."

And hung up on Freeman, picking up the receiver immediately to telephone his wife. From Mrs. Freeman she learned the details of his distant enterprise.

Within an hour she had contacted Freeman's business manager, her business manager, her lawyer, her agent, and her banker. By the following day every facet and detail of the operation had been checked. Arranging a meeting in her house for that night, she called Freeman and asked him to come over.

When he arrived at Fanny's house together with his wife, who mysteriously insisted on accompanying him, Fanny gestured at the assembled legal, banking, and business talent.

"All right, sucker," she said, "listen."

Freeman listened. Within five minutes he realized he had been taken. Within ten minutes his face was beet-red with embarrassment. Within fifteen minutes the wolf of Wall Street slunk sheepishly out of the house, his wife in tow.

On the patio, Freeman had begun to perspire from the sun. "She just knew," he said, "knew it in her bones, that I was being taken. She knew everything that way: by instinct and something more than instinct, some sixth or seventh or tenth sense that I've never found in any other human being."

She had it in her radio show as well. At rehearsal she invariably gave a desultory, bored reading of the script. "I never got a performance from her during the rehearsal," Freeman said, "and I never knew what to expect. But she never disappointed me on the air. She'd say: 'I can't do a show until it's on the air, kid. Don't worry.'

"She couldn't stop me from worrying," Freeman said, "but she was right as usual. She *knew* she'd be good once we were on the air."

Jess Oppenheimer, who now produces and writes the *I Love Lucy* television show, and was for many years a Baby Snooks writer, said recently: "It wasn't until I had my own children that I realized how good she was. My three-year-old is just like Fanny as Baby Snooks. She had kids down perfectly, with an amazing attention to detail."

Freeman insists it was more than an imitation of a child that made Fanny such a successful Baby Snooks. "While she was on the air," he explained, "she *was* Baby Snooks. And after the show, for an hour after the show, she was still Baby Snooks. The Snooks voice disappeared, of course, but the Snooks temperament, thinking, actions, were all there. She was at her sweetest, and I loved Fanny then more than any other time."

Freeman remembers that in the early days of their relationship he would constantly ask Fanny's opinion on each script. Then, as her replies to his questions became more and more perfunctory, he realized that he was the boss.

"She had the ability to spot someone whom she believed in. Then she trusted him completely."

Fanny's trust, however, did not eliminate her interest in any proceeding with which she was concerned. For many years the show was broadcast on Thursday. Occasionally Fanny would telephone Freeman on Sunday.

"Hello, kid," she would begin, "Fanny."

"Hello, Fanny."

"What's new, kid?"

"Nothing much," said Freeman, waiting.

"How do you feel?"

"I feel fine, Fanny."

"I don't feel so good. I woke up this morning feeling oogly-boogly. It's too hot."

"Yes, it is hot, Fanny."

"So . . . what else is new?"

"Nothing much," said Freeman, waiting.

"How's the baby?"

"Fine, Fanny, fine."

"That's fine," Fanny said, very little-girlish and, from the start of the conversation, as sweet as honey. "What are you doing, Everett?"

"Having breakfast."

"Oh, did I interrupt your breakfast?"

"No, Fanny, not at all."

"What's on for today?"

"Well, I've got some work to do on the script."

Then, finally, it came. "Is it going to be good, kid?" Fanny asked.

"I don't know. I haven't written it yet."

"Yeah. Well, good-bye, kid."

Freeman would hear no more until Tuesday, when the first rehearsal was always held—and never in the morning.

Fanny wanted afternoon rehearsal. Freeman soon learned that it was best to level with Fanny at all times. When she appeared with the cast, her first question was invariably: "How's it look, kid?"

"Fanny, I think I let you down this week," Freeman would say, if he thought the script was a stinker.

"Okay."

"Do the best you can, will you, Fanny?" Freeman would ask.

"You know I will, kid."

And she did. But if Freeman—or anyone—gave her a bum steer, trying to coddle her into thinking a weak script was great, they heard about it, brother. They heard it loud and clear. Sometimes even hardened stagehands covered their ears.

Other times Fanny would purr like a kitten, and this was most nerve-racking of all, for she seemed almost disinterested. She used glasses for reading, but she would never wear them before an audience. As a result, special scripts were prepared for her, printed in big capital letters on cardboards that she held in her arms before the microphone like a little girl hugging her schoolbooks.

"The deadly period of my life," says Freeman, "came between the time of the dress rehearsal, a few hours before the show, and the show itself. Fanny would stand on the stage during the dress, bored with it all, reading the lines flatly, her eyes wandering. Often she read a line that had been cut.

"That's out, Fanny," Freeman would say.

"Okay."

"Can't you give me a little life in the reading?" he would ask desperately.

"Don't worry."

"I can't help worrying. I'm the nervous type."

"Come on inside and we'll play gin rummy."

With the dress rehearsal finished, Fanny would return to her dressing-room. Several moments before show time, she would appear in the wings to stand beside Freeman.

"I'd look at this woman," Freeman remembers, "seeing this dignified lady in the best clothes, the height of fashion. I'd watch her holding her cards in her hand, not knowing what was printed on them, and I'd break out in a sweat. Then I'd get the signal from the engineer.

"All right, Fanny," I'd say. "You're on."

"She'd nod and leave me. And when she went out in front of all those people she was suddenly a little child, clothes and coiffure and high heels forgotten.

"When she went on, something happened. I saw it happen, but I can't tell you what it was. She just needed that audience in front of her and she was trouping. It didn't make any difference whether she lost her place or read Hanley Stafford's line. She was Snooks."

Freeman began to walk from one end of the Stark patio to the other as he spoke. It was hot. The Stark cook appeared, interrupting to ask whether iced tea would help. Freeman nodded shortly and returned to his chair in the sun, leaning forward, elbows on knees, to continue talking of Fanny.

"Being the star she was, we couldn't just give her a soap-opera story—we had to invent block comedy routines and conceal them within the general conformation of a story. Lancelot and Vera Higgins—Baby Snooks's Daddy and Mommy—were a typical American pair. They lived in a typical American home, had a typical American life, enjoyed typical American friends, and had typical American fun. Where they differed, where they were not typical, and where they became worthy of a weekly biography of their life, was in their daughter, Baby Snooks. She was as typical as a tornado."

Freeman reached for the briefcase beside the chair and from it extracted a mimeographed script of twenty-seven pages. "Here is a show Fanny did," he said. "In it Daddy has to make a speech at a dinner. It is an important speech for him. It may make his career. Nothing very funny or odd about that, right?

"But as he dresses, Baby Snooks wanders into his room:

SNOOKS: *Hello, Daddy.*

DADDY: *Snooks, please don't come in here now.*

SNOOKS: *Why?*

DADDY: *Because I'm trying to rehearse a speech.*

SNOOKS: *But I got a problem, Daddy.*

DADDY: *For Pete's sake, Snooks, can't you understand that this speech is very important to your Daddy's career?*

SNOOKS: *It is?*

DADDY: *Yes. In two hours, I'm gonna be standing up at a banquet table, looking into a bunch of stupid faces. I've got to get into the mood for that.*

SNOOKS: *Is that why you're rehearsing in front of a mirror?*

DADDY: *That settles it! Out you go! Shoo! Beat it!*

SNOOKS: *Lemme listen, Daddy.*

DADDY: *Okay* (CLEARS THROAT) *Mr. Toastmaster, ladies and gentlemen—thank you!*

SNOOKS: *You're welcome!*

DADDY: *I told you to keep quiet. I was thanking the toastmaster.*

SNOOKS: *Who's he?*

DADDY: *He's the master of ceremonies. He introduces the speakers.*

SNOOKS: *Don't they know each other?*

DADDY: *Yes, but it's customary to acknowledge the toast-master's introduction.*

SNOOKS: *Does he get mad if you don't?*

DADDY: *He gets burned up.*

SNOOKS: (LAUGHS)

DADDY: *What are you laughing at?*

SNOOKS: *Burned toastmaster.*

After the first commercial, Daddy continues to rehearse his speech with Snooks in attendance.

DADDY: *Well, I still have a few minutes left—I think I'll work on my diction.* (ENUNCIATING) *Yes, ladies and gentlemen, we are gathered here tonight to* (MOUTHS UNINTELLIGIBLY)

SNOOKS: *What did you put in your mouth, Daddy?*

DADDY: *Towf fowa foof—marbles. See? Three marbles.*

SNOOKS: *Are you hungry?*

DADDY: *No, I'm merely doing what all the great orators have done to help them with their diction. Take Demosthenes. Demosthenes practiced speaking with a mouthful of marbles.*

SNOOKS: *He did?*

DADDY: *Yes, and Daniel Webster put a cork between his teeth.*

SNOOKS: *Why did he do that?*

DADDY: *Who, Webster?*

SNOOKS: *No—the mouse with knees.*

DADDY: *Not mouse with knees—Demosthenes.*

SNOOKS: *Who's he?*

DADDY: *What's the difference? If you can put these marbles in your mouth and talk intelligibly, you're a great orator.*

SNOOKS: *I'll bet I can do it, Daddy.*

DADDY: *If I can't how can you?*

SNOOKS: *Lemme try it.*

DADDY: *All right, Miss Smarty. Here's some more marbles. I'll put one in your mouth. Now try reciting something.*

SNOOKS: *Mary had a little lamb.*

DADDY: *Not bad. Here, try another one.*

SNOOKS: *Her father shot it dead.*

DADDY: *Funny, I didn't do that well. Here, try a third one.*

SNOOKS: *Now, Mary takes that lamb to school—*

DADDY: *This is fantastic. Three marbles in her mouth! Here, try a fourth.*

SNOOKS: *Between two hunks of bread!*

DADDY: *Amazing! Four marbles and she talks plainly.*

SNOOKS: *It's easy, Daddy.*

DADDY: *How is that possible?*

SNOOKS: *I swallowed 'em!"*

Mummy assures Daddy that four marbles in Snooks's stomach are not enough to keep him from his speech. She hustles him off to the dinner, calls the doctor, and, after another commercial, Snooks is being examined by the physician.

SNOOKS: (SUSPICIOUSLY) *What are you gonna do?*

DOCTOR: *Well, do you see this big apparatus here? It's called an X-ray.*

SNOOKS: *I'm scared of it.*

DOCTOR: *There's nothing to be scared of. It's just like a camera. All you do is lie here on this table and the machine snaps your stomach.*

SNOOKS: (CRIES)

DOCTOR: *What's the matter?*

SNOOKS: *Snap your own stomach.*

DOCTOR: *Now listen here, Snooks—*

MUMMY: *Er—Doctor—I think perhaps you worded that a little unfortunately. Let me explain to her. Snooks, you trust Mummy, don't you? You won't feel a thing. The doctor just presses this little button and then he goes into the other room.*

SNOOKS: *What does he do in the other room?*

MUMMY: *Well, he looks at your ribs on a plate.*

SNOOKS: *WAAAAAAAAAAAAHHHHHHHHHH!*

The marbles remain in Snooks's stomach while Daddy stammers, stutters, and splutters through his speech. The doctor is thwarted, Mummy is helpless, and Snooks is delighted with her importance until Daddy returns from the dinner, learns that an operation to remove the marbles will cost some three hundred dollars, seizes Snooks's ankles, inverts her, and shakes the marbles free.

Freeman sipped his iced tea slowly. "She was just immense," he said. "You had to hear her do that 'WAAAAAAAAAHHHH!'—hear her and watch her—to believe her. It never failed to convulse an audience. How can you explain Fanny? In her fifties, incomparably dressed, making you feel—not believe—but *feel* as though you were watching a child."

In those Hollywood years Fanny was identified only as Snooks in the nation's show-business firmament. Occasionally a Sunday supplement writer would devote a page to Fanny's past: the Follies, Nick, Billy Rose; but to an entire generation of Americans Fanny Brice was Baby Snooks, the bawling, battling, bombastic brat they heard once a week on the nation's radios.

During the war a huge benefit show was held at the El

Capitan theater in Los Angeles. Fanny agreed to appear
with Hanley Stafford, the Daddy of the radio show, in a
brief skit.

As she and Daddy began their sketch before a packed
house, Fanny noticed that he was standing beside her all
right, but about a yard nearer the footlights. Slowly, without missing a word of a line, she drew abreast of him, only
to glance to her left after another minute and see him once
more ahead of her. Again she came forward, and again he
left her behind.

Taking a step ahead, Fanny stood shoulder to shoulder
with him. As she smiled at her audience and he delivered a
line, she whispered: "You start downstaging me, you sonofabitch, and I'll walk you right through that audience!"

Daddy stayed put.

☀ 22 ☀

KATHARINE HEPBURN: *"We Are a Very Curious People."*

KATHARINE HEPBURN came into her Hollywood home the way Katharine Hepburn should enter: a little late, a little breathless, hair piled atop her head and a little disheveled; taking long strides and flashing the quick smile; showing the extended hand with its square-cut, unpainted fingernails; offering the firm handshake, the sincere apology, all of which made you her obedient servant from that moment forward, forevermore.

This was Charles Boyer's house, which she had rented while making a picture for Metro-Goldwyn-Mayer. A house with terrazzo floors and low ceilings, and big, big rooms furnished sparsely so that everywhere was the feeling of space and more space, like the feeling you have in walking through a museum on a rainy Monday afternoon.

She took a cigarette, ordered tea, lit her cigarette, turned her head quickly to avoid the smoke, and said: "Fanny was a fabulous character, you know. The frankest human being I've ever known. She had a smell for what was good and true in a thing," Hepburn continued. "She had a kind of peasant-like, absolute honesty about her own work, and about others' work. I brought all my scripts to her and read them aloud. If Fanny didn't like a script, I was frightened."

The Hepburn was not alone in her fear of Fanny's displeasure with a script. Beverly Hills and Manhattan abound with actors, actresses, scenarists, playwrights, composers, and lyricists who came alone to Fanny carrying their brain-children to her with no less trepidation than a mother who brings her infant to a famous pediatrician. Moss Hart read his plays to her and to each—as with Hepburn or Hart or Hecht, or whoever the talented man or woman—Fanny gave her full and complete attention, the two of them alone, she having cleared the room of possible intruders, reserving judgment until the very end, and then at last offering criticism swiftly and succinctly.

"If Fanny liked it," said Sylvia Kaye, wife of Danny Kaye, and composer of much of his material, "I was sure of it. I would come home to Danny and tell him we could use the song or sketch or whatever I'd read or sung for her. If Fanny said: 'Oogly-boogly,' shaking her head at me, I went home and went to work."

Hepburn rose and strode to the windows looking down into the Hollywood hills, talking steadily and doing, with tact, with graciousness, and with consideration, what must be the most difficult task of all for her: disregarding the stares of her caller, who could not lose the spine-tingling, stomach-trembling knowledge that he sat with Katharine Hepburn.

She ignored her visitor's knowledge. His discomforture and embarrassment and stuttering had become, by some rare osmosis, her problem and she set about solving it as though it were her only responsibility. Solve it she did, gathering to herself another unwanted champion.

"Fanny had," Hepburn said, turning quickly and returning to the fireplace, "a consideration for . . . for . . ." she gestured with her hand like a speaker driving home a point, only now she searched for the only word that would fit the thought, "for artistic integrity that I've never encountered elsewhere. She had something else: the rare quality that made women like her as much as men. She was not masculine, you know. Hardly. She was quite the most feminine woman I've ever known, but she could meet a man on his own terms. She could tell a good story. And she could listen. How many woman can *really* listen?"

Hepburn knelt before the fire, setting a match to the kindling, and was motionless for a moment, waiting for the flames to feed. She rose and turned, her back to the fire and her hands behind her.

"No one in our business is particularly happy," Hepburn said. "We are a very curious people, you know. Once Fanny said: 'Any man I would want, wouldn't want me, and any man who would want me, I wouldn't want.'

"She talked of herself a good deal," Hepburn said, "but only when you had finished talking about yourself. She had an amazing—an absolutely amazing—curiosity to know, to really know things. And she could not do anything half-heartedly. Whether it was decorating or watching television, Fanny did it completely, with all of herself."

Idleness was Fanny's great enemy and she gave it no quarter. In June 1945 she was hospitalized for a time with a slight heart attack and within a few days was well on the way to recovery, with an enforced convalescence of several weeks ahead of her. Fanny had been confined to a hospital bed only twice before in her life, each time for the birth of a child. Fanny had not been sick long then, she was not sick now, and since the fear of all fears in her life was the prospect of being left alone—absolutely alone—during any wak-

ing instant, she summoned every friend and acquaintance
to her bedside.

Once when Orry-Kelly, the dress designer, was walking
down the hall to her room, he found himself behind two
well-dressed middle-aged matrons who were shocked at the
language issuing from an open door ahead.

"Who," one of the ladies asked her companion, "is that?"

Orry-Kelly took a step forward, bowed, smiled, and said:
"Baby Snooks, madam."

Learning that a well-known Las Vegas gambler was in an
adjoining room, himself recuperating from a heart attack,
Fanny sent her nurse in with a bet on the third race at Hollywood Park, where the annual meeting had just begun.

That gentleman took her money, wrote the name of the
horse and the size of the bet on a sheet of Kleenex, and sent
it to Fanny with the nurse. When Fanny won the bet, the
gentleman, true to the code, immediately sent in her win-
nings with *his* nurse, thus establishing the first—and last—
bookmaking concession to flourish at Cedars of Lebanon
Hospital. Every day thereafter, shortly before the first-race
post-time, there began a flurry of activity along the halls of
the hospital, with the nurses acting as runners between bet-
tor and bookmaker, that continued until the last race went
to the post.

After she was discharged from the hospital she went to
her beach house to convalesce.

At the sight of the ambulance stopping before Fanny's
beach house, a gang of kids gathered. The attendants opened
the rear door. While Fanny's stretcher was being slowly
lifted out of the ambulance, one of the kids shouted: "It's
Baby Snooks! It's Baby Snooks!"

"Are you nuts?" another asked. "Baby Snooks is on the
radio."

"Yeah, but that's her right there! I know that's Baby

Snooks. Isn't that Baby Snooks, mister?" the lad asked
Bill.

Hoping to end the debate and scatter the youngsters, Bill
nodded.

"See?" said the first boy. "Didn't I tell you?" he said, and,
pushing his way forward, he looked down at Fanny and
asked: "What's the matter with you, Baby Snooks?"

"I had a baby," said Baby Snooks, who was then in her
fifty-fourth year.

When her convalescence was complete, Fanny returned
to the big house. Her enthusiasms, her intuitive, strongly
vocal reactions to anyone and anything, continued unabated.
Bill remembers escorting her to the premier of a motion picture. For some reason Fanny was in a particularly bad mood
when they left for the theater, but an evening with her son
never failed to cheer her up. They were shown to their seats,
and soon after the start of the picture Fanny began a running commentary.

"Get that, kid," she said to Billy of a particular scene.

Followed by: "Oh, I'm sick!" as the heads began to turn.

Followed by: "This picture is a dog!"

Followed by: "I'm dying!" as she slapped her neck vigor-
ously.

Bill leaned closer and whispered: "Mother, the star of the
picture is sitting in front of you."

"I don't give a hoot in hell *where* she's sitting!" Fanny
shouted, drowning out the screen dialogue.

Bill ran. He went up the aisle as fast as his feet would
carry him, and he was out on the sidewalk, smoking a cigarette, when Fanny joined him.

"See?" she said victoriously. "You couldn't even sit through
that picture, it was so lousy."

More are more now Fanny began to withdraw from Hollywood society. She wanted old friends around her. Bea Lillie

was in California for a few weeks, and Fanny insisted that
the English comedienne stay with her. They went to the
track together one day, laughing and giggling like a pair of
schoolgirls, both dressed in slacks and turbans.

Before one race, as they stood in line waiting to place
their two-dollar bets, a woman suddenly recognized Fanny.
Trembling with excitement, the woman touched Bea's
shoulder.

"Is that . . . is that really her?" the woman asked.

"Is that who?" asked Bea.

"Miss Bruce?" [sic]

"Yoos," said Bea, turning her back on the woman.

Now and then Fanny would accept an invitation to an
evening at someone's home. Once Ethel Barrymore invited
Fanny, George Cukor, Katharine Hepburn, Greta Garbo,
and one or two others to a dinner party. Miss Ethel enter-
tains rarely, and a summons to her home is not taken lightly
in Hollywood. An hour before Cukor was to pick up Fanny
and drive her to Miss Ethel's home, his telephone rang.

"George, it's me," Fanny said. "I can't go tonight."

"Are you sick, Fanny?" Cukor asked.

"I'm not sick. It's my hair, George. I can't go out with my
hair looking like this. Tell Ethel I can't . . ."

"You tell her," Cukor said. "I'll be damned if I'm going to
do your dirty work."

"Well, I'm not going," Fanny said.

"Don't go. But you should call her, Fanny."

"I can't, George. You do it," Fanny said, and hung up.

Cukor arrived at Miss Ethel's home while the hostess and
her guests were having cocktails. "Where is Fanny?" demanded Miss Ethel.

"Something about her hair," Cukor said, uncomfortably.

"What about her hair?" demanded Miss Ethel.

"Something about how awful it looked," Cukor said.

"Why didn't she come without her hair?" Miss Ethel asked.

At what Bill remembers as the last large formal evening in Fanny's home, the dinner guests were New York society expatriates. It was a black-tie affair, and for days before the event Fanny was busy supervising the preparations for her gala.

On the day of the party, when Fanny's dining-room was a model of taste, Polly Moran appeared at the door carrying her battered drugstore suitcase. Polly, who never needed an invitation to Fanny's house, had decided to come up from Laguna Beach for a few days.

The two embraced for a full moment, and then Fanny led her guest upstairs. They were alone together for several hours. The servants scurried about downstairs, completing the arrangements for the formal dinner.

At one point the maid who was to serve the dinner was summoned to Fanny's room and told to fetch one of her uniforms. A short time later Kaye Brewer, Fanny's secretary, was told to change the orders of the day: instead of serving dinner that night, the maid was to be given the evening off —and no questions asked.

Kaye relayed her mistress' commands and retired to her room shortly before the first guests arrived.

After the cocktail hour Fanny led them into the dining-room and took her place at the head of the table. She pressed the buzzer at her foot, and there emerged from the serving-pantry one of the strangest sights to grace Hollywood since the days of Lon Chaney, Boris Karloff, and Bela Lugosi.

It was Polly. She wore a uniform, the white apron of which covered her thigh and buttock. Her bonnet hid her left ear. Her cheeks were inundated with rouge, her mouth was hidden behind lipstick, and her teeth were safe in

Fanny's bathroom upstairs. Her stockings sagged, and in
each hand she juggled a plate of soup.

She set one down before Cobina Wright, Sr., and another
before Lionel Atwill. The first was a victorious venture, the
second only seventy-five per cent successful, since one fourth
of the contents settled on the late Lionel Atwill's shirt front.

"Sorry, Buster," said Polly, and made for the kitchen.

Soon to reappear with two more plates of soup which she
deposited before two other diners with a cheery: "Helluva
night, isn't it?"

Fanny's guests, paragons of social graces all, leaped into
small talk with no less ferocity than a pack of hounds following a spoor, while the sound of a bottle being tipped in
the serving pantry was heard with the regularity of an artil-
lery barrage.

When at last Fanny led her guests to the barroom for
coffee and liqueurs, Polly appeared with a broom and dustpan and fell to her knees before one crowded sofa as she
began to sweep.

She scattered dust about her like a Model T Ford on a
country road. "Where were you raised?" she snarled at one
woman.

And: "Lift your feet, Mabel," to a second.

And: "Out of my way, gents," to several other guests.

"Thank you," Fanny said.

Polly looked up, pushing her bonnet back from her eyes.
"Huh?"

"You may go now," Fanny said sweetly.

"Okay," said Polly. She reached behind her to pull at her
girdle, raised the broom high, waved the dustpan, and said:
"So long, gang," as she left the room.

And with a vast sigh of relief, the guests relaxed.

Until Polly, who had rid herself of dustpan and broom,

and re-entered the barroom through a door in a far corner, raised a glass half full of brandy and began to sing: "God Bless America!"

In those days Fanny talked more and more of leaving money to the children. One day, when her oldest grandchild, Peter Stark, was visiting and making more noise than usual, she pointed a long finger at him.

"One more crack out of you, kid," she said, "and the dough goes to U.C.L.A."

About this time she wrote: "I wouldn't care as much about leaving money if I was a painter or a writer, but what do I leave when I go? I leave nothing. But the money really shows what I did in my life. It's kind of a proof that I did all right. I think the saving thing got very big with me when the children were born. If I never had any children, I might have been more careless with money. But there was nothing I wouldn't buy if I saw it and wanted it. I have never said to myself: 'I want that but I won't spend the money.' If I wanted it, I never cared for the cost of it."

If she had done nothing else in her life, Fanny's interior decorating during her Hollywood years would have earned her a secure spot in the artistic firmament. She was, now, more than a woman for whom house furnishing was a hobby; she had become a master craftsman and between her and the Beverly Hills decorators there were only two differences:

1. She would accept no fee.
2. She would accept no suggestions.

The question of payment was one she would not even discuss. Woe to the citizen who offered it. The problem of suggestion, however, was made clear to the "client" at the outset. Fanny would do the house, but Fanny would do it her way.

She was a woman possessed when she took over a decorating job. To Sam Jaffe, the Hollywood agent, she confided one night when he and his wife were visiting: "Your office looks like hell."

"Come fix it," he promptly replied.

"You got a deal," she said, and over her shoulder: "Kaye! Remind me tomorrow morning: we're going to Jaffe's office."

Twelve hours later the invasion had begun. Jaffe occupies a building on Sunset Boulevard. His clients are almost exclusively among the highest-priced people in show business, a group marked by constant traveling along the emotional roads of artistic temperament, most of it spent in Jaffe's office.

Jaffe, a high-domed, slender man, was accustomed to these forays, but the appearance of Fanny the following day was something he had never experienced before. She went through the floors and offices of his establishment like a swarm of locusts; noticing nobody, talking to nobody but Kaye, who followed with the tape measure, the pad, and the pencil. Then, as suddenly as she had appeared, she disappeared.

To return several hours later with a painter to whom she gave orders that could be heard in Santa Monica; with whom she left abruptly to return a second time with several swatches of fabric which she draped over Jaffe's chair while the latter held the telephone and tried to talk a producer into hiring one of his writers.

The furnishing of Jaffe's building took several weeks. When at last the painters and upholsterers and other craftsmen had departed, when new lamps, chairs, coffee tables, graced the premises, when some semblance of sanity had returned to his establishment, Jaffe came into the lobby one afternoon with a New York lawyer, and saw Fanny on her knees beside a table, trying to pull the carpet flat beneath it.

Knowing from long and bitter experience with her that it was the better part of valor not to offer even a hello, Jaffe passed her silently. But Fanny, in a burst of rare civility, said: "Hello, Sam," and continued pulling at the carpet.

Jaffe, loath to press his luck, just nodded at her and continued across the lobby. The lawyer tugged at his sleeve. "Who's that?" he asked.

"Who's who?" Jaffe countered, playing for time to be far enough removed from Fanny so that he might not be the victim of a sudden change of her heart.

"Who's that dame on her knees?"

"Oh, her," said Jaffe, opening the door of his office, and showing his guest inside, "that's Fanny Brice."

While Fanny never volunteered her services as a no-fee decorator, and usually complained of the number of homes and apartments waiting for her capable hands, she was as acutely conscious as a tigress of what she considered a betrayal of friendship. When Richard Haydn, the actor, bought a home in Pacific Palisades, Fanny waited patiently while he rebuilt the house to suit himself. Now and again she would listen to a progress report from him, but merely accepted the intelligences without comment.

"I wanted the house to be mine," Haydn explains, somewhat apologetically, "and I didn't care how it looked. If I wanted a chair here or a sofa there, I was going to put it here or there, and the devil with how it blended, or with groupings."

Haydn's home is a model of comfort and taste, although it might not pass the rigid tests of the decorating boys. Fanny, aware that Haydn was thus flouting their long friendship by not asking her to wear herself out furnishing his home, sulked in solitude and silence, showing the world— and Haydn—a stiff upper lip.

She even accepted an invitation to call on Haydn when at last the house was ready for visitors. "Very nice," she murmured, when he asked what she thought, and even sat down gingerly on one of the chairs, rigid and straight-backed as though touching something unclean.

"She *thought* she was not showing her hand, you know," Haydn remembers, "but she was boiling mad. She said not a word for six months until one night we were at a party together."

It was a party celebrating another house Fanny had just done. For hours she received the plaudits of the guests until, at a moment when she stood alone with Haydn, she leaned toward him and whispered: "You know you blank-ed *your* house up, don't you, kid?"

It became her standard greeting to Haydn. Never, whether in her house, or his house, or at some friend's to which they had gone together, would she let an evening escape without reminding him of the tragic error he had committed by furnishing his own house.

"You see," she wrote, "if I go to do somebody's house, I tell them this: 'I want you to know I am doing this for me, not for you! You can't have anything to say. I have to do it my way. If I want to use green, I want to use green.' If they say, 'I like pink better,' too damn bad. Green is my plan, and you have to have it that way. I always tell them before I start: you are leaving it all to me. It's the only way I could do it. If I did it their way, how the hell could it be any expression of *mine*?

"When I do someone's house, I always like to do it better if they have less money. It's a challenge. And I'd get such a kick out of it. I think that what brought that on out here [California] is that going in radio like I did, you never get that feeling that you are creating anything, and naturally I have to—something has to happen every day in creation with me.

"Now I have gone very modern with furnishing. I believe in the modern. I'll tell you why modern is right: when you do an early American house, what makes it is all those little knick-knacks and those cute little things. That makes it warm. In a modern house you have very few pieces, but very large. In an early American it's all hanging shelves and spinning wheels and quaint goddam things.

"And if you go to clear this room, it takes you three or four hours to dust everything. In a modern house, you can even eliminate a servant. You can dust it off and in two minutes it's clean.

"You don't have those damn drapes that are interlined. The interlining and the lining hold the odor of the house, of the cooking. When I took the drapes down in my barroom, the room was four feet larger. They close in a room. Every building they're building now is modern. Everything will be modern. It is very practical and very wonderful.

"I like to make good buys. Not for myself. I mean when I am buying for someone, I keep saying: 'Look at this! Two dollars!' I love to say how little it cost. I did Danny Kaye's house. And I went to a little place where they build furniture for me. I design it. I did a lot of designing for them free. With Danny Kaye's house, I took a tortoise-shell cigarette box to this finisher there. And I said: 'I want you to finish in lacquer with this tortoise-shell finish.' I was in there with the finisher five hours. Finding out how to do it, because of course I have a need to know everything about anything I do. We'd put the mottling on, and then tip the table to let it run. Let that dry, then lacquer it. Well, they (the Kayes) have a seven-foot long table about twenty-four inches wide and thirteen inches off the floor. The whole table cost eighty dollars with the finishing and everything.

"I like to buy an old sewing-machine with iron legs. You take the two sides, and just get this nice, thick piece of bleached wood, and make a long table. And I like it not costing anything much. I don't know whether anyone remembers, but in old ice cream parlors there were tables that had a center column that was iron. You get two of those, with a slab of bleached wood, and there is a beautiful table. That's what I get a kick out of doing. To create something myself. To go and buy a lamp that is made up—no kick. I did some lamps for the Kayes. I got those big crockery jars that have a glaze on them, they were three dollars each. And I got raw silk to match that, and had the lampshades made."

When she was not busy with someone's house, she was somewhere in the Los Angeles metropolitan area, hunting for buys. A friend remembers accompanying her one afternoon to a kind of cheap auction shop. In a bookcase Fanny saw several stacks of china. "It's good," she whispered to her friend, and waited until the owner of the shop appeared beside them.

"What kind of funny-looking stuff is this?" Fanny asked.

"Who knows?" he shrugged. "Some kind of crazy stuff."

"Boy, you'd have to be nuts to put food on that, wouldn't you?" Fanny asked him.

"Well," said the owner, "it's according to taste. Now my wife could like such stuff, but I already got her beautiful white china. Do you like it, lady?"

"Me? I hate the stuff."

"I could give you cheap prices on that junk," the owner offered.

"You couldn't give it to me altogether," Fanny replied. "Who wants it?"

Fanny started to walk away, but the owner said: "Lady, lady, just a minute. Is there a fire somewhere? Stay a minute," he insisted, counting the china, taking it out of the bookcase and stacking it. He counted fifty-seven pieces. "Have you got a patio, lady?" he asked Fanny.

"Yes," said Fanny, who had a huge terrace looking out on the swimming-pool. "I've got a kind of patio."

"This would go very nice on the patio, lady."

"Sure," Fanny said. "If you're blind."

"How much?"

"How much what?"

"How much do you offer?" the owner asked.

"Not me."

"Give me an offer."

"I don't want it," Fanny said.

"I'll give *you* an offer. A dollar a piece and take it away for fifty-seven dollars. For fifty-five dollars."

"Not me."

"Seventy-five cents. Lady, you couldn't buy in the dime store china that cheap."

"But it would be clean," Fanny reminded him.

"Take it for fifty cents apiece."

"I don't know. I'll give you a quarter."

"For a quarter I'll put it on *my* patio."

Fanny bought the fifty-seven pieces for fifty cents apiece. The next day she took one plate to a dealer on La Cienega Boulevard. "I'll give you twenty-five dollars each for these plates," he told her.

Fanny wrote: "When I met Johnny Schwartz (who is now one of Hollywood's topflight decorators), he was selling damask, and doing curtains for synagogues. Just a little business. And I said to him: 'I want you to get me some provincial prints.'

"He said: 'Provincial prints?' and looked at me like I was crazy.

"I said: 'Just go to the wholesale house, get all the samples of provincial prints—American, French—and bring me the samples.'

"So he goes and brings them and he says to me: 'What do you want with this? It's cotton!'

"I said: 'I like cotton.' And I explained to him about decorating, about *feeling* what is right, about how one thing will
clash with another thing, and a second thing won't clash. I
changed his whole life."

Schwartz agrees. He is a stocky little man of about sixty
whose regard for Fanny is not unlike an Indian's for Gandhi.
"She built me a forty-thousand-dollar home," he says flatly.
And nodding for emphasis, says: "She did it through the
people she got for my clients. Right now I am doing a house
for Spencer Tracy.

"When she asked me for provincial prints, I was in the
racket thirty-seven years already and never even heard of
them.

"Every place she furnished, she got me the business. I'd
walk upstairs into her bedroom like I'd walk into my own
home. If I came in around noon, she'd take me down to the
kitchen and cook me lunch. I'd say: 'Fanny, there is a cook
and a butler.'

" 'To hell with them,' she would say. 'I want to cook you
lunch.'

"I would take a look at her," Schwartz remembers, "and I'd
see in a minute whether she was in a mood to talk business.
If she wasn't, I'd say: 'I got an appointment. I have to leave,'
and I'd have no place to go. If I stayed and she didn't want
to talk business, she would tell the story of her life. I knew
that woman like I know my ten fingers.

"Many times she would say: 'Johnny, how's business?'

" 'More than I can handle,' I would tell her, which was the
God's honest truth.

" 'Wonderful, Johnny, wonderful,' she would say.

" 'You did it, Fanny. You gave me the chance to prove myself,' I would tell her.

" 'You're crazy,' she would tell me.

"Four years ago I built a home, and after it was done I took her up there. She loved it. 'It's all thanks to you, Fanny,' I told her.

"She didn't want to hear that or have any credit for it.

"When we went to a wholesale house, she would act like a poor woman, like a person who didn't know where their next bite of bread was coming from, to get it cheaper for the clients. She would say: 'Johnny, it's too much. We got to cut.'

"I would say: 'Fanny, you cut.' "

While Fanny was proclaiming to all who asked for her services that they had nothing to say about how their own homes should look once she went to work, she was particularly closemouthed about another condition she imposed: that any gifts she bought for the house must be accepted without thanks.

Invariably, when someone whose house she was doing was at last permitted to see it, he or she would find there something that did not appear on the bills. In the case of Phil Weltman, who was the William Morris office's liaison with Fanny in the last years of her life, she ordered at wholesale a sofa costing a hundred dollars, for which she would not let Weltman pay.

Then, after a tortured week during which she was plagued by the thought that Weltman, a bachelor, would be entertaining guests with the flatware he owned, of which she distinctly disapproved, she ordered a complete set of stainless steel cutlery, to round out what she considered a job well done.

Weltman returned to his apartment late one afternoon to discover Fanny arranging his table for a dinner to which he had invited no guests. Helping her was Phil's houseman, whose aid and loyalty she had enlisted during her first visit to the apartment.

"How do you like it, kid?" Fanny asked, stepping back from the table and beaming at the flatware.

Weltman, whose bachelor's psyche rebeled at such possessions, managed a faint smile. "Looks fine, Fanny," he said.

"It's yours," Fanny said abruptly. She asked the houseman for her coat.

Meanwhile Weltman, who had served Fanny loyally for four years as buffer, and complaint department, made bold to ask: "How much is that set, Fanny?"

Fanny whirled, confronting him in sudden anger. "What business is it of yours?"

Weltman shrugged and rubbed one hand in the other. He backed away. He perspired. He ran his tongue over his lips. To this point their decorator-client relationship had been a placid one. He had no wish to evoke a display of the Brice temper now. "All right," he said to himself, "so I'll pay for the silver and be done with it. All right," he continued to himself, "I just don't want trouble with her."

"Nothing, Fanny," he said, standing still at last behind the table, protected by distance, if nothing else. "It's none of my business, Fanny."

"Then don't ask stupid questions," Fanny said. "Somebody buys you a present, it's none of your business what it cost," and smiled at the houseman, who escorted her to the door, bowing her out.

For several moments Weltman was too shaken to move. After the sofa, after the change she had wrought in his apartment, he had been pondering for days the choice of a suitable gift for *her*. That she might buy him another present had never occurred to him.

"She never let me talk about it," Weltman remembers. "I'd come to see her often, as much because I wanted to as for business. But I couldn't talk about the silver, or the sofa, or the apartment, except to say I liked it. She wanted to hear that, all right: that I was enjoying the apartment, but nothing else.

"Then, a few weeks after she died, I got tired of some plants she'd brought into the apartment. One morning I told my houseman to get rid of them. That night when I got home I saw the plants.

"The next morning I said to my houseman: 'Didn't I tell you to get rid of those plants?'

" 'Yes, sir.'

" 'Well, why didn't you get rid of them?'

" 'Can't get rid of *them* plants, Mr. Weltman.'

" 'Why can't I? Is there a law? What do you mean I can't get rid of those plants?'

" 'Miss Brice put them plants there, Mr. Weltman. I'm not moving any plants Miss Brice set up. Not me. *No*, sir.'

"Those plants are still where she put them," Weltman reports. "He won't do anything but water them every morning, and I'll be blessed if I'll move them."

Even in death, as the poets say. Even after she was gone, nobody dared tamper with Fanny's groupings.

☼ 23 ☼

NICK ARNSTEIN: *"A Variable*
Oriental Fairy-Land."

THREE months after the death of his last wife, on New
Year's Day, 1950, Nick Arnstein telephoned Fanny and
made an appointment to call on her.

As Fanny hung up on Nick she said excitedly: "Kaye!"

And picked up the telephone to call Frances.

She reached for a cigarette while she dialed, trying to
strike a match, with her elbow holding the telephone stationary and her head cocked to keep the receiver in place as
Kaye Brewer entered.

"What is it, Fanny?" Kaye asked.

Frances said: "Hello."

Fanny dropped the unlit match.

"Fran?" Fanny said. "Hold on."

"Nick called," she said to Kaye. "He's coming over tomorrow afternoon."

"Here?" Kaye asked, for she had heard about Nick often
since entering Fanny's service.

"Right here, in this room," Fanny said. "Give me a match,
kid," and to Frances: "Your father just called me."

"Nick?" Frances asked.

Fanny leaned forward to accept the light from Kaye. "Yes, Nick," Fanny said. "Coming here tomorrow. 'Bye, kid, I'm busy." She hung up on her daughter.

"Get Edna Cantor for me," Fanny said, shoving the telephone at Kaye. "How do you like that?" Fanny asked, as Kaye started to dial. "What the hell does he want? He has something on his mind. He is not just making a . . . give me that telephone," seizing the instrument.

"Edna! One guess who's coming over tomorrow. *Who?* Who do you think? Nick! Yeah, here. Wait a minute, kid." She pressed the receiver to her bosom.

"Kaye!" Fanny shouted at the nurse beside her. "Where's Bill?"

"I suppose he's in the studio, painting," Kaye said.

"Get him. Don't tell him why. Just tell him I want to see him right away. Yeah, now." She turned away from Kaye, moving the receiver to her ear.

"Well, Edna," she said, "and how do you like it? I don't know what he wants. I'll call you later, 'bye."

She hung up on Edna, and dialed Frances Lastfogel, the wife of the William Morris Agency head, at the Beverly-Wilshire Hotel.

But hung up almost immediately, before talking to Frances Lastfogel, as her son entered the room. "Nick called," she said to Bill. He nodded as though she had told him the menu for dinner.

By nightfall Fanny, who had become as secretive about her private life as a newscaster is about the day's events, had told everyone she knew of Nick's scheduled visit.

Meanwhile ordering her hairdresser and manicurist to appear at the house on the following day.

Fanny had an early dinner and took to her bed, propping herself up on three pillows and summoning people to come and talk to her. Long after midnight, with Kaye asleep, with several hours of wakefulness before her, Fanny telephoned Eddie Cantor.

When the phone rang, Cantor quickly took the receiver from the cradle so the bell would not wake Ida. He whispered: "Hello," and Fanny said: "Eddie? Fanny."

"What is it, Fanny?"

"Can you come right over, Eddie?"

"What's the matter, Fanny?" asked Cantor. "What's wrong?"

"Eddie, please come over. Don't ask questions. I have to see you."

"I'm on my way," Cantor told his old friend, replacing the receiver in the darkness and groping his way out of the bedroom. He pulled pants over his pajamas, found a tweed jacket which he got into as he ran, and flung the garage doors open.

As he sped toward Fanny's house, Cantor saw her in her terrible trouble, and running across the lawn, pushing open the door and leaving it open, taking the steps two and three at a time, he came at last to Fanny's room, where he found her high up in the bed, her hands atop the covers, her eyes wide with pleasure, and her face smiling at him as she smoothed the blankets beside her.

"Tell me something," she said.

Cantor collapsed. He fell down on the bed. He tore at his hair. He pressed the palms of his hands against his face and moved his fingers slowly to his chin. Holding his face thus, he shook his head back and forth, back and forth, while Fanny waited patiently.

Then: "Are you crazy, Fanny?"

She watched him affectionately.

"Fanny, have you lost your mind altogether?"

She giggled.

He extended his hand, fingers together, pointing at the floor. "Calls me three o'clock in the morning. I'm just falling asleep," extending his other hand. "What should I think? I think you're dying, God forbid. I think maybe you had news that . . ."

"Nick's coming tomorrow," Fanny said.

"I *know* Nick's coming tomorrow," Eddie said. "So what is it with you? Do you have to scare me half to death? Look at me, Fanny, I'm shaking like a leaf," offering his hands for inspection, but Fanny lit a cigarette.

"You remember that time in Cleveland, kid?" she asked.

Cantor rose. "I'm going home," he announced.

"When I wouldn't let you and Bill Fields eat on the diner?" she asked.

"You shouldn't call people this hour of the night, Fanny," Cantor said, taking a stride toward the door.

"And the spaghetti I made," Fanny said as Cantor stopped, stood motionless with his back to his hostess, and turned to face her finally, the smile spreading over his face.

"I never believed you, and I don't believe you to this day," he said, sitting down on the chair beside her bed.

Fanny raised her right hand. "May I be struck dead this minute," she said, "if I did it on purpose."

What they remembered, sitting together in the middle of the night, was the tour of the Follies of 1918. They were a few hours out of Cleveland when W. C. Fields and Cantor decided to have dinner. Passing Fanny's compartment, they invited her to join them. "Wait until we get to the hotel," Fanny said. "I'll make us something in the room."

"Why can't we eat here?" Cantor asked.

"Will you do what I say?" Fanny asked. "Why should you spend good money on the train? Let me make dinner."

"I'm starving," Cantor protested.

"Here, have a mint to tide you over," Fanny suggested.

The train was an hour late. It was after nine o'clock when they reached the hotel and rendezvoused in Fanny's room. When at last she appeared with three plates of spaghetti, the trio fell to like kids at a bean feed.

And very nearly began foaming at the mouth.

Fanny's maid had somehow sprinkled soap flakes on the spaghetti, mistaking them for cheese. In her bedroom half a continent and thirty-two years later, Cantor could not yet understand how anyone could make such an error. So these two old, old friends sat talking while the night faded away into a thousand memories, and the years left them both; for a few fast hours they were young, looking ahead to life.

She let Cantor go home with the morning sun, and slept fitfully for a few hours. Fanny remained upstairs all morning, eating nothing except a piece of toast, which she washed down with several cups of coffee. When at last the doorbell sounded through the house, Kaye went to welcome Fanny's guest.

"I am Mr. Arnold," Nick said, using the name by which his California friends knew him.

"Please come in, Mr. Arnold," Kaye said. As Nick stepped across the threshold Kaye said: "Will you wait in the barroom, Mr. Arnold? Miss Brice will be down in a moment."

"I wait for nobody," Nick said. "Kings and queens have waited for me."

Kaye said nothing. She showed him to the barroom and left him there, going upstairs to summon Fanny.

Fanny came into the barroom quietly, so that she saw him before he saw her. She stood for a moment looking at the back she knew so well, at the neck she knew so well, at the slope of his shoulders which she had never forgotten, at his well-shined shoes hiding the shapely feet that she had admired. She was in her fifty-eighth year that day and her once-husband was in his seventieth year, but the sight of him could still move her.

"Hello, Nick."

"Fanny, Fanny, Fanny," Nick said, taking her hands in his hands and bending his head to kiss her.

Nick kissed her, and she kissed him. There was in the kiss the clear, never-forgotten memory of two people who had lived through more than most; who had shared in love, in anger, in jealousy, in laughter, in sorrow and quarrels and tears those years which were the most important part of their lives.

"How do you feel, Fanny?" Nick asked. "I heard that you were ill," he said, following her across the room and sitting in the easy chair to which she gestured. She sat on the sofa, which rested at right angles to the chair.

"I'm all right, Nick. How are you?"

"Fine, Fanny, fine, thank you. Never better," he said, hooking a thumb in his vest pocket.

"You look wonderful, Nick," she said.

"*Feel* wonderful, old girl," he said, patting his flat stomach. "Been keeping busy, have you, Fanny?"

"Ah," she said, "it's too much. Running around all the time."

They continued thus until Nick said: "You know, Fanny, my wife died on New Year's Day."

"I *didn't* know that, Nick," Fanny said. The concern she showed him was real concern. "I'm awfully sorry to hear that, Nick."

"Yes," he said, "she's gone. She was a fine woman, Fanny. I spent twenty-five happy years with that woman. I learned things; many, many things. I've changed a great deal since the old days in New York. I don't think I've held a deck of cards in my hand for nearly twenty-five years. Now there's something that's hard to believe, isn't it?" he asked, and wouldn't wait for an answer. "Perhaps it was the kind of life my wife and I had here in this land of *mañana*."

"The Arnstein residence was located in Pasadena; a gorgeous estate, beautifully landscaped; several fountains and a spray pool adorned the formal Oriental garden," Nick wrote in his autobiography. "The former owner had travelled extensively through the Orient, and loved Japan. The Japanese Tea House in a corner of the spacious grounds had been imported in sections from Japan, and the miniature garden surrounding the pagoda was quite authentic in detail; the beauty of the spot often intrigued the curious to wander at will through the grounds.

"Nicky learned," Nick continued in his autobiography, "that many important and distinguished Nipponese had been entertained in this unique summer-house in the past. Frequently, the entire grounds had been turned into a variable [sic] Oriental fairy-land for some garden party or lavish entertainment."

In Fanny's barroom Nick was silent for a moment.

"That house is gone," he said heavily. "My wife is gone. Many things are gone. Where have the years gone, Fanny?" he asked, as she watched him carefully.

"I'm alone now," he said.

Fanny was silent.

"Alone," he repeated. "You know, Fanny, when I was a young man, long before you and I met, I was often alone. I liked the lonely road and chose it in preference to traveling with the pack. I've made I don't know how many ocean crossings without a companion, spending the days at sea by myself. I've lived in hotels for months at a time, moving among strangers, content to speak to no one. I can't do it any more." He shook his head. "Can't do it any more."

"Can I get you a drink, Nick?" Fanny asked.

"That would be fine, Fanny. Brandy . . ."

". . . and soda," she said, and went to the bar. She made him his drink, remembering how much brandy and how much fizz, and she brought it to him. He was standing when she returned from the bar and he waited until she sat down before he sat down.

He drank slowly, waiting for Fanny to speak, who waited for Nick to continue.

"This is a beautiful home, Fanny," Nick said, looking about him, holding the glass in his right hand. "You've done a magnificent job with it."

"Thanks, Nick. I like it."

"It's a long way from the Albany in New York, old girl, isn't it?"

"Yes."

He chuckled. "Do you remember how that place was furnished?" he asked.

"Sure."

"We fixed *that,* didn't we, Fanny?"

"You fixed it, Nick," she reminded him.

"So I did. So I did." He rose suddenly. "I'm afraid I must be running along. It's been wonderful seeing you, my dear. I am most grateful to you, Fanny, for having me."

And Nick left.

Bill Brice found his mother slouched deep in the chair Nick had vacated, her long legs stretched out before her, and her elbows resting on the chair arms. Fanny did not turn to see who had entered. "I told you he wanted something," she said. "His wife is dead, Bill."

"I'm sorry . . ."

"He's looking around to get married."

"Maybe he just dropped in to say hello," Bill said.

"Not Nick," Fanny said. "Don't tell me about Nick." She waited until Bill sat down in the chair opposite her. "I know Nick," she declared.

"Of course you do," Bill assured her.

She nodded. "He figures he'll just step in now and take over," Fanny said.

"How do you know that, Mother?" Bill asked.

"I know it," she said. "I don't know how I know it. I just know it."

Nick telephoned ten days later and asked Fanny to go to dinner with him that evening. He arrived as dusk was falling over a splendid southern California day, walking to the door with a bounce that belied his years. He was wearing a double-breasted blue suit and a white shirt, and the knot of his handsome tie was geometrically perfect. When Fanny opened the door for him, he held his broad-brimmed gray fedora in his left hand and a box of candy in his right.

"This is for you, Fanny," he said, offering the candy.

"Thanks, Nick." Fanny opened the box, and after Nick had refused a sweet, she munched happily on a nougat.

"You'll spoil your dinner, Fanny," he warned.

"Not me," she declared.

Nick helped her on with her coat and led her out to his car, a gleaming new convertible. He made her comfortable and as he got in behind the wheel, asked: "How do you like it, Fanny?"

Fanny, who could not recognize her own automobile on the street, said: "Gee, it's a swell car, Nick."

"Bought it last week," Nick said, as they drove away from Fanny's house. "Mine was in need of work and I felt the urge for a change. I drove it into a garage and walked out on the sales floor. There sat this convertible. I liked it right off and bought it, paying cash."

"That's swell, Nick."

"Where would you prefer to dine?" Nick asked.

"There's a Chinese place on Sunset Boulevard I like,"

Fanny said, mentioning a restaurant where she was certain none of the Hollywood hierarchy would see her.

"You're the captain of my fate, little lady," Nick said. "I'm the mate taking orders." He waited for her reaction. Then: "You know, Fanny, I'm in the shipping business now. Oh, yes. A ship is tied up at Long Beach being fitted as a banana carrier. I'm looking for big things to come from this venture of mine, Fanny."

It was an old, old song, and Fanny knew the words very, very well. Big things were to have come from his shirt factory more than a quarter of a century ago. From the shirt factory, from the advertising business, from the casino in Chicago, from all the various ventures she had witnessed and paid for.

"That's wonderful, Nick," Fanny said, thinking now of spare ribs and egg roll and chow mein. "It sounds swell, Nick."

"Yes, Fanny," he said, as they crossed town to the bright-lights boulevards, "I think that Lady Fortune is going to smile at me finally. It's about time, isn't it, my dear?"

"Sure, Nick."

"You sound a touch pensive, old girl," Nick said. "Remembering the old days, are you? Other times and other towns and that first trip we took to England? Weren't those the times, Fanny? Didn't we have . . ."

"I'm hungry."

Nick chewed his lip. After a moment he said: "Well, we can certainly remedy that, Fanny. I'll just put the heat on this runabout."

In the parking-lot beside the restaurant Nick handed the attendant a dollar. "Keep an eye on her," he ordered, nodding at the convertible. "She's brand new, you know."

"I'll watch it," the attendant promised.

"Do that, my boy, do that," Nick said, dismissing the man

and taking Fanny's arm. He escorted her into the chow mein place as if it were Rector's, pausing briefly inside the doors to survey the rows of booths flanking both walls of the establishment. He gave orders to the Chinese waiter as if that chop suey specialist had served the crowned heads of three continents. He left instructions not to be disturbed as if he and Fanny were the cynosure of all the eyes and all the ears in the restaurant. He demanded cocktails, and when he was told there was no liquor served he demanded wine. When he was told no wine was served he demanded—and got—beer, pouring the amber fluid with the careful care devoted to the most delicate vintages.

Holding the menu with one hand, he adjusted his pince-nez with the other. He ordered dinner slowly, pausing after the selection of each dish to counsel the waiter regarding its preparation.

Watching him, Fanny said to herself: "Look at the old faker. He's still handsome, with the glasses and the deep voice, and the beautiful hands. As she wrote later: "Nick didn't change at all. He was still the same Nick. He was old, but he was good-looking old, just like he had been good-looking young."

When the waiter was gone, Nick sipped the beer appreciatively. He set the glass down to light Fanny's cigarette and he said: "Just you and me, Fanny."

"Yeah."

"Fanny, I've been thinking about us."

"Oh."

"I've been thinking that we're two lonely people in this bitter world."

"I'm not alone, Nick. I've got my kids."

He seemed not to have heard. "Why should we live alone, Fanny, you and I? We've only got a few years left to us, you know."

Taking a grip on herself, an unprecedented move, Fanny said calmly: "Now, Nick, forget it. We're not getting together. Nick, I know you too long and too well."

"Why, Fanny, what are you talking—?"

"Stop it, Nick."

He looked out into the restaurant. He pulled at his mustache. He laced his fingers. He nodded. "How is Bill's painting coming along, Fanny?" he asked.

Fanny leaned forward eagerly. "Just fine, Nick. He's working hard and he's been offered a teaching job."

Nick devoted himself to the soup that was placed before him. They finished their dinner. As they sipped their final cups of tea, Nick said: "What would you like to do now, Fanny?"

"I don't want to do anything, Nick," she replied.

"How about a film, my dear?"

"I don't care."

"Perhaps we could find something good."

"If you want to go, Nick, I'll go."

He gestured for the waiter, paid the check, and accepted the change without counting it, leaving a large tip, after which he escorted Fanny to the movies.

Driving home in the cool, clear California night, they were silent. Nick whistled aimlessly and Fanny sat quietly, her head back against the leather cushions, feeling the wind on her face and thinking, now on this lovely, lovely evening thirty-eight years after walking into Nick's Baltimore hotel suite, of nothing—not of him, not of herself, not of her children, not of the years alone with her children—but lulled into utter relaxation.

As they entered Beverly Hills and Nick turned into a darkened street, they seemed for a few moments to be driving in a world where those two were the only people alive, where they had been thrust together here in his convertible with its newness smelling unmistakably, with the canvas top creating a warm, safe sanctuary against all who threatened their peace and safety on the outside.

Nick turned into the drive before Fanny's house and sat back in the seat. She reached for the door handle and Nick said: "Don't go."

Nick said: "There's no hurry, Fanny."

"Can't we talk, Fanny?" Nick said.

"Sure, Nick. Talk about what, Nick?"

"About you and me, my dear. About . . ."

"There is nothing to talk about, Nick."

"Couldn't we make a go of it once more, my dear?"

Fanny reached for the door handle. She pressed down on the door handle, and Nick said: "I've learned, Fanny. Believe me, old girl, I'm a different man."

"No, you're not," she said, and the door swung open.

"I am, Fanny. I swear I am."

"All right," she said, wearily and finally. "You're a different man. I'm a different woman. I'm tired, Nick. I'm going."

"Fanny!" he cried.

And she turned to look at him. He was facing her and his hat was in his hand. His hair was thin and gray. His shoulders were slightly stooped, and his skin was wrinkled, and he was seventy years old.

Seventy years old and not different at all.

He waited while she studied him and then she put her purse under her arm. She didn't shake her head. She didn't sigh. She didn't say: "I'm sorry," or: "Forget it, Nick," or: "What's the use?" or: "It's too late."

She said: "Good night, Nick," and left him.

Alone in his shiny new convertible with his hat in his hand.

Nick called the next morning. He telephoned early. He said it was urgent and the maid, who could take orders like a Kamikaze pilot, disobeyed her mistress' order that she was never to be awakened. The maid woke Fanny and said it was Mr. Arnold.

"Nick?" Fanny said sleepily.

"Mr. Arnold, Miss Brice. He said it was urgent."

"Urgent?" Fanny said, and she was no longer sleepy.

"That's was he said, Miss Brice."

"Yes, indeed," Fanny said, and she lay back against the pillows. "Urgent," she repeated, and turned to the maid. "Tell Mr. Arnold I'm not in."

The maid started to leave, but Fanny stopped her. "From now on I'm never in when he calls," she said.

"Yes, Miss Brice."

"Tell the others," Fanny said.

"Yes, Miss Brice," the maid said, and left the room.

She left Fanny in the half-dark room.

Alone and finished with Nick.

Finally and for the last time. For the last time in her life.

✳ 24 ✳

FANNY: *"We See the Funny
Side of Everything."*

===

S HE died on May 29, 1951, five days after a cerebral hem-
orrhage had struck her. A few weeks earlier Fanny Brice
had written:

"I have noticed something about comedians. I have always found them the most honest people. We see the funny
side of everything. We are not sensitive. If we have a fault,
we are the first to point it out.

"And I went out to honest people wherever I found them.
If they were not chi-chi or phony, then I liked them for that.
It could be anyone: a butler or society. Once I went to a
party here [in Hollywood] and Sir Charles Mendl was there.
He was very, very old; white hair and thin. I don't think I
ever knew anybody as old as Sir Charles. And when I saw
him, I hadn't seen him for a long time, so when I saw him,
I grabbed him and I said: 'Charles, you look wonderful.
How do you keep yourself looking like that?'

"And he twirled his mustache and looked me straight in
the eye.

" 'Blank-ing, my dear Fanny,' he said. 'Blank-ing.'

"I always tried to be true to myself, not to fool myself by thinking I was something else than what I was. I remember after I had the detectives following Nick and they reported that he was seeing this woman, and I told him I knew about this woman, well, he started to pack. This was in New York before the divorce, but the beginning of the end with Nick.

"I was on the chaise lounge and he was packing. He was packing awfully slow. Stalling. I was watching. I thought of a tortoise-shell comb in the bathroom. I liked that comb better than any other comb. And it was Nick's favorite comb.

"I said to myself: 'I hope he is not going to take that comb.'

"He was folding shirts into his suitcase. I got up and went into the bathroom. I closed the door. I got the comb and put it under the mat. After he left that night, I thought: 'If you really loved him, why did you think of that comb?' I don't know why I thought of it. I could never figure it out. I never saw Nick again without thinking of it, that comb. And it is upstairs right now. All those years and I'm still using the same comb.

"When I think back, I know I was the same person at all times. Right from the beginning, from the minute I could think, I know my brain worked the same way and I wanted the same things. And I was never ashamed of myself. I was practically raised in a saloon, and I never had any feeling about that. I guess I knew it was better to be honest. If you are honest, it makes the sailing so much easier. The most dangerous thing in the world is not to be honest. I think you can only get in trouble. You are either something or you are not. When I came to Broadway and was meeting all those people; society people, royalty, and the like, I never thought to myself: 'Gee, kid, you are really there now. You are with the important people now.' I never said that. I never thought it. Money never impressed me if there wasn't the person to go with it.

"If I am passing a beggar, and you know when you pass a beggar you look for the smallest change you have, it's natural; so if I stop in front of a beggar and I see there is nothing smaller than fifty cents in my purse, I'll stop in front of him and watch his face. I want to see that smile when he gets the four bits. But if I am putting a few pennies in, I just put it in quick and keep walking.

"And with honesty goes another thing: that you don't like things in people that you don't like in yourself. If someone comes in, lays down, and puts their feet on a nice clean couch, I don't like that: whether it's my couch or somebody else's couch. I couldn't do that. If I want to lay on the couch at somebody's house, I would take my shoes off. I hate anyone who has no regard for that, who dismisses you like that. I hate the word 'hate.' Every time I say that word I say to myself: 'Don't use that word. Use "dislike."' I'm always conscious of using that word. It jars me. If you wanted to ask me: 'Is there anybody that you hate?' I'd say: 'No. There is nobody that I hate.' I never hated Nick, with all I went through. Maybe having children with a man would have something to do with that. When I think about Nick, I am still glad that he is the father of my children. I wouldn't want anyone to have been their father but Nick.

"I know I feel that way because there was really nothing bad in Nick at all. I can only say he was just a fool. He had such courage and such strength at the right time, like when he had to go to jail. There was no breaking down. He wasn't sorry for himself, or pitying himself. I didn't hear a word out of him about that. He never greeted me in the jail without a smile and a big hello. And I liked that, how he took it. That is the mark of a man, I think. But with other things, he wasn't good, I guess.

"I have always been embarrassed discussing sex. If you will talk to a comic, you will find out that comedians and comediennes all feel the same way about sex. There are two things you can't really be funny about. They are sex and religion. If you can talk about sex easily, then your feelings aren't very profound about it.

"And what makes me know I am very self-conscious about sex is that once I did a strip-tease dame on the stage. I found I couldn't get out on that stage and do it unless I took a big drink of whisky first. I can really do hot dancing, but I could never do it on the stage when it had something to do with sex. If anybody talks about their sex life, I laugh and listen—fine. But if I am also in the conversation I can only say something funny about sex with me. I couldn't seriously talk about my sex life with anybody. I can't, that's all.

"Another thing: there has always been two people within me: the Fanny that's in action and the Fanny that's looking at her. Almost like a mother and child. I have felt like I was my own mother, and when I would think about Fanny I would always think about myself as a child. There were always two people: the mother and the child. I am the mother of Fanny and Fanny is the child.

"Being a funny person does an awful lot of things to you. You feel that you must never get serious with people. They don't expect it and they won't take it from you. You are not entitled to be serious. You are a clown. And maybe that is what made me dislike emotion. Once I cried in the movies and I covered my face and bent my head. I admired the Chinese all my life because they would never show any feeling.

"Years ago I was playing San Francisco and went to dinner at somebody's house, and they had Chinese help. And I thought the help were just wonderful. So I went to an employment agency and hired three Chinese and paid their fare to New York. And I wired my secretary to get rid of the servants because these three were coming. When I got

back, four or five weeks later, the chef was the head guy of
the three. And whenever I wanted one of them to do something, I had to go through the chef. So I thought: 'You're
paying these blanks and you have to ask *permission*? Out!'

"When I am in a hotel, in a suite of rooms, now you know
I am not paying for the lights, I have to put out every light
before I leave. If I take a bath, and use a nice, lovely, clean,
Turkish towel, I'll fold it up and put it back the way it was.
That towel is clean. I can use it once more. In my own bathroom I never use guest towels. I have them hanging there,
but right in my shower behind the curtain, I have a Turkish
towel. If I come in and see someone has used the guest towels, it annoys me. If they are friends of mine, I tell them. I
say: 'If you want to dry your hands, kid, there's a towel in
the shower.'

"I don't think making money affected me at all. At one
time I was making eighty-five hundred dollars a week, doing
four shows a day at the moving-picture houses, for eight
weeks, and all I could eat was celery and carrots, so what
the hell did the money mean? I saved it, but I can honestly
say it wasn't me. I was always smart enough to surround myself with smart people. They knew what I didn't know. I was
never paid in cash. I never saw a cent. The check was given
to my secretary or my business manager and deposited. I'll
bet nobody in the world will believe this, but at any time in
my life, if anybody asked me: 'How much money have you
got?' I couldn't tell them. I get a monthly statement from
my business manager and my secretary in New York sends
me a statement of my affairs every six months. I never look
at it. I never said: 'Oh, I'll see how much I'm worth.' I never
wanted to know, and I don't know to this day.

"And I find now that I am thinking of the old, old times.
I am thinking more and more of when I was a real small
kid. When we lived on the East Side, my nickname was

'Blank-Behind-the-Coal-Box.' And the reason for that is that there was a store and the name of the store was Stafford's. They had a coal box in front of the store. The top would open and people would buy coal from them. And once when I really had to go and I was too lazy to go home, I lifted the top of the coal box. The kids knew about it, and that was my nickname.

"And on the boat, when my mother took us to Europe, that first time, I used to beg oranges. There was a staircase going up to another deck and one day I saw a woman sitting there eating an orange. I wanted an orange. I stood there looking at her. I don't know how I looked, but she gave me an orange. And every day she would give me something, because I would just stand there until she did.

"Now, here is something. On the boat, I remember somebody gave me a doll. A broken doll. And I took it to bed with me. But it was stolen in two days. Now that is probably fifty years ago, but here is a funny thing: I miss that doll. I couldn't remember people's names that I met yesterday, but I can describe that doll to you from head to foot. And I will tell you another funny thing: I still want that doll. Now what does that mean?

"Next door to the saloon in Newark, there was a furniture store. When the owner would get his Christmas stock in, he didn't have enough room. And he rented my mother's attic. And he put all those children's toys: little tables and things, up there. When I saw that stuff going into the attic, I shook like a leaf. Because I knew a way to get into the attic. And I would go up and play with all this children's furniture. One day, I was running up the steps and the point of a table was sticking out and it stuck in my forehead. There is still a scar there. I put a big hole in my head. I know my mother beat the hell out of me. I was *never* to go up there again. *Never.* So what happened? So—the next day I'm up there.

All my life it was like that: I didn't like when anybody told me what to do.

"In the Follies showgirls were not popular until they had a millionaire. They only became big with the public when they were being kept by some guy on Wall Street. The showgirl who had the richest man could get more money in the show. And of course when they got popular, that would make them popular with these rich guys too; so they would leave a sucker with five million dollars for one with maybe ten million dollars. Funny the way it worked back and forth. But very few of them finished with a family and a happy life.

"In 1917 I was around with Peggy Hopkins Joyce. I flew around with her because she was very amusing to me. We went to the races one day in my electric car. And on the way to the track it started to run out of juice. I'm driving and I'm saying, 'God is love, God is love,' and the car goes a little further each time. Finally I see this electric garage, where you took your car and they would recharge it. We left the electric and got to the track, taking a taxi. And at that track we met Arnold Rothstein. So when he saw Peggy, he starts out being very much of a personality. And Peggy said: 'Oh, dear, if I could get just enough money to buy a Stutz sport car. I wish I could win enough money to buy one.'

"So he told her he was putting a bet on a horse for her. You see, he knew her, and I knew him, how they both operated, so I just stood by. 'What horse is it?' Peggy asked, but Arnold wouldn't tell her. Not until the race was over. Then he said: 'Well, Peggy, you won that race and you have two hundred dollars which I am betting for you on the next race.' But he wouldn't tell her the name of the horse, and she thinks she is winding up with the Stutz, until the last race when Arnold told her she lost. Here she had thought he might make a good prospect.

"I never liked chiselers. I liked thieves if they were thieves, but not angle guys. One time in Chicago we were playing poker: Polly Moran, Bill Fields, me, Sophie Tucker, and two agents. Bill is losing, Sophie is losing, Polly is losing. I am out eight hundred dollars so far. This night I say to myself: 'It is very funny why all of us have been losing. I am going to watch.' I saw what these two agents were doing. If one of us would raise the pot, the other guy would raise and put his cards face down on the table. The guy dealing would say: 'For Christ's sake, why don't you turn them up!' and he would reach over for them and would palm off another card. If the guy had two jacks, he would give him a third jack, and like that. I saw it and I knew I couldn't say anything. You can't say: 'You're cheating,' when you're losing. I knew I had to show him up. So, I am sitting there, and the first guy lays his cards down, face down, and the dealer reaches over to pick them up with the palm card ready. I jumped up and grabbed both their hands and started to holler.

"I couldn't say anything. I just made noises, I was so mad. The other players thought I had slipped my trolley. I couldn't talk. I turn over the guy's hand and there is a third king. I got up and I said: 'I'm going upstairs. If I don't get my eight hundred dollars in ten minutes, I'm going to call Albee (Edward F. Albee, of the Keith-Albee vaudeville circuit).' Those two agents would be out of business in twenty-four hours, because if they couldn't book their acts, they couldn't get commissions. I go upstairs and in ten minutes the dealer walks in with the eight hundred dollars. The others kept playing. They just wanted to play. It's like that story where one guy said to the other: 'Did you go to that gambling house?'

" 'Yeah, I went,' said the other guy.

" 'Jesus, didn't you know that's a crooked house?' the first guy said.

"'Yeah, I know,' said the second guy, 'but it's the only gambling house in town.'

"And that gambling-house story is the story of everybody's life. We know we are going the right way or the wrong way, but we do it all the time. I wanted to call my book *I Knew What I Was Doing—I Think,* because whatever happened to me in my life was not a surprise when it happened.

"I made most things happen for me, and if they were good, I worked to get them. If they were bad, I worked just as hard for that.

"But I am not sorry. I will tell anybody that, and it is the truth. I lived the way I wanted to live and never did what people said I should do or advised me to do. And I want my children to do the same. Let the world know you as you are, not as you think you should be, because sooner or later, if you are posing, you will forget the pose, and then where are you?

"And in what I've said for my book, I've said the truth. And if people will read about Fanny Brice they might remember that they thought she was very un-funny. They might open the book and throw it away and it can be a big flop, my book.

"But one thing it won't be: a lie."

A NOTE ON THE TYPE

The text of this book is set in CALEDONIA, *a Lino-type face designed by* W. A. DWIGGINS. *It belongs to the family of printing types called "modern face" by printers—a term used to mark the change in style of type-letters that occurred about 1800. Caledonia borders on the general design of Scotch Modern, but is more freely drawn than that letter. The book was composed, printed, and bound by The Plimpton Press, Norwood, Massachusetts.*